lonely planet
MEXICO
Nellie Huang, Joel Balsam, Jennifer Fernández Solano, John Hecht, Anna Kaminski, Mara Morhees, Liza Prado, Brendan Sainsbury, Regis St Louis, Iain Stewart, Paul Stafford, Phillip Tang

Meet Our Writers

Nellie Huang

@wildjunket

On Nellie's last research trip to Copper Canyon, she went on a sunrise hike up to the highest point of the canyon. Standing on the cliff edge, she watched in awe as the golden sun slowly peeked above the canyon rim, bursting into a million rays that splashed the entire valley in a sea of gold.

Joel Balsam

@joelbalsam

Joel didn't know what to expect from 'snake place' near the town of Atotonilco. He soon found himself peeking into buildings that felt like being underwater with SpongeBob Squarepants. 'I guess I probably should've expected the unexpected, especially from the Northern Central Highlands – a region of Mexico well-known for its surrealism'.

Jennifer Fernández Solano

@mexicantravelwriter

Huamantla's pulque-producing haciendas were the highlight of Jen's latest trip to Mexico. This tiny town comes alive once a year during La Noche Que Nadie Duerme. Each August, streets roll out intricate, colorful sawdust carpets, made all the more beautiful by their ephemeral nature.

John Hecht

@john_hecht

Just when John thought he had seen Bahía Concepción's prettiest beaches, along came another sublime cove, then another, leaving him in a constant state of awe. Whether he was swimming in gentle turquoise waters or kayaking out to uninhabited islands, time just seemed to stand still.

Anna Kaminski

@anna.cohen.kaminski; Bluesky @askmainski.bsky.social

Anna finds the Western Central Highlands utterly beguiling: some of best volcano trekking she's ever done; wildlife tours that let you witness the remarkable spectacle of millions of migrating butterflies; timeless pueblos mágicos in spectacular mountainous locations.

Liza Prado

@liza.prado

Liza Prado is a corporate lawyer turned travel writer and the author of over 60 books. Stepping onto Playa Conejos, the curving beach bathed in sunset, she whispered to herself 'How can a place so beautiful exist?'

Dallas
USA
Houston
New Orleans
Monclova
Monterrey
Reynosa
Saltillo
Gulf of Mexico
Northern Central Highlands 196
San Luis Potosí
Tampico
San Miguel de Allende
San Miguel de Allende 4hr
Pachuca
Mexico City 44
Pico de Orizaba
Cuernavaca
Puebla
Veracruz
Veracruz 82
Around Mexico City 68
Tehuacán
Oaxaca 8hr
Chilpancingo
Acapulco
Oaxaca
Oaxaca 140
Bahía de Campeche
Villahermosa
Tuxtla Gutiérrez
Chiapas & Tabasco 124
Golfo de Tehuantepec
Chichén Itza 2¼hr
Cancún
Mérida
Campeche
Reserva de la Biosfera Sian Ka'an
Yucatán Peninsula 96
Chetumal
Reserva de la Biosfera Calakmul
Caribbean Sea
Belmopan
BELIZE
Flores
GUETAMALA
Guatemala City
HONDURAS

Get blown away by ancient cities and towering pyramids that have withstood the test of time. Meet indigenous people who continue to practice the traditions passed down from their ancestors. Strap on your boots and go on wild adventures in remote, virgin jungles. Come face to face with unique wildlife and marine animals. Frolic at sun-kissed beaches, spearmint natural pools and dreamy waterfalls. Chow down on sizzling street tacos or dine in style at Michelin-starred restaurants. Down mezcal and tequila in old-school cantinas.

This is Mexico.

TURN THE PAGE AND START PLANNING YOUR NEXT BEST TRIP →

Ensenada
Tucson
Nogales
Ciudad Juárez
Baja Peninsula 212
Hermosillo
Chihuahua
Reserva de la Biósfera El Vizcaíno
Ciudad Obregón
MEXICO
Los Mochis
Copper Canyon & Northern Mexico 222
Sea of Cortez (Golfo de California)
Torreón
Culiacán
La Paz
Durango
Los Cabos 2hr
Mazatlán
Zacateca
PACIFIC OCEAN
Islas Marías
Tepic
Western Central Highlands 180
Puerto Vallarta
Guadalajara
Puerto Vallarta 4hr
Islas Revillagigedo
Colima
Central Pacific Coast 158
0 500 km
0 250 miles

Brendan Sainsbury

𝕏 @sainsburyb

With its cobbled streets and pastel-shaded buildings, the low-rise town of Zihuatanejo reminds Brendan of the Italian Riviera. He likes standing dockside watching the fishers: 'This is my abiding memory of Zihua: the smell of fish, sunlight on silvery scales, and congenial banter in Spanish.'

Regis St Louis

@regisstlouis

Bacalar is one of the most enchanting places to start the day. Regis loves watching the sunrise over the lagoon. By late afternoon, the sleepy streets of town come to life, with a near palpable feeling of joie de vivre amid the banter of street food vendors on the plaza.

Iain Stewart

@iainstewart79

Iain finds Xalapa's astonishing Museo de Antropología a beauty to behold and a delight to visit. Not only are its exhibits outstanding, covering the entire history of Mesoamerica from the Olmecs onwards but the modernist building is elegant, the displays well-organized and the adjacent gardens beautiful.

Paul Stafford

@paulrstafford

Paul loves that you can casually stroll across the border into Guatemala at the Lagos de Montebello and nobody will bat an eyelid. It's a side of Chiapas few will see: wild, undeveloped, friendly and with all the state's hallmarks wrapped into one national park: nature, adventure, cenotes and Maya ruins.

Phillip Tang

@mrtangtangtang

Phillip believes eating *tacos al pastor* in Mexico City is a ritual. Pinched in your hand, you tilt your head as if listening to its regal history from other seas. A tale of migrants blending their spices into Mexico's recipes. Mexico City is fusion. On the streets here, every juicy bite sizzles with these stories.

Contributing Writer

Mara Morhees

Havetwinswilltravel.com

Mara's favourite place is Hormiguero, a rarely visited Maya site that dates back two millennia. Often you can explore the ruins in complete solitude. Mara contributed to the Yucatán Peninsula chapter.

FIRST SPREAD: SIMON DANNHAUER/SHUTTERSTOCK

Contents

Best Experiences 6
Calendar 20
Trip Builders 28
7 Things to Know About Mexico 40
Read, Listen, Watch & Follow 42

Mexico City **44**

Underground Mexico City 50
In the Footsteps of Frida & Diego 52
Architectural Wonders in Centro Histórico 56
Find Your Taco Personality 58
Listings 62

Around Mexico City **68**

Pre-Hispanic Food in Tepoztlán 72
Mexico's Smallest State 74
Listings 80

Veracruz **82**

Along the Malecón 86
Road-tripping the Coast 88
Touring Coffee Country 90
Listings 94

Yucatán Peninsula **96**

Undersea Adventures off Cozumel 102
Mysteries of Chichén Itzá 104
Beach-Hopping the Riviera Maya 106
Swimming in Cenotes 108
Wilderness Adventures in Calakmul 110
Strolling Mérida's Historic Center 112
Exploring Uxmal & the Ruta Puuc 114
Listings 122

Chiapas & Tabasco **124**

A Mighty Wild Rift 128
Cacao and Chili in Chiapas 130
Maya Monuments Road Trip 132
Listings 138

Oaxaca **140**

Art of Oaxaca City 146
Oaxaca's Sea Turtles 148
Zapotec County Hiking 150
Listings 156

Central Pacific Coast **158**

Artistic Ingenuity 162
See Acapulco's Cliff Divers 164
Surf's Up in Troncones 166
Soporific San Blas 168
Tropical Style in Old Mazatlán 170
Puerto Vallarta from the Water 172
Zihuatanejo Coastal Hop 174
Listings 178

Western Central Highlands **180**

Tequila Tasting in Tequila 184
Millions of Marvelous Monarchs 186
Trekking in Volcán Nevado de Colima 188
Exploring Guadalajara's Centro 190
Listings 194

Northern Central Highlands **196**

Boho & Beautiful in San Miguel 200
Art-chitecture in the Hills 202
Wine & Mezcal Tasting 204
Guanajuato Alleys & Architecture 206
Listings 210

Baja Peninsula **212**

Hit the Wine Trail 216
Venture off Baja's Beaten Path 218
Listings 220

RUBI RODRIGUEZ MARTINEZ/SHUTTERSTOCK

Above Hierve El Agua (p156) near Oaxaca

Copper Canyon & Northern Mexico 222

All Aboard the Chepe Train 226
Pancho Villa's Mexico 228
Listings 234

Practicalities 236

Arriving 238
Getting Around............... 240
Safe Travel 242
Money 243
Responsible Travel 244
Accommodations 246
Essentials 248
Language........................ 250

ESSAYS

Pulque's Sacred Origins ...78
The Arrival of the Spanish............................ 92
Maize & the Maya........... 118
Return of the Jaguar 120
The Birth of Mesoamerican Civilization 136
Día de Muertos 154
Acapulco & the Manila Galleon............................ 176
Folk Art of the Western Central Highlands 192
How Mexico Broke Free 208
The Evolution of Monterrey 232

VISUAL GUIDES

Mesoamerican Treasures 60
Lesser-Known Ruins Around Mexico City 76
Maya Icons 116
Indigenous Crafts in the Chiapas Highlands..........134
Oaxacan Artesanía..........152
Northern Mexico's Natural Landmarks 230

ANCIENT **TREASURES**

Pre-Hispanic sites are scattered across Mexico, revealing the secrets of past civilizations that built them. Many of these impressive sites have been restored to their full glory, while others have only been explored in part, but thousands of others remain untouched, buried beneath the earth. These are some of the most extraordinary ancient treasures in Mexico, both in their settings and history.

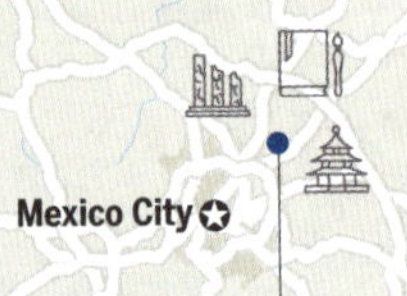

Teotihuacán

Largest pyramids in Mexico

This was once the largest city in ancient Mexico, serving as the capital of the Teotihuacán empire. Featuring ornate mosaics and impressive temples, **Teotihuacán** is most celebrated for its towering pyramids, the Pirámide del Sol (Sun) and the Pirámide de la Luna (Moon).

1hr northeast of Mexico City ▶ p29

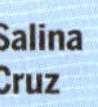

Monte Albán

Zapotec ruins with a view

Graced with astonishing views of Oaxaca's valleys and mountains, it's easy to see why the ancient Zapotecs built their capital, **Monte Albán**, on this hilltop location 2700 years ago.

20min west of Oaxaca City ▶ p156

FROM LEFT: SANTIAGO CASTILLO CHOMEL/SHUTTERSTOCK, KLARA BAKALAROVA/SHUTTERSTOCK, VACLAV SEBEK/SHUTTERSTOCK

Uxmal

The best of the Puuc

The most important site along the Ruta Puuc (a forested region dotted with Maya temples), **Uxmal** features a slew of fascinating structures in good condition and some elaborate ornamentation.

1hr south of Mérida ▶ p114

Chichén Itzá

Most famous Maya site

While tremendously crowded, **Chichén Itzá** is the most well-restored of Yucatán's Maya sites. Visit during the equinox to see the shadow of a serpent descending the steps of **El Castillo** (The Castle).

45min west of Valladolid ▶ p104

Palenque

Jungle-clad temples

Soaring pyramids rise from the dense forest, alongside maze-like palaces and temples swathed in hanging roots. The most iconic is the **Templo de las Inscripciones** (Temple of the Inscriptions).

2½hr southeast of Villahermosa ▶ p132

Yaxchilán

Hidden ruins

Ensconced deep in the Selva Lacandona (Lacandón Jungle) of Chiapas, **Yaxchilán** is dramatically set around a horseshoe loop in the Río Usumacinta (pictured right), a river that divides Mexico and Guatemala.

4hr southeast of Palenque town ▶ p133

Cancún
Mérida
Valladolid
Playa del Carmen
Tulum
Campeche
Yucatán Peninsula
Reserva de la Biosfera Sian Ka'an
Chetumal
Caribbean Sea
Ciudad del Carmen
Reserva de la Biosfera Pantanos de Centla
Reserva de la Biosfera Calakmul
Villahermosa
Palenque
Belize
Belize City
Reserva de la Biosfera Maya
Presa Nezahualcoyotl
Flores
San Cristóbal de las Casas
Maya Mountains
Tuxtla Gutiérrez
Guatemala
Sierra Chiapas
Comitán
Presa La Angostura
Honduras
0 100 km
0 50 miles

THE UNDERWORLD

The Yucatán Peninsula is sprinkled with an estimated 10,000 cenotes, natural sinkholes formed when limestone caves collapse.

The ancient Maya believed that some of these sinkholes were entrances to the underworld, known as Xibalba, a place of great importance in Mayan mythology.

WATER WORLD

Thanks to its rich jungle areas and intense rainy season, Mexico features a plethora of dreamy waterfalls, hot springs and mystical cenotes (incredible water-filled sinkholes). Many of them lie way off the well-trodden tourist trail and can be hard to reach, while some are popular spots in tourist hubs. One thing is for sure: they all promise a world of adventure.

NAILOTL/SHUTTERSTOCK

Left X'Canché Cenote, Yucatán Peninsula (p108) **Right** Waterfall, Huasteca Potosina region (p211) **Below** Cave diving, Cenote Dos Ojos (p109)

→ SEASONAL SAFETY

Check the best time to visit each inland water experience. Rainy season makes these off-limits because of high water levels and impassable roads in some locations.

ENVIRONMENTAL IMPACT

Avoid wearing sunscreen when visiting cenotes and waterfalls. The oil collects on the surface, pollutes the water and can kill fish that live in the cenotes.

FROM LEFT: JULIAN PETERS PHOTOGRAPHY/ SHUTTERSTOCK, MAYUMI.K.PHOTOGRAPHY

↑ CAVE DIVING

Some of the cenotes extend for miles underground and make for exhilarating scuba diving experiences. Float past illuminated stalactites and stalagmites in an eerie wonderland in Cenote Dos Ojos.

▶ (p108)

Best Water-Based Experiences

▶ **Plunge from one cenote to another in the Yucatán Peninsula, enjoying what makes each one unique.** (p108)

▶ **Frolic in the waterfalls dotted all over the region of Huasteca Potosina.** (p211)

▶ **After exploring the temples of Palenque, cool off in the spearmint cascades of Agua Azul and Misol-Ha.** (p138)

▶ **Venture out of Creel in the Copper Canyon, where hot springs are a day's hike away.** (p234)

▶ **Watch the sunrise on an early morning paddle along Laguna Bacalar.** (p107)

SEAWEED EPIDEMIC

Sargassum seaweed begins washing onto the Caribbean beaches in April (through to September), though resorts and beach clubs do their best to clean it up.

SANDY **STRANDS**

Mexico is up there with the best when it comes to beaches, from small bays packed to the gills with partying beachgoers to remote stretches blanked in white-silky sand and cerulean water. The Pacific Coast's Baja California and Oaxaca are lined with relatively uncrowded beaches with decent but unpredictable swells; families with children are better off sticking to shallow and calm beaches off Riviera Maya.

Left Isla Holbox (p122) **Right** Isla Mujeres (p122) **Below** Tropical thunderstorm, Playa del Carmen

→ BEACH SAFETY

Be aware that lifeguards are only present on town-fronted beaches or stretches that form part of resorts.

PACIFIC RIP CURRENTS

Use extreme caution if you're swimming in the Pacific. Rip currents and rogue waves are common, and even experienced surfers and swimmers have reported issues.

↑ HURRICANE SEASON

In Mexico, hurricanes and tropical storms are most prevalent between July and October (the hottest months of the year), with September and October usually the worst hit.

Best Beach Experiences

- **Hike to a panoramic viewpoint overlooking Playa Balandra in Baja California and soak in the knee-high water.** (p220)
- **Swim, kayak or bird-watch at Playa La Mancha, north of Veracruz City.** (p89)
- **Stroll along the sandbar and wriggle your toes in the confectioners'-sugar sand of Isla Holbox.** (p122)
- **Rent an old convertible VW Beetle and explore Cozumel, stopping at coastal reserves like Punta Sur.** (p102)
- **Surf the swells of Puerto Escondido along Oaxaca's largely unspoiled Pacific Coast.** (p32)

ENDANGERED SPECIES

More than 60% of Mexico's wildlife species are classified as endangered and include the vaquita porpoise, leatherback sea turtle, Mexican gray wolf, scarlet macaw and jaguar.

WILDLIFE ENCOUNTERS

From breaching whales in the Sea of Cortez to migrating butterflies in hilltop forests, Mexico is home to an impressive array of wildlife and marine animals. Scientists estimate that almost 15% of Mexico's wildlife is endemic, meaning it is found nowhere else on Earth. For close-up wildlife encounters, look for responsible tour operators and check the best seasons, which vary for different animals.

Left Olive ridley turtles, Oaxaca (p148) **Right** Axolotl **Below** Humpback whale, Baja California (p218)

→ MEXICO'S ICONIC ANIMAL

The axolotl is a unique salamander endemic to Mexico, sporting a dragon-like head and external gills, originally from the freshwater lakes underlying Mexico City.

MASLOV DMITRY/SHUTTERSTOCK

PROTECTED RESERVES

Nearly a fifth of Mexico's land is protected from development by law. One of the most famous is the wildlife-rich Sian Ka'an Biosphere Reserve.

FROM LEFT: AURORA OPEN/GETTY IMAGES. DOMINGO SAEZ/SHUTTERSTOCK

↑ WHALE SEASON

Whale-watching season in Mexico falls between late November and March (stretching to April at times). Keep your eyes open as you cruise the coast.

Best Wildlife Experiences

- **Be awed by migrating butterflies in the forests of Reserva Mariposa Monarca in Michoacán.** (p186)
- **Swim alongside larger-than-life whale sharks as they feed in shallow waters off Isla Holbox.** (p122)
- **Witness thousands of turtles coming ashore to nest at Playa Escobilla in Oaxaca.** (p149)
- **Spot humpback whales from a boat in the gorgeous, rugged bays of Huatulco.** (p157)
- **Go bird-watching in San Blas on the Nayarit coast to spot the area's 250 endemic species.** (p168)

↘ INDIGENOUS PEOPLE OF MEXICO

The biggest indigenous groups in Mexico are:

Nahua Descendants of the ancient Aztecs/Mexicas

Maya Predominantly live in Yucatán and Quintana Roo states

Zapotec Make up a big portion of Oaxaca's indigenous population

CULTURE VULTURE

Mexico has one of the largest and most diverse indigenous populations in Latin America. Statistics show that 2.5 million people in Mexico are *indígenas*, the indigenous descendants of Mexico's pre-Hispanic inhabitants, and they speak more than 63 languages. Many of these groups are rich in culture and traditions, eager to share their practices with visitors, in the form of dance, food and craft.

Best Cultural Experiences

- **Explore the pyramids and ball courts of the ancient Totonac city, El Tajín, in Papantla.** (p89)
- **Visit traditional Tzotzil and Tzeltal indigenous villages near San Cristóbal de las Casas.** (p30)
- **Learn about the Mennonite community's history in Mexico at the Museo Menonita north of Cuauhtémoc.** (p235)
- **Get spiritually cleansed by a Mesoamerican healing ritual in a temascal or shamanic sweat lodge.** (pictured above; p143)

SPACE_CAT/SHUTTERSTOCK

JUNGLE ADVENTURES

About 25% of Mexico, mainly in the east and south, is covered in jungle. The Lacandón Jungle, the country's largest swath, runs from Chiapas south to Honduras, incorporating the southern portion of the Yucatán Peninsula. Journeys into these precious regions and local communities are a privilege.

RUBI RODRIGUEZ MARTINEZ/SHUTTERSTOCK

★ GO PREPARED

We can't stress it enough: when traveling to remote jungle areas, pack lots of water, sunscreen and insect repellent.

WAYAK/SHUTTERSTOCK

Above Puente de Dios, Huasteca Potosina (p211) **Right** Lacandón people, Chiapas

Best Jungle Experiences

▸ **Delve deep into the Selva Lacandona in Chiapas where Lacandón people live in small communities.** (p133)

▸ **Hike in the cloud forests of Querétaro's Reserva de la Biosfera Sierra Gorda.** (p211)

▸ **Discover the under-visited archaeological site in Calakmul, miles from civilization in the jungle of Campeche.** (p110)

▸ **Road-trip through Huasteca Potosina, a lush jungly area brimming with dreamy waterfalls and jungle retreats.** (p211)

← RESPECTING INDIGENOUS PEOPLE

When visiting indigenous communities, book a homestay to learn more about their culture and experience life in the jungle.

MEXICAN STAPLES

Mexican cuisine has three staple ingredients: corn, beans and chilies. These crops were all grown before the Spanish arrived and continue to form the basis for many dishes, even in the most upscale restaurants.

TACOS, MOLE **& BIRRIA**

It would be no exaggeration to say that Mexicans live for their food. The culinary culture can be experienced from the ubiquitous street taco stands to world-class Michelin-starred restaurants. Mexico truly has one of the world's most diverse and exciting cuisine scenes. Whatever your food preferences, you won't leave Mexico hungry.

Left *Birria* tacos **Right** *Gorditas*
Below Quesadilla de comal con queso y nopales

→ STREET FOOD

For many Mexicans, the best food is found on the streets. Local favorite street snacks include *gorditas* (stuffed dough pockets) and *tamales* (steamed corn mixture).

JROMERO04/SHUTTERSTOCK

CONTEMPORARY MEXICAN GASTRONOMY

Having ranked among the World's Best 50 Restaurants several years in a row, **Quintonil** *(quintonil.com)* in Mexico City focuses on traditional Mexican flavors prepared with modern techniques.

FROM LEFT: BRENT HOFACKER/SHUTTERSTOCK, SERGIO HAYASHI/SHUTTERSTOCK

↑ VEGETARIAN FARE

Many traditional Mexican snacks are vegetarian: order quesadillas stuffed with *nopales* (cactus leaf) or *huitlacoche* (corn fungus) and *flor de calabaza* (squash flowers).

Best Food Experiences

▸ **Join a taco tour in Mexico City and sample all kinds of tacos – from *carne asada* to *al pastor*.** (p58)

▸ **Between August and September, try *chiles en nogada*: stuffed chilies in walnut sauce and pomegranates.** (p71)

▸ **Head to Yucatán and enjoy *cochinita pibil*, pork with Maya *axiote* spice.** (p101)

▸ **Try Oaxaca's famous *mole* – a rich, thick sauce prepared with a chili base, nuts and spices.** (p145)

▸ **Jalisco is most famous for *birria*, braised kid-goat stew with herb-filled tomato broth.** (p183)

MEXICAN FOLK ART

The Museo de Arte Popular in Mexico City (p65) gives a crash course on Mexican folk art. The museum has a curated collection of textiles, pottery, glass, *alebrijes* (figurines of mythical animals) and piñatas.

ARTS & CRAFTS

Mexico's dexterity and passion for vibrancy and traditions are translated into extraordinary *artesanías* (handicrafts). Many traditional techniques have been adapted from pre-Hispanic times and the country's indigenous peoples continue these important practices. Throughout Mexico, you'll find all kinds of ceramics, masks and beadwork, as well as lacquerware and woodwork, with techniques and decorations unique to each region.

Left Traditional *alebrije*, Oaxaca **Right** Man wearing a leopard mask, Mexico City **Below** Handcrafted Talavera pottery, Puebla

→ MASK MEANINGS

For millennia, Mexicans have worn masks in dances, ceremonies and rituals. The wearer becomes the creature or deity represented by the mask.

CLICKSDEMEXICO/SHUTTERSTOCK

TREE OF LIFE

One of the most famous sculptures of Mexican culture is the *árbol de la vida* (tree of life), which traditionally represents the biblical scene of creation.

FROM LEFT: BERNARDO RAMONFAUR/SHUTTERSTOCK, EYEPIX GROUP/FUTURE PUBLISHING VIA GETTY IMAGES

↑ A VISUAL FEAST

The beautiful full-color book *The Crafts of Mexico* by Margarita de Orellana and Alberto Ruy Sánchez covers the full gamut of Mexican crafts.

Best Art & Craft Experiences

- **Shop for Mexico's famous Talavera (tin-glazed earthenware), which originated in Puebla.** (p178)
- **Wander Oaxaca's workshops for black pottery and *alebrijes* in Valle de Zimatlán.** (p156)
- **Hone your textile knowledge at Centro de Textiles del Mundo Maya in San Cristóbal de las Casas.** (p139)
- **Circle Lago de Pátzcuaro and hop from one historic art town to another for Purépecha handicrafts.** (p193)
- **Visit Teotitlán del Valle near Oaxaca for intricate Zapotec rugs and tapestries.** (p156)

Summer is a great time to visit because it's never cold, even when it rains, and the sun often makes an appearance.

Jornadas Villistas

In the week of July 20, the town of Hidalgo del Parral commemorates the death of national hero Pancho Villa with a series of literary events and a grand parade.

Hidalgo del Parral, p228

↖ Guelaguetza

On the last two Mondays in July, the people of Oaxaca celebrate the biggest festival of the year with vibrant costumes and traditional dances.

Oaxaca, p156

▸ guelaguetza.oaxaca.gob.mx

Rainy season kicks in June to August, bringing luscious green and flowering plants to the highlands and making some jungle areas inaccessible.

JUNE

Average daytime max: 26°C (78.8°F)
Days of rainfall: 16

JULY

Mexico in SUMMER

FROM LEFT: ITZAVU/SHUTTERSTOCK, ALXMENDEZR/SHUTTERSTOCK, ULISES RUIZ/AFP VIA GETTY IMAGES, BACKGROUND: CK-TRAVELPHOTOS

↘ International Mariachi Festival

At the end of August, mariachis head to Guadalajara to 'battle' with their trumpets, guitars and voices.

Guadalajara, p190

▸ mariachi-jalisco.com.mx

↗ Feria Huamantla

Parades, cyclists and music flood the streets of Huamantla, Tlaxcala, every August. On the final evening, locals blanket the streets with elaborate flower and sawdust *tapetes* (carpets).

Huamantla, p74

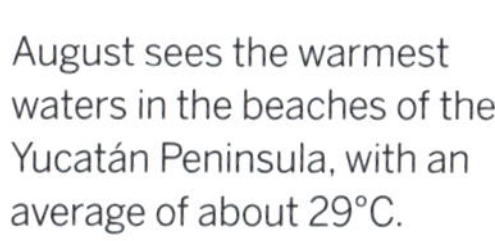

August sees the warmest waters in the beaches of the Yucatán Peninsula, with an average of about 29°C.

AUGUST

Average daytime max: 24°C (75.2°F)
Days of rainfall: 20

Average daytime max: 25°C (77°F)
Days of rainfall: 19

Demand for accommodation peaks in August. View tours and overnight adventures in advance at lonelyplanet.com.

Packing Notes

A hat and sunscreen are obligatory, but also a rain jacket because it's rainy season in the highlands and coastal areas.

September is hurricane season on the Yucatán Peninsula. Check the weather forecast and keep updated with the latest news before visiting.

Mexican Independence Day

Every September 16, the country comes together to commemorate the day Mexico gained independence from Spain with fireworks, music and the traditional cry of independence: *¡Viva México! ¡Viva la Independencia!*

↗ Autumnal Equinox

For a week preceding and following each equinox, the sun casts shadows on El Castillo, the tallest pyramid at Chichén Itzá, in the form of a serpent. Visitors mob the archaeological site to witness this phenomenon.

Chichén Itzá, p104

↗ Festival Cervantinos

October sees the city of Guanajuato partying hard during this annual international arts event.

Guanajuato, p206

▸ festivalcervantino.gob.mx

SEPTEMBER

Average daytime max: 25°C (77°F)
Days of rainfall: 17

OCTOBER

Mexico in AUTUMN

FROM LEFT: SOMATUSCANI/SHUTTERSTOCK, EYEPIX/NURPHOTO VIA GETTY IMAGES, MOAB REPUBLIC/SHUTTERSTOCK, CHRIS ALLAN/SHUTTERSTOCK. BACKGROUND: BIGC STUDIO/SHUTTERSTOCK

↘ Día de Muertos

From late October to the first two days of November, Día de Muertos (Day of the Dead; p154) is celebrated with fervor throughout the country with live music, processions and night vigils in cemeteries.

Beautiful weather with sun and mild temperatures in the highlands brings down the snowbirds from North America, but few tourists.

↗ Día de Revolución

On November 20, almost every town and city in Mexico celebrates Revolution Day with military parades involving the army, community organizations and schoolchildren.

NOVEMBER

Average daytime max: 24°C (75.2°F)
Days of rainfall: 9

Average daytime max: 23°C (73.4°F)
Days of rainfall: 4

Packing Notes

Bring cotton layers and quick-dry items for the beach, and a warm jacket or sweater for chilly evenings anywhere beyond that.

December sees the Christmas crowds everywhere, both local and foreign.

↗ Las Posadas

Over nine nights of Las Posadas, locals recreate the journey of Joseph and Mary to the church. It culminates with the birth of Jesus at Christmas followed by a midnight feast in people's homes.

Nochevieja

At the stroke of midnight on New Year's Eve, Mexicans count down by eating 12 grapes, one for each chime of the clock's bell. This tradition, known as *las doce uvas de la suerte*, is thought to bring good luck in the new year.

Los Reyes Magos

January 6 is Epiphany Day, a Christian holiday commemorating the baptism of Jesus. Mexicans gather to eat the Rosca de Reyes, a ring-shaped cake with a small figurine of baby Jesus hidden within; whoever finds the baby Jesus will buy tamales on February 2, Día de la Candelaria.

DECEMBER

Average daytime max: 23°C (73.4°F)
Days of rainfall: 2

JANUARY

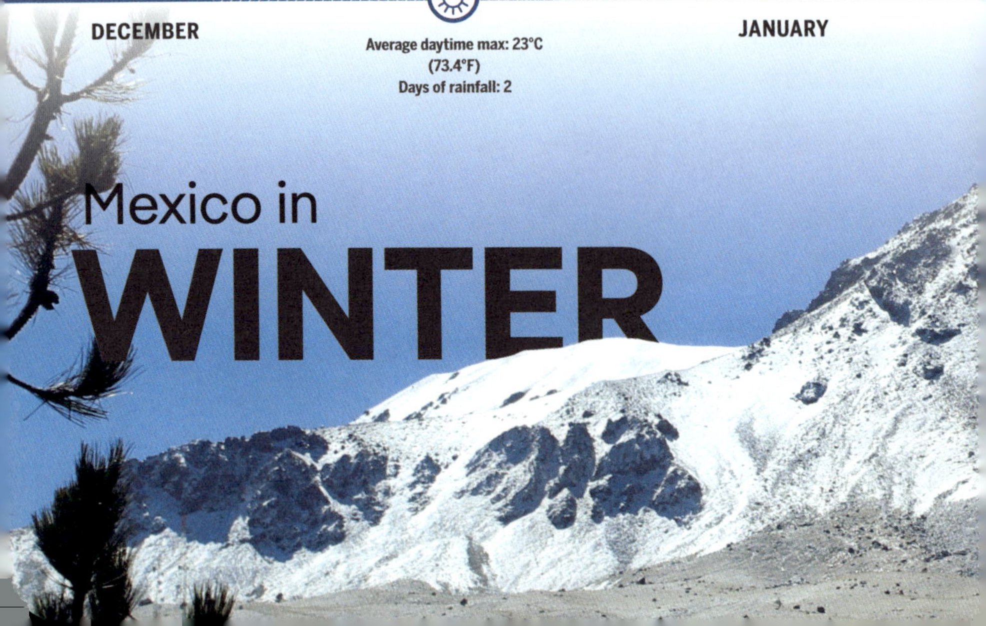

Mexico in WINTER

↓ Fiesta Grande de Enero

Chiapa de Corzo celebrates the Fiesta Grande de Enero, a 12-day festival in January with regional food, music and the famous Parachico masked dance.

Chiapa de Corzo, p129

→ Carnival

Carnival is celebrated throughout the country, with parades, floats and people dressed up in costumes. The largest and most famous celebrations take place in Mazatlán and Veracruz (pictured).

While average temperatures range between 10°C and 32°C (50°F to 89.6°F), don't be fooled. Temperatures can drop significantly at night, and it sometimes snows in the Copper Canyon in February.

FEBRUARY

Average daytime max: 22°C (71.6°F)
Days of rainfall: 2

Average daytime max: 23°C (73.4°F)
Days of rainfall: 1

Winter is the driest time in Mexico, so prepare for cloudless skies and strong sun.

Packing Notes

Bring layers and a winter jacket if you're visiting Mexico City, and central and northern Mexico.

April is the busiest travel season all over the country. Coastal towns tend to be packed, and prices are considerably higher. It's worth reserving your accommodation and tours ahead.

↓ Semana Santa

Easter Week sees church services, solemn processions and age-old rituals. Enormous crowds attend the re-enactment of the Crucifixion in Iztapalapa.

Mexico City, p44

↗ Spring Equinox

Crowds flock to Chichén Itzá to witness the Descent of Kukulkan, when the shadow of a serpent is seen descending the main staircase of El Castillo.

Chichén Itzá, p104

MARCH

Average daytime max: 26°C (78.8°F)
Days of rainfall: 3

APRIL

Mexico in SPRING

↘ Whale Shark Season

Whale sharks start migrating through Isla Holbox and the northeast coast of the Yucatán Peninsula in May (through to September).

Yucatán Peninsula, p122

↗ Cinco de Mayo

Mainly celebrated in Puebla, this holiday commemorates the day a small Mexican army won a battle against the French military, double its size, in 1862.

Puebla, p71

May ushers in low season but also humidity in the south.

MAY

Average daytime max: 26°C (78.8°F)
Days of rainfall: 11

Average daytime max: 27°C (80.6°F)
Days of rainfall: 19

Packing Notes

Thin, breathable gear is a must to combat the increased humidity in the south.

CENTRAL HIGHLANDS
Trip Builder

TAKE YOUR PICK OF MUST-SEES AND HIDDEN GEMS

This classic journey goes from Mexico's beating heart to its glorious historical towns and surrounding hot springs and wineries. The itinerary gives a good glimpse of the exciting capital city, and then takes you along much of Mexico's 'cradle of independence' route, with stops at monuments, museums and archaeological sites.

Trip Notes

Hub towns Mexico City, San Miguel de Allende and Guanajuato

How long Allow 10 to 12 days

Getting around There are reliable and frequent bus services between the towns, and taxis or ride-shares are readily available for day trips outside of town.

Tip Driving in the cities isn't recommended; traffic can be hectic in Mexico City and the narrow cobblestoned streets of Guanajuato are not easy to navigate by car.

FROM LEFT: RUBI RODRIGUEZ MARTINEZ/SHUTTERSTOCK, PHOTOSTOCK BY LEONARDO EM/SHUTTERSTOCK, BRESTER IRINA/SHUTTERSTOCK

Guanajuato
Get lost in the colonial-era center, wander the pedestrian streets and colorful houses, and head up via narrow alleyways to Monumento Al Pípila for sweeping views.
1½hr from San Miguel de Allende

León

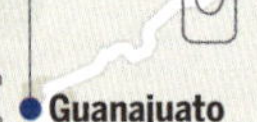

Guanajuato

San Miguel de Allende

San Miguel de Allende
Wander the romantic cobblestoned streets and pop into art galleries, boutiques and rooftop bars. Venture out to the nearby hot springs or wineries.
1hr from Querétaro

Pátzcuaro

0 — 50 km
0 — 25 miles

Dolores Hidalgo

Shop for local ceramics and visit the independence museum, where Padre Hidalgo freed locals from prison after launching his famous *El Grito* (The Cry) for independence.

1hr from San Miguel de Allende

Reserva de la Biosfera Sierra Gorda

Tamazunchale

Mexican Plateau

Sierra Madre Oriental

San Juan del Rio

Teotihuacán

Take a day trip to the capital of ancient Mexico's biggest empire. Marvel the country's largest pyramids, Pirámide del Sol (Sun Pyramid; pictured) and Pirámide de la Luna (Moon Pyramid) and visit the on-site museum.

1hr from Mexico City

Querétaro

Admire the amazing art galleries, aqueduct and coffee scene. Do a side trip to the wineries of Tequisquiapan and Bernal (p204), both an easy one-hour drive away.

4hr from Mexico City

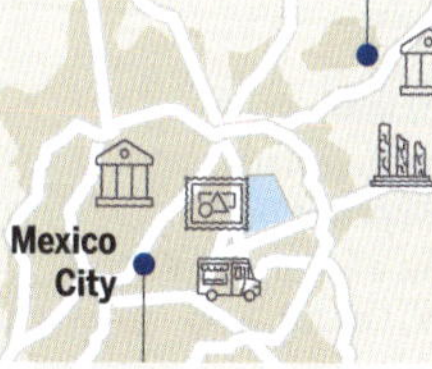

Mexico City

Explore the Centro Histórico, Museo Nacional de Antropología and Palacio de Bellas Artes. Tuck into street food tacos, visit Frida Kahlo's home and wander the neighborhoods of Roma and Coyoacán.

4hr from Querétaro

Puebla

Presa Manuel vila Camacho

YUCATÁN PENINSULA & CHIAPAS
Trip Builder

TAKE YOUR PICK OF MUST-SEES AND HIDDEN GEMS

This itinerary is for outdoorsy and adventurous folks, combining the best of Mexico's beaches with ancient sites and jungle adventures. You will get plenty of time to bask on the Caribbean beaches, explore archaeological sites, splash in cenotes (natural sinkholes) and have fun in jungle-clad eco-parks.

Trip Notes

Hub towns Cancún, Mérida and San Cristóbal de las Casas

How long Allow 2 weeks

Getting around The major towns are connected by reliable and regular bus services, but the newly completed Tren Maya (Maya Train) provides a faster way of getting around the Yucatán Peninsula. To travel at your own pace, hire a car.

Tip Avoid traveling around this region during the peak holiday season because the beaches can get overcrowded.

FROM LEFT: ATOSAN/SHUTTERSTOCK, PATRYK KOSMIDER/SHUTTERSTOCK, EDUARDO FONSECA ARRAES/GETTY IMAGES

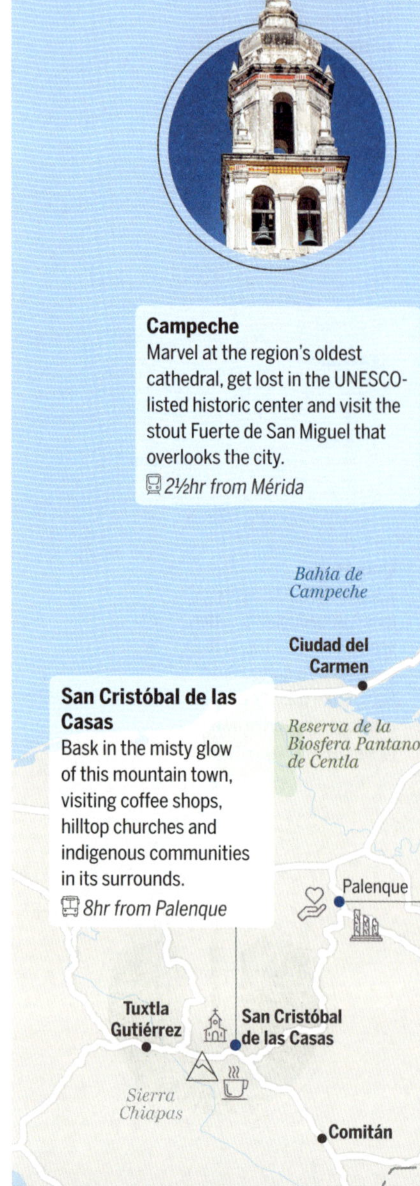

Chichén Itzá
Base yourself in Valladolid and spend a full day at Chichén Itzá, the most celebrated of all the Yucatán's Maya sites.
2½hr from Cancún

Cancún
Let your hair down at this unabashed beach resort and explore the nearby cenotes, or bypass it for Isla Holbox, a pristine car-free island two hours away by car.
1¾hr from Tulum

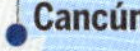

Mérida
Wander the cobblestone streets of Yucatán's cultural capital, visit the region's best museums, and take side trips to the amazing ruins of Uxmal and other sites along Ruta Puuc (p114).
4hr from Cancún

Tulum
Explore the waterfront Tulum Ruins in the verdant Parque del Jaguar, kick back at spiritual wellness retreats and enjoy shoreline activities – from basking at beach clubs to snorkeling the reefs just offshore.
1½hr from Cancún

Palenque
Climb the pyramids of this stunning ancient Maya city and head into the Lacandón Jungle to visit local communities and the remote little-known Yaxchilán ruins.
4½hr from Campeche

Cancún
Yucatan Channel
Mérida
Valladolid
Playa del Carmen
Tulum
Campeche
Yucatán Peninsula
Reserva de la Biosfera Sian Ka'an
Chetumal
Reserva de la Biosfera Calakmul
Caribbean Sea
Belize
Maya Mountains
Guatemala
Gulf of Honduras

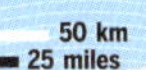
0 50 km
0 25 miles

OAXACA & VERACRUZ
Trip Builder

TAKE YOUR PICK OF MUST-SEES AND HIDDEN GEMS

This all-encompassing itinerary takes you on a journey through Mexico's arts and gastronomy while giving you plenty of beach time. Starting from the underrated city of Veracruz, travel south to the colonial-era city of Oaxaca, the misty mountains of Sierra Sur and Oaxaca's rugged coast.

Trip Notes

Hub towns Veracruz, Oaxaca and Puerto Escondido

How long Allow 2 weeks

Getting around Buses and private shuttles serve the region with regular departures, with some making stops in the mountain towns.

Tip Driving the winding Sierra Sur route between Oaxaca and the coast can be slow and vomit-inducing, but the Puerto Escondido highway (completed in 2024) has cut journey time in half and made travel smoother.

Xalapa
See giant Olmec stone heads (pictured) in Museo de Antropología, or venture north to Papantla to watch the flying *voladores* put on a show and explore the often empty ruins of El Tajín.

2hr from Veracruz

Oaxaca
Feast on Oaxaca's culinary delights in its markets, hang in cool mezcal joints, explore the Monte Albán Ruins, and take day trips to the clifftop mineral springs, Hierve El Agua.

6hr from Veracruz

Puerto Escondido
Surf the swells at Playa Carrizalillo by day and immerse in the nightlife scene as the sun goes down in this ultra-cool beach town.

3hr from Oaxaca

0 — 50 km
0 — 25 miles

FROM LEFT: JOSEPH SORRENTINO/SHUTTERSTOCK, LAURA JACOME/SHUTTERSTOCK, ASCENT/PKS MEDIA INC./GETTY IMAGES

Xalapa

Pico de Orizaba

Córdoba

Veracruz

Veracruz

Embrace the art-deco architecture of Mexico's oldest European-founded settlement, see evening folk dances at the *zócalo* and go beach-hopping along the coast.

6hr from Oaxaca

Gulf of Mexico

Orizaba

Ogle Eiffel's art-nouveau Palacio de Hierro or hop on the cable car to Cerro del Borrego, where you can peek at Mexico's highest mountain, Pico de Orizaba (pictured).

2hr from Veracruz

Tehuacán

Tuxtepec

Coatzacoalcos

Istmo de Tehuantepec

Sierra Madre del Sur

Oaxaca

San José del Pacífico

Make a detour en route to the coast and stop at this cloud-capped mountain town for a stay in the wooden cabins and nearby coffee plantations.

3hr from Oaxaca

Sierra Chiapas

Juchitán

Bahías de Huatulco

Explore the wildlife-rich jungles, wetlands and sublime beaches of the surrounding national park from your base in Huatulco.

2hr from Puerto Escondido

Golfo de Tehuantepec

Puerto Escondido

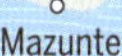

Mazunte

CENTRAL PACIFIC COAST & HIGHLANDS Trip Builder

TAKE YOUR PICK OF MUST-SEES AND HIDDEN GEMS

Retrace Mexico's cultural roots on this unconventional route, where mariachis, tequila and Día de Muertos rituals originated. The journey starts in the popular coastal city of Puerto Vallarta, then heads inland to the metropolis of Guadalajara, and further east to the butterfly reserves of central Michoacán.

Trip Notes

Hub towns Puerto Vallarta, Guadalajara and Morelia

How long Allow 10 days

Getting around Long-distance buses connect the major cities but the Michoacán highlands are best explored on your own wheels. Pick up a hire car in Puerto Vallarta to drive up to the highlands.

Tip Wallet-friendly and efficient water taxis connect the beach towns north and south of Puerto Vallarta.

FROM LEFT: CHUCK COHEN/500PX, NORADOA/SHUTTERSTOCK, MEL GONZALEZ/SHUTTERSTOCK

Sayulita
Beach-hop your way along the coast to charming Sayulita, where you can surf or paddleboard and shop at fair-trade boutiques.
1hr from Puerto Vallarta

Sierra Madre Occidental

Tepic

Puerto Vallarta

Puerto Vallarta
Go snorkeling or whale watching, check out the weekly Art Walk and browse the numerous art galleries and street sculptures.
4½hr from Guadalajara

0 50 km
0 25 miles

Tequila

Take a tequila tour, wander the agave plantations and even stay in a barrel at this quirky *pueblo mágico* and UNESCO World Heritage Site.

1hr from Guadalajara

San Luis Potosí

Mexican Plateau

Sierra Madre Oriental

Guadalajara

Discover the world of mariachi music, *charros* (Mexican cowboys) and excellent cuisine in Mexico's second-biggest city.

4½hr from Puerto Vallarta

Reserva de la Biosfera Sierra Gorda

Morelia

Get lost in the historic center of Michoacán's capital, shop for artisanal folk art and admire the stunning cathedral.

3½hr from Guadalajara

Guadalajara

Querétaro

Lago de Chapala

Lago de Pátzcuaro

Explore the lakeside *pueblo mágico,* Pátzcuaro, and tour villages where age-old Purépecha traditions abound, especially during Día de Muertos (p154).

1hr from Morelia

Morelia

Pátzcuaro

Reserva de la Biósfera Santuario Mariposa Monarca

Colima

Tecoman

Sierra Madre del Sur

Presa del Infiernillo

Reserva Mariposa Monarca

Brace yourself for millions of monarch butterflies (pictured left), cool mountain air and pristine pine forests in this cluster of reserves that sprawl across central Michoacán.

2½hr from Morelia

Lázaro Cárdenas

Zihuatanejo

BAJA CALIFORNIA Trip Builder

TAKE YOUR PICK OF MUST-SEES AND HIDDEN GEMS

Driving the 1690km along Hwy 1 from Tijuana to Los Cabos is an epic Mexican road trip, passing deserts, dramatic coastlines, rock canyons and a number of colonial towns. Along the way, you might spot whales, swim alongside whale sharks, try surfing, sample wines and taste extraordinarily good fish tacos.

Trip Notes

Hub towns Tijuana, La Paz and Los Cabos

How long Allow 2 weeks

Getting around Rent a car, go off the beaten path and stop at remote beaches. Camper vans are a popular option here, where it's allowed to park on certain beaches.

Tip Driving distances can be long in Baja California, so stock up on supplies. Gas stations and grocery stores can be few and far between.

FROM LEFT: TRAVELNERD/SHUTTERSTOCK, VG FOTO/ SHUTTERSTOCK, ARLETTE LOPEZ/SHUTTERSTOCK

Tijuana
Soak up the lively atmosphere, stroll along the famous Av Revolución, and eat at the many fantastic restaurants in the tourist zone.
3hr from Mexicali

Ensenada
Savor fresh-from-the-sea fish tacos in this beach town. If time permits, drive up to the Sierra de San Pedro Mártir to experience a beautiful conifer forest and dense alpine scrub.
2hr from Tijuana

Loreto
Cross the Desierto de Vizcaíno to the leafy oasis of Laguna San Ignacio and continue to Santa Rosalía, before exploring the missions of Loreto and its wildlife-rich marine park.
4½hr from La Paz

0 100 km
0 50 miles

Valle de Guadalupe

Take a scenic drive to Mexico's prime wine region for wine tasting and gourmet meals at world-class wineries.

1½hr from Tijuana

Guerrero Negro

Drive south via the Carretera Transpeninsular to this important whale-watching destination that sits halfway down Baja on the Pacific coast.

8½hr from Tijuana

La Paz

Spend a day or two enjoying the laid-back *malecón* (beach promenade), and book a day tour to the island of Espíritu Santo (pictured above) where you can kayak, snorkel or visit its sea lion colony.

2hr from Los Cabos

Todos Santos

Feel the spiritual energy of this artsy, bohemian beach town, browse the numerous art galleries, snap photos at Hotel California, or release baby turtles at Playa Los Cerritos.

40min from Los Cabos

Los Cabos

Head to mellow San José del Cabo for its historical center, art galleries and chic cafes. Take a water taxi or glass-bottomed boat from tourist-favorite Cabo San Lucas to Land's End and marvel at the majestic stone arch and sea lion colony.

2hr from La Paz

COPPER CANYON
Trip Builder

TAKE YOUR PICK OF MUST-SEES AND HIDDEN GEMS

Traverse the spectacular Copper Canyon by train, hike rugged trails with Rarámuri (Tarahumara) guides, and descend to the Pacific Coast. This itinerary leads you on an offbeat route through a little-visited part of Mexico, characterized by impressive mountains and vast deserts.

Trip Notes

Hub towns Chihuahua, Creel, Los Mochis and Mazatlán

How long Allow 1 week

Getting around El Chepe is a scenic train that stops at various mountain towns in Copper Canyon, but buses run more frequently and are cheaper.

Tip A direct journey on the Chepe (without any stops) only takes 10 hours, but we recommend making stops along the way to explore the Copper Canyon.

FROM LEFT: NATALIAST/SHUTTERSTOCK, BILL PERRY/SHUTTERSTOCK, KYLIE NICHOLSON/SHUTTERSTOCK

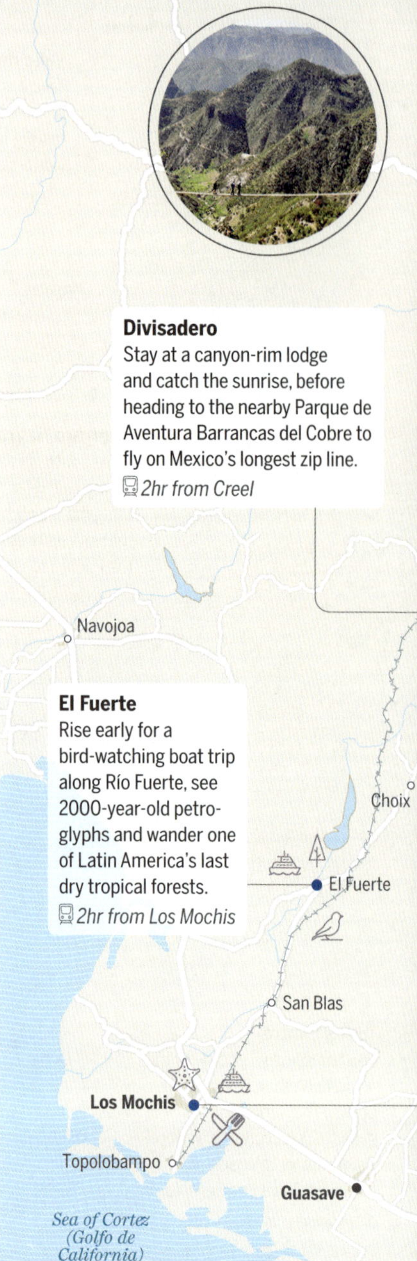

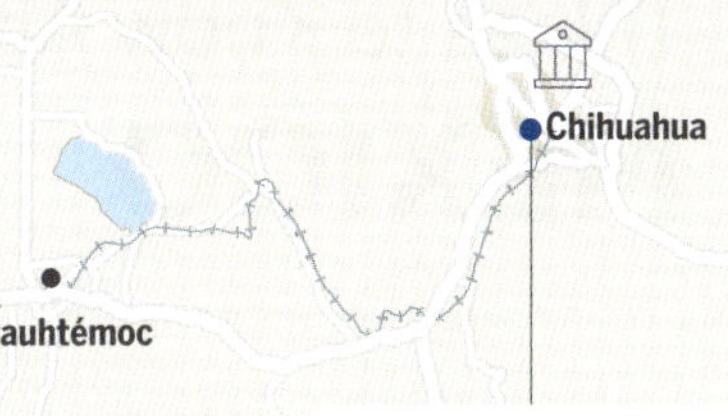

Creel
Hop on the El Chepe train at this quaint highland town, after hiking in its rock valleys and marveling at one of Mexico's tallest waterfalls.
4hr from Chihuahua

Chihuahua
Learn about the city's revolution history in its numerous museums, visit Villa's mansion, and rub shoulders with cowboy-hatted ranchers.
4hr from Creel

Delicias

Creel

Cerocahui
Stop at Bahuichivo train station and make a beeline for Cerocahui to see its yellow-domed church and take in the glorious views at the Mirador Cerro del Gallego.
4hr from Creel

Bahuichivo

Urique

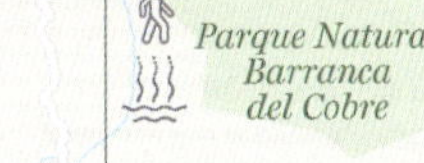

Hidalgo del Parral

Urique
Descend to the bottom of the canyon via dizzying switchbacks to experience lush foliage, riverside hikes and natural pools.
7hr from Creel

Guachochi

Los Mochis
End your rail journey at Los Mochis, enjoy fresh seafood at nearby Topolobampo and do a boat trip to Isla Farallón to see its sea lion colony.
5½hr from Mazatlán

Guamuchil

0 50 km
0 25 miles

Things to Know About MEXICO

INSIDER TIPS TO HIT THE GROUND RUNNING

1 Let's Celebrate!

In Mexico, there's always a celebration happening every other month. Music, food, drinks and fireworks are almost always involved, whether it's a religious holiday or feria (fair). The most iconic of all Mexican festivals, Día de Muertos (Day of the Dead), is celebrated with fervor all over the country. Mexicans honor and remember their loved ones by setting up *ofrendas* (altars) decorated with marigolds and photos.

▶ See more about Día de Muertos on p154

2 It's Not Always Hot in Mexico

Mexico is a huge country, with diverse topography ranging from snowcapped volcanoes to tropical coastlines. Mexico's driest season – December to April – means sizzling hot temperatures in the tropical south, but freezing weather in the mountains of the north (where it snows sometimes). The rainy season – June to August – brings luscious green to the highlands and tropical storms to the coast. November is an ideal time to be anywhere in the country.

3 Hidden Areas

As parts of Mexico battle overtourism, the country still has pockets of wild, pristine areas that remain under the radar. Yucatán's impressive Calakmul ruins (p110) are still being excavated, while Chiapas' Lacandón Jungle (p15) is hardly known.

4 Families Are Welcome

Mexico is a welcoming place for kids, and children are well received at almost every hotel. Kids dig the colorful plazas, fun-filled parks and wildlife-watching.

▶ See more about family travel on p249

5 Social Life

Mexico has a strong sense of community, with family and social gatherings occupying much of their calendar. In general, Mexicans are super warm, welcoming, open and friendly to outsiders. They love to laugh and socialize – it's common to get together in friends' or relatives' homes, with music, food and drinks. The fun often lasts until the wee hours.

6 Local Lingo

Think you know how to speak Spanish? Wait until you talk to Mexicans. Pick up some Mexican slang to understand the locals.

¿Qué onda? – Use this to say 'what's up?' and ask how someone is, in a casual way.

¡No mames! – It's a commonly used phrase that means 'no kidding!'

¡Órale! – A spirited exclamation to express amazement or approval.

¿Neta? – Use this to seek confirmation, and ask 'really?' or 'seriously?'

¿Mande? – A polite way of asking someone to repeat what they said.

¿A poco? – A colloquial way of expressing doubt or surprise.

Güey – This word, meaning 'dude,' is used to refer to pals or buddies.

¡Qué padre! – This phrase means 'how cool!' and is used very commonly by Mexicans of all ages.

Ahorita – Translated to mean 'in a moment,' this word can sometimes mean a lot longer than you'd imagine.

▶ See more on language on p250

7 Tipping Culture

Many workers in Mexico's service sector depend on tips to supplement miserable wages. It's customary to leave gratuities for grocery baggers and gas station attendants (M$10 to M$20). The standard tip for a restaurant meal is 10% to 15%, but some unscrupulous restaurants may tack on a 'service fee' to a bill. This practice is illegal.

▶ See more about the tipping on p243

Read, Listen, Watch & Follow

READ

Like Water for Chocolate (Laura Esquivel; 1989) Captures the flavors of love and Mexican cooking.

Mañana Forever: Mexico and the Mexicans (Jorge Castañeda; 2012) A take on the culture and politics of Mexico.

De perfil (José Agustín; 1966) The struggles and joys of adolescence in 1960s Mexico.

The Labyrinth of Solitude (Octavio Paz; 1950) Mexican Nobel laureate poet looks at Mexico's search for identity.

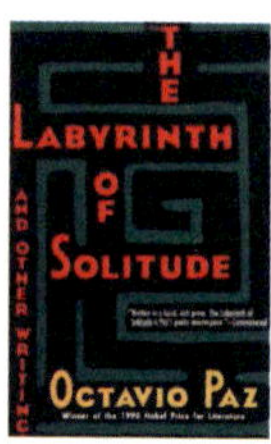

LISTEN

Mexico Matters (CSIS; csis.org/podcasts/mexico-matters) An intellectual podcast covering Mexican economics, trade and security.

Sincerándome (Carlos Rivera; 2023) After winning a singing competition, Carlos Rivera has risen to become a pop sensation.

Error (The Warning; 2022) The Warning, a trio of Mexican sisters, has hit the hard rock scene since 2013.

Lo Mejor de José Alfredo Jiménez (José Alfredo Jiménez; 1990) Even after his death, the much-loved singer is still considered the King of Mexican country music.

PHOTO BY RODRIGO VARELA/GETTY IMAGES

Vestido de Etiqueta por Eduardo Magallanes (Juan Gabriel; 2016) Mexico's pop icon Juan Gabriel (pictured) released this weeks before his death.

WATCH

Amores perros (2000) Three interlinked stories that put the Mexican director Alejandro González Iñárritu on the map.

Roma (2018) Follows the life of an indigenous housekeeper of a middle-class family in Mexico.

Coco (2017; pictured top right) Humorous children's animation based on Día de Muertos (Day of the Dead).

Y tu mamá también (2001; pictured bottom right) Coming-of-age road trip movie about two teenagers from Mexico City.

La reina del sur (2011) Fictional TV series following the rise of a Mexican drug lord.

LIFESTYLE PICTURES/ALAMY

UNITED ARCHIVES GMBH/ALAMY

FOLLOW

Visit Mexico (visitmexico.com) Official website of the Mexico Tourism Board.

Mexico Travel Blog (mexicotravel.blog) Practical travel guides and tips.

Mexico News DAILY

Mexico News Daily (mexiconewsdaily.com) Daily news from Mexico in English.

CDMX Secreta (cdmxsecreta.com) Culture, music, food from Mexico City.

@ChampiTravels Inspiring, mindful travel ideas around Mexico.

Sate your Mexico dreaming with a virtual vacation at lonelyplanet.com/mexico

MEXICO CITY

CULTURE | ART | EDGY

RESEARCHED BY PHILLIP TANG

- Trip Builder (p46)
- Practicalities (p48)
- Underground Mexico City (p50)
- In the Footsteps of Frida & Diego (p52)
- Architectural Wonders in Centro Histórico (p56)
- Find Your Taco Personality (p58)
- Mesoamerican Treasures (p60)
- Listings (p62)

Decode the mysteries of the **Aztec Sun Stone** (p60)
40min from Roma

Rio Hondo
Av Presidente Masaryk
POLANCO
Calz Mariano Escobedo
Av Industria Militar
Paseo de la Reforma
Arquímedes
Paseo de la Reforma
Lago Mayor
Lago de Chapultepec
LOMAS DE CHAPULTEPEC
Lago Menor
Calz Chivatito
Av Constituyentes
Av Paseo Bosque de la Reforma
TACUBAYA
Av Patriotismo
Av Revolucíon
Av San Antonio
Río Mixcoac
Av Revolución
Av Insurgentes Sur

MEXICO CITY
Trip Builder

Have it as spicy or mild as you like. Linger in gorgeous leafy Condesa, Roma and Coyoacán. Explore Frida Kahlo's life and art, and fascinating ancient artifacts – or find underground experiences in dance halls and art collective parties. Mexico City is endlessly fascinating.

Bathe in the art-deco glow of **Palacio Postal** (p57)
3min from Palacio de Bellas Artes

Get down in underground dance hall **Salón Los Ángeles** (p51)
15min from Centro

Gawk at the gorgeous tiled **Casa de los Azulejos** (pictured bottom left; p57)
3min from Palacio de Bellas Artes

Get close to open-air Diego Rivera murals at **Museo Vivo del Muralismo** (p55)
10min from Zócalo

Drink a local-only pre-Hispanic tipple at **Pulquería Las Duelistas** (p51)
18min from Zócalo

Explore the Mexican witchcraft aisles of **Mercado de Sonora** (p51; pictured right)
2min from Zócalo

Enter the home and mind of an artist at **Museo Frida Kahlo** (p53)
40min from Centro

Practicalities

COLINMTHOMPSON/SHUTTERSTOCK

ARRIVING

Aeropuerto Internacional Benito Juárez Official, safe taxi counters upon exiting customs charge a flat fee (about M$300 to Roma or Condesa; 25 to 45 minutes), less for Centro. Use available free wi-fi for Uber/DiDi (about M$170). Taxis hailed from the street are unsafe.

Metrobús (M$30) *Línea* 4 goes to the Zócalo (45 minutes) from *puerta* (gate) 7 in terminal 1 and *puerta* (M$30) Línea 4 goes to the Zócalo (45 minutes) from *puerta* (gate) 7 in terminal 1 and *puerta* 3 in terminal 2, but requires a bus change at San Lázaro station.

WHEN TO GO

MAR–MAY
Last warm, dry weather in May before rainy summer; empty at Easter.

JUN–AUG
Hot daytimes with afternoon downpours, making traffic stand still.

SEP–OCT
Spots of rain but without heat; Independence Day celebrations.

NOV–FEB
Rainy season ends; early November Día de Muertos events.

HOW MUCH FOR A

Taco
M$15–30

Mezcal cocktail
M$175

Metro ride
M$5

GETTING AROUND

Metro The metro system is the quickest way to get around Mexico City and costs only M$5 a ride. Trains arrive every two to three minutes during rush hours. All lines operate from 5am to midnight on weekdays, 6am to midnight on Saturdays and 7am to midnight on Sundays and holidays. With crowded conditions, pickpocketing occurs.

Taxi The safest and cheapest cab option is using the ride-share apps DiDi or Uber using a smartphone or device with internet. Use secure taxis; never hail from the street.

Walking Subway stations are close in Centro Histórico and Alameda Central; save pesos and see more by walking if you only need to go one stop.

EATING & DRINKING

Mexico City's dining scene expertly balances fine dining with street eats. From world-class restaurants where Oaxacan *mole* goes all out, to the world's only Michelin-starred taco stand. There are plenty more praise-worthy joints in Roma, which sizzles up some of the best taco magic in the country. Party-like bistros, late-night stalls and vegan restaurants get creative with fillings in handmade tortillas. In Roma, you'll also find bars and cafes hewn from Parisian mansions serving mezcal cocktails and Mexican pastries and dishes – only in Mexico City.

Best craft cocktails
Licorería Limantour (p63)

Must-try tacos
Taquería Orinoco (p62)

CONNECT & FIND YOUR WAY

Wi-fi Free wi-fi is available in nearly all accommodations and cafes, at every metro station and in many public parks and plazas. Easily buy and activate a good-value data-only *chip* (SIM card) from convenience stores without ID.

Navigation Google Maps works well for finding your way and includes accurate metro and *metrobús* information.

WHERE TO STAY

Accommodations in Mexico City tend to cluster in neighborhoods by type, from hip hostels and designer B&Bs to five-star towers, so location is everything.

Neighborhood	Pros/Cons
Centro Histórico & Alameda Central	Near main sights; accommodations at all budgets. Characterless hotels; deserted at night.
Roma	Stylish and foreigner-friendly; vibrant restaurants. Business and love hotels.
Condesa	Gorgeous residential area with parks; boutique B&Bs. Overpriced restaurants and bars.
Juárez & Zona Rosa	Asian restaurants; LGBTIQ+ clubs. Seedy at night; business and chain hotels.
Polanco & Bosque de Chapultepec	Museums; fine dining; international chain hotels. Isolated and sterile.
Coyoacán & San Ángel	Near Frida Kahlo sights; far from others. Few accommodations. Beautiful town atmosphere.

MUSEUM DISCOUNTS

Most museums offer free admission on Sundays (sometimes Wednesdays) to everybody, and close on Mondays. For student discounts, non-Mexican university ID is often accepted.

MONEY

Mexico City is one of the few cities in the world where the *casas de cambio* (money exchange booths) at the airport actually offer better rates than banks and booths downtown.

01 Underground MEXICO CITY

LOCAL | ALTERNATIVE | QUEER

Venture to less-touristed backstreets where Mexican subcultures feel preserved in gritty amber. Go cheek-to-cheek dancing with locals in cinematic dancehalls as they have for decades, or shake it in sweaty queer clubs. Find out where local artists shop and meet, sipping on drinks that are only served locally. You might just want to check your bill carefully.

ANDREW HASSON/ALAMY

How to

Getting around Take a secure taxi, Uber or DiDi to these edgier neighborhoods.

When to go Nighttime events get going late, throughout the year, regardless of the weather.

Foreigner tax Check your bill carefully but expect to pay a little more than locals if you don't speak Spanish. Cash is safest.

Meet and greet Many Mexicans speak some English but a good icebreaker always starts with a friendly *hola* (hello).

FRANZ MARC FREI/GETTY IMAGES

Top left Salón Los Ángeles
Bottom left Mercado de Sonora

Dance on the Wild Side

Transport yourself to another era in a dancehall rippling with silver streamers and orchestras playing salsa, *merengue* and *chachachá*. At cabaret-style **Barba Azul** you'll see *ficheras*, women who dance with men for work, as they have done since the 1950s. In the rough Guerrero neighborhood at **Salón Los Ángeles**, graceful older dancers parade the vast 1937 ballroom.

The grittiest gay dive bar isn't in Zona Rosa; it's **Tom's Leather Bar**, with explicit dancers, visuals and a darkroom.

By day, fans of goth, punk and alternative music gather at **Tianguis Cultural del Chopo**. Outdoor stalls sell clothes, tattooing and piercings while hungry bands play to an often high audience.

Dark Arts

Understand alternative beliefs in CDMX in the **Mexican witchcraft aisles** of **Mercado de Sonora**, which hawk voodoo dolls, amulets and fresh ingredients for concocting potions. Then enter notoriously dangerous Tepito at your own risk to visit a **Santa Muerte altar** (death skeleton clutching a scythe), worshipped by outcasts in a fast-growing cult.

Creative Communities

Santa Maria La Ribera is a hotbed for niche artistic communities. The queer-art collective of **Eucalipto 20** gathers for artisanal pizza and wine nights, exhibiting and selling art. Join up-and-coming artists and locals over a craft beer at art hangout **Casa Equis**, or at an intimate exhibition party by **Galería Rab 63**.

Pulque Pride

Pulque, a sacred Aztec drink that ferments all by itself on maguey plants, has gone from a quaint rural drink to a mark of Mexican resistance against the beer of foreign elites. Young artists and musicians in CDMX have reclaimed classic *pulquerías* (pulque bars) such as **Pulquería Las Duelistas** near Palacio de Bellas Artes and **La Hija de Los Apaches** in rough Doctores. Expect graffiti art, plastic tables and the people's tipple dispensed straight from the barrel. Pulque doesn't keep well and has to be pasteurized outside of Mexico, so you can only try this zingy potion here.

02 In the Footsteps of FRIDA & DIEGO

ART | MURALISTS | FEMINISM

Step inside Frida Kahlo's house and understand her art and pain through her art studio with Diego Rivera, and her iconic works. Get up close to Rivera's murals without picture frames or crowds, and go Frida-spotting in his paintings.

ALEXANDRA LANDE/SHUTTERSTOCK

Blue House

Start where renowned Mexican artist Frida Kahlo was born, lived and died: **Casa Azul** (Blue House), now **Museo Frida Kahlo** in Coyoacán.

Built by Frida's father Guillermo three years before her birth, the Blue House is littered with mementos and personal belongings that evoke her long, often tempestuous relationship with her husband Diego Rivera, and the leftist intellectual circle they often entertained here. Kitchen implements, jewelry, outfits and objects from the artist's everyday life are interspersed with art and pre-Hispanic crafts.

The house dispassionately reveals Kahlo's pain, with her wheelchair and prosthetics on show. The most intimate section is her bed-studio where a bedridden Kahlo would

ALEXANDRA LANDE/SHUTTERSTOCK

How to

Getting here Coyoacán metro is a pleasant 1km walk; an Uber is about M$120 and 35 minutes from Roma.

When to go Visit on weekdays and early mornings to avoid the crowds.

Artist's mind Get inside Frida's head by watching the movie *Frida* (2002) before your trip. It features locations listed here.

Hop on Turibús (*turibus.com.mx*) buses stop at most of the locations here.

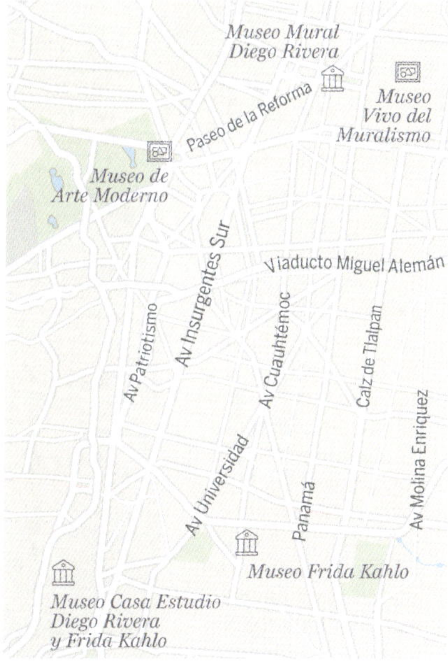

Top left Museo Frida Kahlo, Casa Azul
Bottom left Courtyard of Casa Azul

work on self-portraits using a mirror installed above her bed while recovering from multiple back surgeries.

The Other Blue House

Head to San Ángel to Frida Kahlo and Diego Rivera's other blue house, **Museo Casa Estudio Diego Rivera y Frida Kahlo**. They lived here from 1934 to 1940, but the walkway linking their studios is a metaphor made concrete of their connected yet separate lives.

It was here that Kahlo painted two works that established her true artistry: *Lo que el agua me dio* (What the Water Gave Me; depicting her whole life in a bathtub) and *El difunto dimas* (The Deceased Dimas; depicting a deceased child in a tunic). You can visit Kahlo's austere space with a kitchenette, single bed, dark bathroom and studio. Head to the mezzanine to see the green armchairs where Kahlo rested from her back pain, overlooking Rivera's handicrafts-filled studio.

Pain, Art & Frida

Frida Kahlo was born in Coyoacán in 1907. She contracted polio at age six, leaving her right leg permanently thinner than her left. In 1925 she was horribly injured in a trolley accident that broke her right leg, collarbone, pelvis and ribs. During convalescence, she began painting. Pain – physical and emotional – became a dominating theme of her art. Kahlo said: 'I am my own muse.' Kahlo had only one exhibition in Mexico in her lifetime, in 1953. She arrived at the opening on a stretcher, thrilling the Mexican art world. Kahlo died at the Blue House the following year.

Blue House Tickets

Shadeless queues outside the Blue House can take two hours, especially on weekends. Book tickets online to fast-track. Foreign student IDs can provide hefty discounts. Like most museums, it's closed on Mondays. Inside, take a break on a bench in Frida Kahlo's courtyard of floral archways and cobalt-blue walls.

FROM LEFT: BETTMANN/GETTY IMAGES, CLAUDIO BRIONES/SHUTTERSTOCK

The Two Fridas

Head north in an Uber or secure taxi to **Museo de Arte Moderno** to lay eyes on one of Frida's best works. There are also Diego Rivera canvases here, but the piece *Las dos Fridas* (The Two Fridas) is the star, with its own viewing room. You can get up close and examine individual brushstrokes.

Kahlo in Diego's Murals

Head downtown to Centro Histórico and some of Rivera's best works without the crowds. His murals at the free **Museo Vivo del Muralismo** are along open-air halls lining the offices of the Education Department.

The two front courtyards are lined with 120 fresco panels painted by Rivera in the 1920s and forming a tableau of 'the very life of the people,' in Rivera's words. Look for Frida Kahlo as an arsenal worker.

Cross Centro to **Museo Mural Diego Rivera** for Rivera's famous *Sueño de una tarde dominical en la Alameda Central* (Dream of a Sunday Afternoon in the Alameda Central), a 15m-long mural imagining significant figures from colonial times onward, including Hernán Cortés, Benito Juárez, and Frida Kahlo as a maternal figure. All crowd around a *Catrina* (skeleton ridiculing the elite).

ROBERTO MICHEL/SHUTTERSTOCK

Left Frida Kahlo **Top right** Museo Frida Kahlo, Casa Azul **Bottom right** Museo Casa Estudio Diego Rivera y Frida Kahlo

03 Architectural Wonders in CENTRO HISTÓRICO

ARCHITECTURE | ART | SECRETS

Uncover sublime buildings hidden amongst the cobblestoned streets of Centro Histórico. Gaze at exquisite painted or stained-glass ceilings tucked out of sight. Behold golden interiors within a post office and opulent buildings rising above the crowds. Photo ops abound.

NATALIA GOLOVINA/SHUTTERSTOCK

Art You Can Watch

The Danzantes Aztecas (pictured) dance daily in the Zócalo, wearing snakeskin loincloths and shell ankle bracelets and chanting in Náhuatl. Drummers bang on the conga-like *huehuetl* (indigenous drum) and barrel-shaped *teponaztli*. It is meant to evoke the Aztec *mitote*, a frenzied ceremony performed by pre-conquest Mexicans at harvest times.

Trip Notes

Getting here The area is bookmarked by metro stations Zócalo/Tenochtitlan and Bellas Artes. Walking is the best way to see the sights.

When to go Centro fills with crowds on weekends, especially on Sundays when many museums are free. Most museums are closed on quiet Mondays.

Crowd avoider Dodge the flood of humans squeezed through Av Madero and stroll lovely parallel Av 5 de Mayo instead.

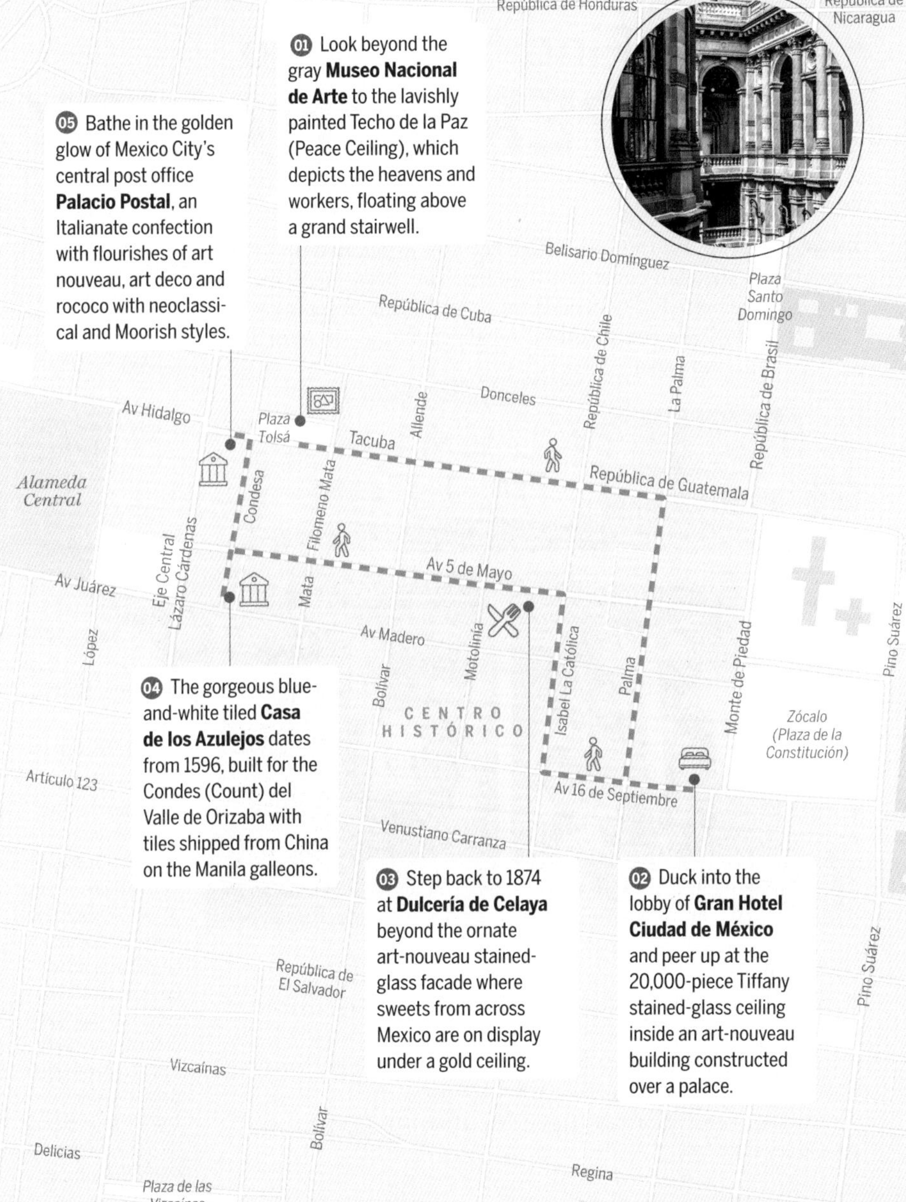

República de Honduras
República de Nicaragua
01 Look beyond the gray Museo Nacional de Arte to the lavishly painted Techo de la Paz (Peace Ceiling), which depicts the heavens and workers, floating above a grand stairwell.
05 Bathe in the golden glow of Mexico City's central post office Palacio Postal, an Italianate confection with flourishes of art nouveau, art deco and rococo with neoclassical and Moorish styles.
Belisario Domínguez
Plaza Santo Domingo
República de Cuba
República de Chile
La Palma
República de Brasil
Donceles
Av Hidalgo
Plaza Tolsá
Allende
Tacuba
República de Guatemala
Alameda Central
Condesa
Filomeno Mata
Eje Central Lázaro Cárdenas
Av 5 de Mayo
Av Juárez
Mata
Av Madero
López
Motolinía
Isabel La Católica
Palma
Monte de Piedad
Pino Suárez
Bolívar
CENTRO HISTÓRICO
Zócalo (Plaza de la Constitución)
04 The gorgeous blue-and-white tiled Casa de los Azulejos dates from 1596, built for the Condes (Count) del Valle de Orizaba with tiles shipped from China on the Manila galleons.
Artículo 123
Av 16 de Septiembre
Venustiano Carranza
03 Step back to 1874 at Dulcería de Celaya beyond the ornate art-nouveau stained-glass facade where sweets from across Mexico are on display under a gold ceiling.
02 Duck into the lobby of Gran Hotel Ciudad de México and peer up at the 20,000-piece Tiffany stained-glass ceiling inside an art-nouveau building constructed over a palace.
República de El Salvador
Pino Suárez
Vizcaínas
Bolívar
Delicias
Regina
Plaza de las Vizcaínas
San Jerónimo
N
0 200 m
0 0.1 miles

04 Find Your Taco PERSONALITY

FOOD | TACOS | TOURS

To get under the skin of the eclectic Roma neighborhood, consult the Mexican constant: the taco. The 'best' tacos are personal preference. Try everything from vegan street-style parcels to sit-down seafood mini-meals enveloped in a tortilla and punctuated with salsa.

GERARDO VIEYRA/NURPHOTO VIA GETTY IMAGES

Trip Notes

Getting here Roma is a short stroll from metro Insurgentes in Juárez & Zona Rosa. Walking is the best way to see the sights.

When to go The main streets are filled with bars and restaurants that buzz on Friday and Saturday nights. Any time of year is taco time.

Fresh is best The busy taco stands are the freshest and best. Approach, order, eat and pay at the end.

On-Trend Tacos

If you want famous tacos, make up your own mind at **Tacos Atarantados** where US pop singer Katy Perry was captured on video chowing down on tacos. For even more opinion-dividing eats, switch neighborhoods to San Rafael for the first Michelin-starred taco stand in the world, **El Califa de León** (pictured).

01 The tattooed staff at **Por Siempre Vegana Taquería** look right at home in rough-around-the-edges Roma Sur (south) and do wonders with soy and other mock meat without the plant-based trendiness.

02 As you enter Roma Norte (north), things get more refined with handmade tortillas and slow-cooked pork at **El Parnita**, a restaurant for those who want more substantial bites.

03 The hip crowds at **Páramo** drink cocktails and knock back tacos of seared tuna in honey or wild boar in a sprawling restaurant-bar that feels more like a house party.

04 On the ritzier side of Roma Norte, the pink-tortilla vegan fried cauliflower (pictured bottom left) or scrambled tofu tacos of **La Pitahaya Vegana** look and taste divine in its cute bistro.

05 Late into the night, Roma's party crowd line up at **Taquería Orinoco** for succulent Monterrey-style pork tacos (pictured top left), befitting the energetic main avenue of Roma Norte.

FROM TOP: MARCOS CASTILLO/SHUTTERSTOCK, INSPIRED BY MAPS/SHUTTERSTOCK

Mesoamerican
TREASURES

01

02

04

03

01 Aztec Sun Stone
The mysterious Mexica sculpture in the Museo Nacional de Antropología (Anthropology Museum; Mexica hall) could represent a calendar, symbol of Tenochtitlán's power or the relationship between humans and gods.

02 Olmec Colossal Heads
Anthropology Museum's two (of 17) giant, cross-eyed basalt sculptures representing Olmec rulers.

03 Disk of Death
Found at the Anthropology Museum (Teotihuacán hall), with a halo representing the cycle of astrological death and rebirth.

04 Jade Mask of Pakal
Funerary mask of Mayan king Pakal the Great, made of 346 jade fragments and obsidian. In the Maya hall of the Anthropology Museum.

05 Penacho of Moctezuma II (replica)
A replica (original withheld in Vienna) in the Anthropology Museum (Mexica hall) of the quetzal-feather and gold-thread headdress worn by the Aztec emperor.

05

06

07

08

09

10

06 Coyolxāuhqui Stone
A stone disc depicting an Aztec goddess being dismembered and decapitated by her brother was found at Templo Mayor.

07 Xōchipilli sculpture
Aztec god of flowers, art, dance, song and poetry. Patron of homosexuals. A figurine in Anahuacalli.

08 Mask of the Bat God
Found in the ruins of Monte Albán (p156), Piquete Ziña is represented by 25 pieces of jade with shell eyes. Now in the Oaxaca hall of the Anthropology Museum.

09 Toltec Atlantean Warrior Column
The Anthropology Museum holds one original 4.6m basalt sculpture (of four) from Tula with a butterfly breastplate, sun shield and spear representing a Mesoamerican military new order.

10 Tlaltecuhtli earth-monster sculpture
The largest Aztec monolith found to date standing at 4m tall at Templo Mayor is a gender-switching deity.

Listings

BEST OF THE REST

Street Tacos

El Huequito $

These old pros near Alameda Central have been churning out delectable *tacos al pastor* (spit-roasted marinated pork) since 1959, thus the higher-than-average price.

Los Cocuyos $

Suadero (beef) tacos abound, but this always-open stand in Centro reigns supreme. Queue at the bubbling vat of meats and go for the heavy *campechano* (mixed-beef-and-sausage taco).

El Flaco $

The menu at this hole-in-the-wall southwest of the Zócalo hasn't changed since the family opened it over 50 years ago. Great spot to try *tacos de canasta* (steamed inside a basket).

Tacos Álvaro Obregón $

The *tacos al pastor* on Álvaro Obregón are some of the best in Roma. The meat is juicy, packed with spice and loaded with onions, cilantro and pineapple.

Tacos El Capote Azul $

Rubén has been slinging *tacos de carnitas* (pork simmered in lard) for more than 35 years, drawing praise from some of Mexico City's top chefs. Try the *costilla* (rib) tacos.

Taco Restaurants

Taquería Orinoco $

For a taste of the north, head to this excellent Monterrey-style taco restaurant buzzing with Roma locals queuing for *chicharrón* (fried pork fat) tacos, the specialty here.

El Parnita $$

Stylish, lunch-only south Roma establishment with a small menu of family recipes such as *carmelita* (shrimp tacos with handmade tortillas) and *viajero* (slow-cooked pork) tacos.

El Tizoncito $

This Condesa institution claims to be the creator of the *taco al pastor*. It certainly is one of the best places to try these Mexico City–born tacos.

Páramo $$

Festive restaurant-bar in south Roma with tacos that set a high bar, like *huasca* wild boar in a beer reduction, and seared tuna in honey. There are also vegetarian hibiscus flowers.

Vegetarian & Vegan

Gatorta $

A busy vegan *torta* (sandwich) stand near Zona Rosa's Metro Insurgentes with soy or wheat-gluten-based Mexican fillings such as *pastor* (spiced pork) and *chorizo* with almond-milk 'cheese.'

MARCOS CASTILLO/SHUTTERSTOCK

Suadero (beef) tacos

Por Siempre Vegana Taquería $

Vegans can join in the street taco action with soy and gluten versions of pastor, *longaniza* (sausage) and chorizo, complete with self-serve toppings – *nopales* (cactus paddles), beans and salsas.

La Pitahaya Vegana $$

Delightfully colorful vegan meals make this a standout in Roma. The knockouts are the *enfrijoladas* (bean-filled tortillas) and pink tortilla tacos with fillings like tofu, spinach curry and pesto yam.

Terra-Nostra $$

A wide buffet selection of Mexican dishes and salads at this traditional restaurant off busy Av Madero in Centro makes it easy to choose what to eat.

India Town $$

Dependably authentic vegetarian Indian curries and *thalis* (tasting plates) southeast of the Zócalo with snacks and mango *lassi* (yogurt smoothies).

Los Loosers $$

Changing vegan menu inspired by Mexican and Asian cuisine, such as *ramen chilaquiles* (ramen noodles in spicy chili sauce) in Condesa.

Green Corner $$

Not vegan but has a rotating daily lunch menu of vegan and healthy organic choices amongst leafy tables. Wonderful for groups with mixed eating choices in Condesa.

Special Seafood

Contramar $$$

Spectacular seafood dining hall with impeccable service specializing in tuna fillet – grilled with red chili and parsley sauces. The creamy tuna tostada topped with avocado is a must-try appetizer.

M.SOBREIRA/ALAMY STOCK PHOTO

Contramar

La Capital $$$

Tasty traditional Mexican dishes with a gourmet twist. Try the incredible *atún fresco* (raw tuna) *tostadas* or duck enchiladas, with the well-balanced house margarita 'Capital' to accompany.

Cozy Cocktails

Felina

In a tranquil corner of Condesa, quiet confidence is felt in Felina's low-level music, and cocktails that don't rely on sweetness but leverage real ingredients, such as fresh juniper berry gin.

Xaman Bar

This is an underground bar, literally. Pass the hidden Zona Rosa entrance and taste sage mezcal served in coconut shells, while smoke, capers and anise materialize from marble vessels.

Xuni Mezcalería

Snack on guacamole with *chapulines* (grasshoppers) while knocking back mezcal cocktails in this cute, relaxed bar away from the chaos of Zona Rosa.

Licorería Limantour

This romantically lit cocktail bar justifiably ranks as one of the top 50 bars in the world and the best bar in Latin America. Arrive early.

Departamento PB

The *planta baja* 'ground floor' bar of Departamento is a stylish place to drink and pose with its mid-century furnishings. It's popular with hip young professionals and international visitors.

Bar Félix

This dimly lit cocktail bar oozes chicness with some of the best cocktails in Roma and a selection of mezcal and craft beer that's sipped by Roma's locals.

Atmospheric Drinks

La Camelia

This restaurant-cantina has been drawing Mexican celebrities to San Ángel since 1931. Tequila or *cerveza mexicana* (Mexican beer) are the other attractions.

El Péndulo Cafebrería

Library-sized cafe-bar-bookstore in San Ángel built around a palm tree ascending over multiple well-stocked levels of books. The ambiance encourages you to spend hours over a coffee, beer or cocktail.

Delicious Views

Terraza Cha Cha Chá $$$

A margarita and *tuna tostada* (crispy tortilla) on the terrace overlooking the Monumento a la Revolución is a real fiesta starter. Families love the roomy ballroom and varied Mexican menu.

Cafeteria Cloister $$

A baguette or salad brunch in the cool air under the cloister of a courtyard within Museo Franz Mayer near Alameda Central is Mexico City at its most atmospheric.

Terraza Alameda $$$

Reserve for brunch on the roof terrace of the Hilton Hotel opposite Alameda Central. The Mexican dishes are good but people come for the views stretching as far as the mountains.

Designer Giftware

Metate

Small Roma boutique specializing in locally designed candles, textiles and woven rugs as souvenirs for the home.

Cafebrería El Péndulo Condesa

Browsing the giftware, Mexican art and history books and novels in English and Spanish is always delightful at this bookstore-cafe.

Happening

A well-curated wide range of gift-worthy designer stationery, jewelry, clothes and elevated Mexican handicrafts you won't find elsewhere except here in Roma.

Jardín del Arte El Carmen

On sunny Saturdays, it's a pleasant local ritual to stroll, browse and chat with some of the artists displaying their work in San Ángel, who include photographers and engravers.

Bunker Bazar

A perfect post-brunch outdoor market for stalls of jewelry, boutique homewares and clothes direct from local Roma designers.

KAMIRA/SHUTTERSTOCK

Artists display their work at Bazaar Sábado

Utilitario Mexicano

You will pay a premium for the curated everyday Mexican basic kitchenware, homeware and stationery in Juárez, but they are certainly artfully displayed.

El Hijo del Santo

Owned by an iconic 1980s *lucha libre* (wrestling) star, this specialty store sells kitschy wrestling portraits, handbags and silver Santo masks in Condesa.

Mexican Handicrafts & Souvenirs

Pingüino México Condesa

Knowledgeable staff can walk you through folk handicrafts with a twist curated from across Mexico with an eye for the special.

Bazaar Sábado

San Ángel's Saturday market showcasing some of Mexico's best handcrafted jewelry, woodwork, ceramics and textiles, including silver from Taxco and psychedelic Huichol beadwork from Zacatecas.

Casa de Luna

Well-considered collection of unique ceramics and handicrafts with refreshingly reasonable price tags and a knowledgeable Coyoacán owner. A fuss-free way to find quality silverware, woven bags and *nichos* (skeleton boxes).

El Arte de la Ratona

A unique toy store in Juárez where all the pieces are handmade, including carved wooden dolls and miniature homewares, knitted animals and decorations.

Museo de Arte Popular

Crafts are thematically displayed from all over Mexico, including carnival masks from Chiapas and *alebrijes* (colorful wooden animal figures) from Oaxaca.

Special Occasion Meals

San Ángel Inn $$$

Classic Mexican meals served in the garden of this historic estate. Try the *pollo con mole almendrado* (chicken with a spiced, almond sauce).

Montejo Sureste $$$

Along a cobbled San Ángel street lined with restaurants, this inconspicuous Yucatecan establishment whips up regional favorites such as *cochinita pibil* (marinated pork) and *papadzules* (tortillas stuffed with eggs).

Taberna del León $$$

Mónica Patiño is a modern, female star chef innovating on traditional cuisine in San Ángel. Seafood is the specialty here, with *róbalo a los tres chiles* (sea bass in three-pepper chili sauce).

Los Danzantes $$$

A contemporary Coyoacán spin on Mexican cuisine with dishes such as *huitlacoche* (truffle-like corn fungus) ravioli in *chile poblano* (peppers) sauce. Accompanied by top-shelf mezcal from its own distillery.

El Cardenal San Ángel $$

Mexican classics like chicken *mole* sit alongside dishes with a twist – think duck tacos. Violinistas complete the atmosphere for a special meal.

Sweet Treats

Churrería General de la República $

Here are Coyoacán's best deep-fried snacks. Get in line for a bag of churros – chocolate-filled or straight up rolled in sugar.

Café NiN $$

This golden Juárez cafe-restaurant looks plucked from belle-epoque Paris with glorious patisserie and bakery treats as part of the

Rosetta Panadería empire. The bar is great for solo egg brunches.

Picnic Helados $

Picnic's organic ice creams and sorbets are miles ahead of the neon icy numbers on Coyoacán's plazas. Try creamy *mamey* (local fruit), dairy-free *guanábana* (soursop) or coffee with cardamom.

Tamales Madre $$

Stylish Tamales Madre in Juárez artfully plates up packets of *mole* with vegan plantain, *hoja santa* (Mexican pepperleaf) and vegan pecan cream. All steamed in a corn husk without *manteca* (lard).

Best Brunches

Farmacia Internacional $$

Perfect brunch spot. Firm favorites are strong coffees, housemade granola with yogurt, or scrambled eggs and bacon on freshly baked biscuits.

El Cardenal Alameda $$

Breakfast *huevos rancheros* fully loaded with fried eggs atop tortillas and bathed in *pico de gallo* tomato salsa at this stately restaurant. The *cazuela* (baked eggs) is hearty.

Café El Popular $

Fresh pastries, *café con leche* (coffee with milk) and good combination breakfasts are the main attractions. A 24-hour Centro stalwart.

Lalo! $$

An elevated brunch spot in trendy Roma for faves including *huevos con chorizo* (eggs with homemade Mexican sausage) and eggs Benedict.

Affordable Eats

Mercado de Antojitos Mexicanos Juanita $

Near Coyoacán's main plaza, this busy market has all kinds of snack stalls, including deep-fried quesadillas, *pozoles* and *esquites* (boiled corn kernels). Look for the red roof.

Tamales Chiapanecos María Geraldine $

Incredible tamales by a Chiapas native at Coyoacán's plazas. Wrapped in banana leaves, stuffed with olives, prunes and almonds, and laced with sublime salsas.

Cafe La Blanca $

Hearty servings of *chilaquiles* (fried tortillas with salsa) and *café con leche* are breakfast fuel until at least late lunch, which Blanca has been serving in Centro since 1915.

Proper Coffee & Cake

Café Negro

The best coffee in Coyoacán with industrial-chic lamps to get some wi-fi-heavy work done. *Nopal* (cactus) ciabatta, fig salad, vegetarian pasta and Mexican pastries are some of the snack offerings.

Café Ruta de la Seda

Baked with love in Coyoacán. Organic cakes infused with lavender or matcha, cardamom lattes and *conchas* (glazed buns).

Qūentin Café

Serious about coffee whether it's dripped, poured over or brewed, with beans from Mexico and beyond. Contender for Roma's best coffee.

Dosis

Patrons sit at outdoor tables at Dosis in Roma using the strong wi-fi and sip espresso, cold brew with soy milk or bottled craft beer.

Casual Bars

La Chicha

Mix one part Mexican vintage decor, one shot of rock vibes and throw in mezcal, beer and snacks, and you have a bar too cool for swanky Álvaro Obregón.

Falling Piano Brewing Co

This spacious Roma Sur bar is one of the few that make beer on-site. Strong IPAs, fruity pale ales and rich porters are all reasonably priced for the area.

Flora Lounge

Condesa is overflowing with bars, but gay-friendly Flora Lounge strikes the right balance between good, fairly priced cocktails and drinks, and a casual-cute bistro atmosphere.

Cantinas

Cantina Covadonga

Echoing with the sounds of clacking dominoes, this brightly lit old Asturian social hall has found new younger fans of its beer and Spanish tapas.

Cantina Riviera del Sur

A grand, converted cantina with rediscovered Yucatán cuisine and mezcal feels like a taste of cinematic old Mexico. A handsome choice for groups.

La Faena

This forgotten relic of a bar doubles as a bullfighting museum in Centro, with matadors in sequined outfits in dusty cases. A new generation of younger drinkers has rediscovered La Faena.

Tour Buses & Walking Tours

Turibús

Red hop-on-off double-decker buses run four routes on one ticket: Centro (downtown), Sur (south, including **Museo Frida Kahlo**; p53), Hippódromo (Polanco and Chapultepec) and Basílica (north).

Eat Mexico

Bilingual guides lead groups on three- to four-hour themed walking tours. Choose between street food, market fare, family-friendly streets and a mezcal crawl; the street food tour departs from El Ángel.

ELOJOTORPE/GETTY IMAGES

Basílica de Guadalupe

Capital Bus

Take a day trip to the Teotihuacán pyramids (includes bilingual guide and entrance fees) and the **Basílica de Guadalupe**, or tour Mexico City hopping on and off.

Dancing & Cooking

Mama Rumba

Managed by a Havana native in Roma featuring contemporary salsa, with music by the house big band and dance instructors to get you started on Wednesdays and Thursdays.

Escuela de Gastronomía Mexicana

If your Spanish is up to it, learn how to cook Mexican dishes in Condesa with popular classes that include *pozole* (hominy soup) and *mole poblano* (chicken in chocolate sauce).

Plaza de Danzón

Learn a few steps of *danzón* (Cuban dance) at Plaza de Danzón near metro Balderas. Couples of all ages (but especially mature dancers) dance every Saturday afternoon and give lessons.

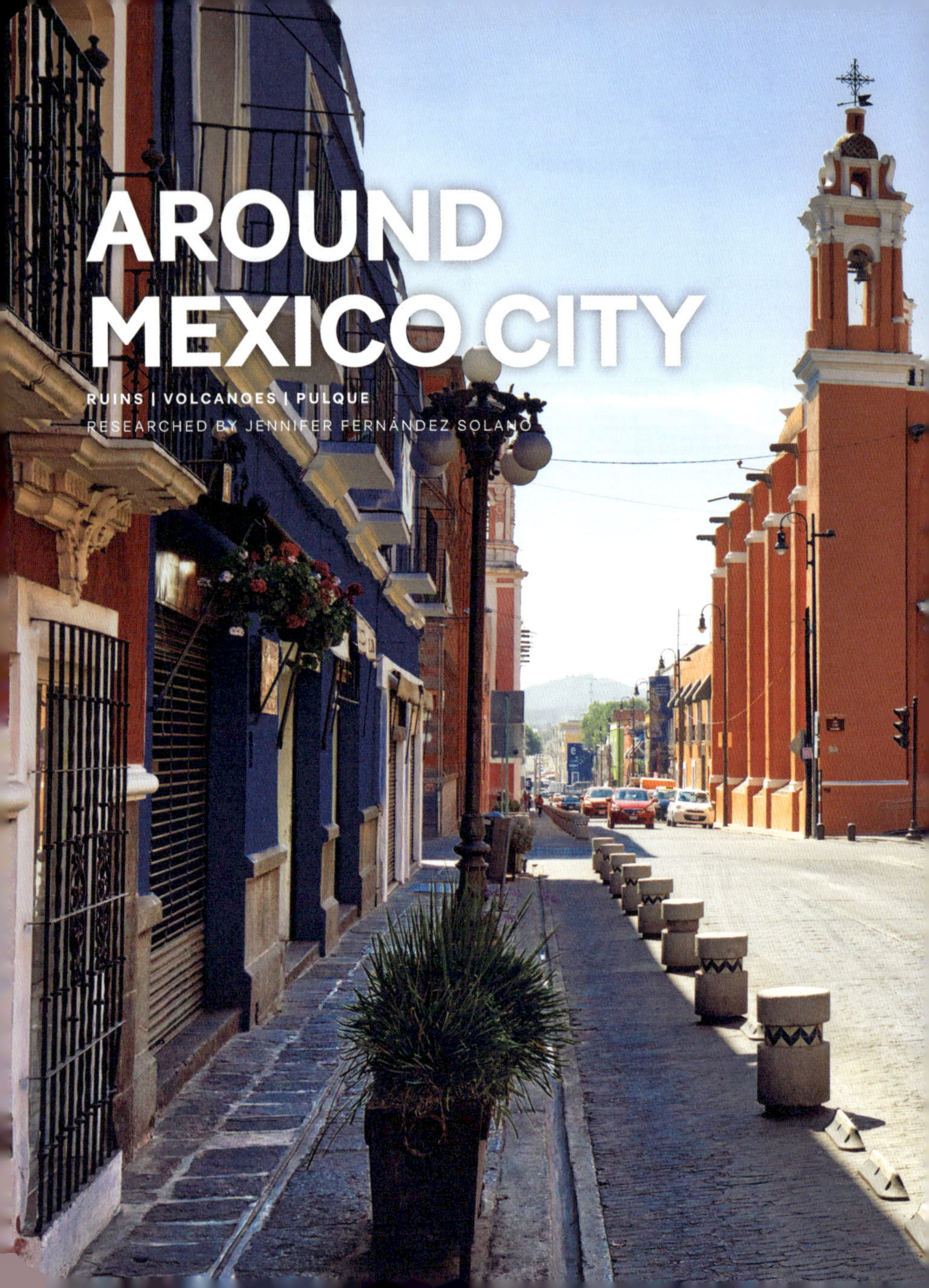

AROUND MEXICO CITY

RUINS | VOLCANOES | PULQUE

RESEARCHED BY JENNIFER FERNÁNDEZ SOLANO

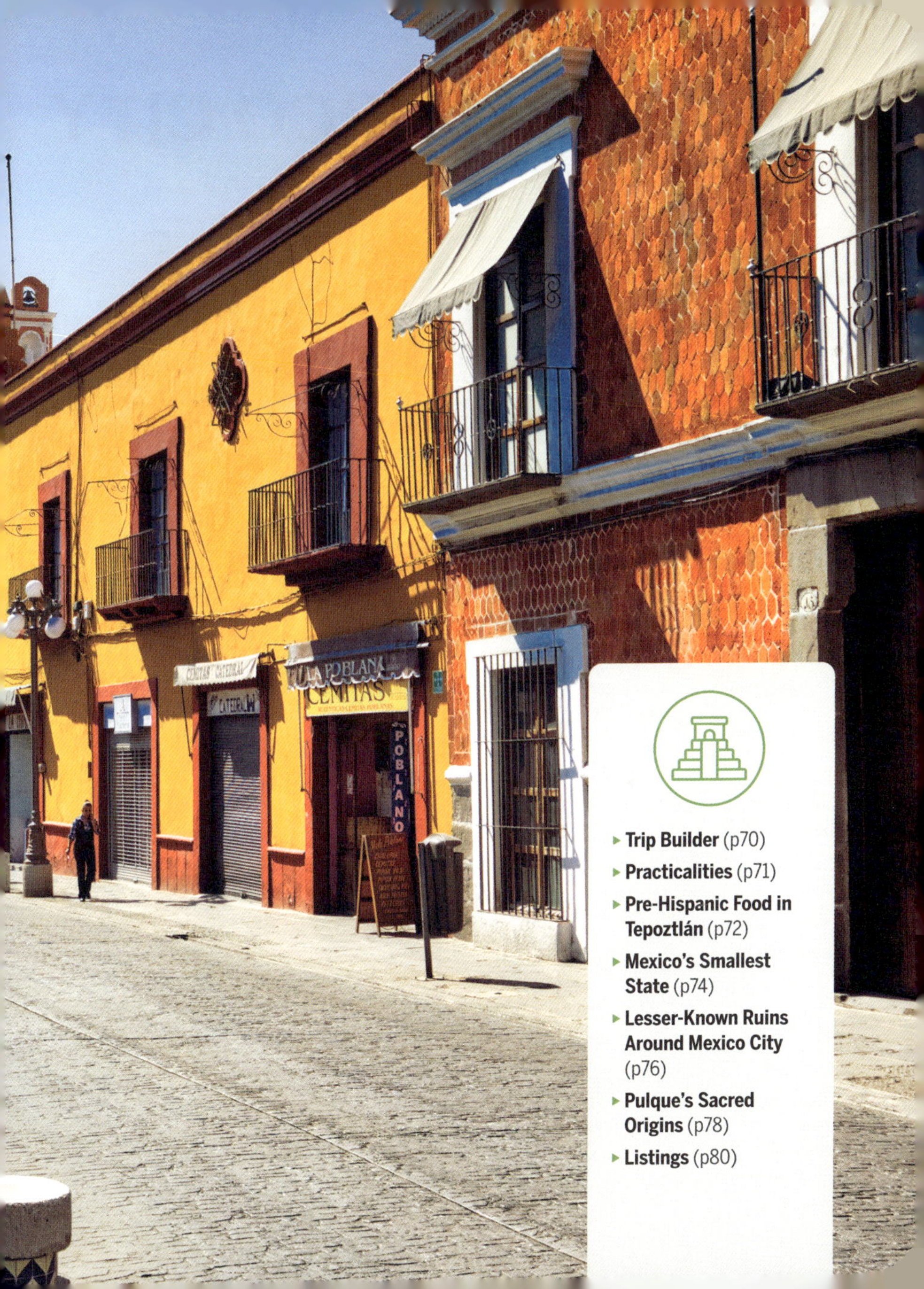

- **Trip Builder** (p70)
- **Practicalities** (p71)
- **Pre-Hispanic Food in Tepoztlán** (p72)
- **Mexico's Smallest State** (p74)
- **Lesser-Known Ruins Around Mexico City** (p76)
- **Pulque's Sacred Origins** (p78)
- **Listings** (p80)

AROUND MEXICO CITY

Trip Builder

Ancient ruins, magical towns and snow-capped volcanoes – both active and dormant – are scattered across the region surrounding Mexico City. With pulque-producing haciendas in Hidalgo, Tlaxcala, Puebla and the State of Mexico, and a wealth of pre-Hispanic food and archaeological sites, adventure opportunities abound.

Drink pulque at a hacienda in **Huamantla** (p75)
1½hr from Puebla

Walk among the fireflies at night in **Nanacamilpa** (p74)
1hr from Tlaxcala City

Venture into chalk mines at the **Minas de Tiza** (p75)
30min from Tlaxcala City

Sample pre-Hispanic food in **Tepoztlán** (p72)
30min from Cuernavaca

Hike **La Malinche volcano** (p75)
1hr from Puebla

Explore ancient ruins minus the crowds in **Xochicalco** (p76)
30min from Cuernavaca

Río San Marcos
Tepotzotlán
Apan
Tlaxco
Mexico City
Parque Nacional Iztaccíhuatl-Popocatépetl
Apizaco
Tlaxcala
Huamantla
Chalico
Parque Nacional La Malintzi
Amecameca
Puebla
Tepoztlán
Cuernavaca
Parque Nacional El Tepozteco
Tetela del Volcán
Atlixco
Presa Manuel Ávila Camacho
Cuautla
Río Atoyac

FROM LEFT: FRENTAN/SHUTTERSTOCK, JENNIFER FERNÁNDEZ SOLANO
PREVIOUS SPREAD: ESKYSTUDIO/SHUTTERSTOCK

0 50 km
0 25 miles

Practicalities

ARRIVING

Aeropuerto Internacional Benito Juárez The main international airport in the region is in Mexico City (p48).

Aeropuerto Hermanos Serdán Puebla's airport offers one international route to Houston.

CONNECT

Get a local SIM card if you're planning to drive. Mexicans rely heavily on the Waze app for directions and to avoid traffic.

MONEY

Always carry a small amount of cash on you. Taxis, smaller shops and street stalls don't take credit cards.

WHERE TO STAY

Area	Pros/Cons
Puebla	Great base along with neighboring Cholula. Lots of options.
Cuernavaca	Wide selection of accommodation. Good base to explore Xochicalco, Malinalco and Tepoztlán.
Tepoztlán	Weekend destination with bohemian vibe. Boutique hotels, cozy guesthouses and camping.
Malinalco	Artsy town with hiking and lively markets. Limited accommodation options due to size.

GETTING AROUND

Bus Different companies operate routes from Mexico City to Puebla, Tepoztlán, Malinalco and Cuernavaca. ADO and Pullman de Morelos are the main ones, with frequent services from TAPO and Terminal Central del Sur (Taxqueña).

Car The best way to explore more remote places and to move freely from one town to another.

TOP: MARCOS CASTILLO/SHUTTERSTOCK
BOTTOM: GUAJILLO STUDIO/SHUTTERSTOCK

EATING & DRINKING

Puebla's regional dishes are plentiful. Try the rich, chocolatey *mole poblano* (pictured top left), the laboriously prepared *chiles en nogada* (served only in the fall) and the shawarma-style *tacos árabes*.

Look out for freshly made pulque (pictured bottom left) – a milky, traditional drink made from fermented maguey plant sap – in towns like Malinalco and Huamantla.

Best chiles en nogada
Casareyna (p80)

Must-try pulque
Museo del Pulque (p80)

JAN–MAR
Cool mornings, clear skies – ideal for exploring ruins.

APR–JUN
Warm days; jacarandas bloom and festivals abound.

JUL–SEP
Rainy afternoons; lush landscapes perfect for hikes.

OCT–DEC
Mild days, vibrant markets and Día de Muertos energy.

05 Pre-Hispanic Food IN TEPOZTLÁN

GASTRONOMY | MARKETS | OUTDOORS

Pre-Hispanic food is often associated with the inclusion of insects as ingredients, but that's not always the case. In Tepoztlán, ancestral recipes passed down from grandmothers are brought to life by local cooks who preserve the traditions of Tepozteco cuisine. Brightly hued edible flowers, seeds and wild herbs feature prominently, and since most are gathered locally, many dishes are not only vegan-friendly but also sustainable.

FERNANDO MACIAS ROMO/SHUTTERSTOCK

How to

Getting there Frequent buses from Terminal del Sur (Taxqueña) in Mexico City. From Cuernavaca, catch a bus at the main terminal.

When to go Dry season (March to May) is the best timing. While April to September brings heavy rains, there's year-round warm weather.

Book ahead **El Tlecuil** relocated to an outdoor spot a 15-minute walk from the main square; by reservation only *(+52 777-4230516)*.

JENNIFER FERNÁNDEZ SOLANO

JUAN PABLO HINOJOSA/SHUTTERSTOCK

Top left Chef selling *tlaltequeadas* **Bottom left** *Tlaltequeadas* on offer at Nonantzin **Right** *Tlaltequeadas* served with mole

Cuisine That Celebrates Mother Earth

What's in a name Tlaltequi, meaning 'love of the earth' in Náhuatl, is the root of the word *tlaltequeadas* – patties that blend regional corn varieties with flowers, natural minerals like *tequesquite*, and lime and wild herbs such as *quelites*, along with other greens well-known in the state of Morelos.

Tlaltequeadas Few are aware of these healthy, colorful pre-Hispanic patties. In Tepoztlán, *itacates* – thick, doughy quesadillas shaped like triangles and filled with *requesón* (a type of fresh cheese) or stews of mushrooms, squash blossoms or meat – have long been favorites. While *tlaltequeadas* have always been part of the regional diet, it was only in recent years that they began to be sold to visitors at the market. Prompted by curiosity and growing interest from those asking what they were eating, some vendors shifted from selling *itacates* to sharing the cherished family recipes passed down from their grandmothers and great-grandmothers.

Dive in Sample a variety of the multihued veggie patties. Squash blossom, *chaya* (a leafy green vegetable) and carrot; hibiscus with rose petals, spearmint and mint; quelites with maguey flower; and jicama with grasshoppers and mezcal are some of the slightly sweet flavors you'll encounter. They're typically served in pairs, drizzled with *mole* sauces containing unique combinations like prickly pear with plum, amaranth or roses, and may come with a side of rice, beans and a stack of tortillas.

Where to Try Tlaltequeadas

Nonantzin $$ Located on the 2nd floor of the new Mercado Municipal, an orange metal and concrete structure opened in 2024 with spectacular views of the hills from a spacious terrace. Nonantzin serves some eight types of *tlaltequeadas* with a variety of *mole* sauces.

El Tlecuil $$ Tlecuil recently moved to a large outdoor space closer to the mountains. The star of the menu is a pattie made with seven seeds, bound together with cactus sap, orange juice and white chia.

El Cuatecomate $$$ A restaurant by the main square plus a stall in Mercado Municipal. Their menu features *tlaltequeadas* along with other pre-Hispanic dishes.

06 Mexico's Smallest STATE

RUINS | HACIENDAS | OTHERWORLDLY LANDSCAPES

As Mexico's smallest state, Tlaxcala has historically been teased by the rest. Good-humoredly, it adopted 'Tlaxcala does exist' as its slogan. But with grand pulque-producing haciendas, ancient ruins, festivals, chalk mines and a firefly sanctuary, it's no wonder this tiny state exudes confidence.

MARIO VAZQUEZ DE LA TORRE/ AFP VIA GETTY IMAGES

Trip Notes

Getting around Rent a car to reach remote places like Minas de Tiza (chalk mines) and to drive between haciendas in Huamantla. Tours can take you hiking up La Malinche and to the Firefly Sanctuary.

When to go In August, locals carpet the streets in colorful sawdust designs in Huamantla. November through February (dry months in central Mexico) are best to hike La Malinche.

Top tip Overnight at Huamantla to hike La Malinche.

Firefly Sanctuary

Overcast, rainy nights from June to August provide an enchanting nighttime spectacle at **Santuario de las Luciérnagas** (Firefly Sanctuary; pictured) near **Nanacamilpa**. Visitors venture into the dark woods without lights, letting their eyes adjust as trees glow with fireflies. Though the woods can get crowded, guides lead small groups to different areas to maintain the whimsical ambiance.

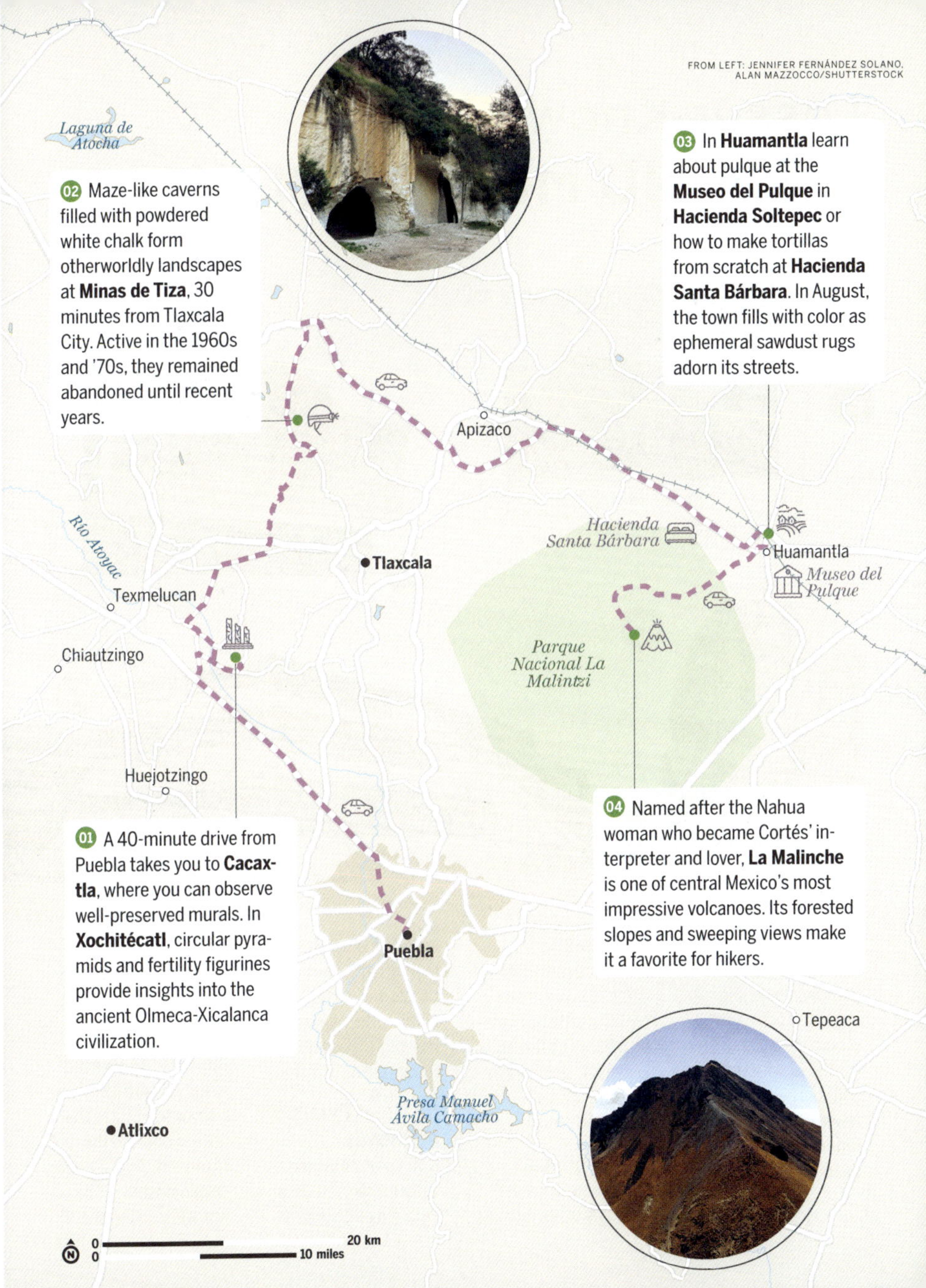
FROM LEFT: JENNIFER FERNÁNDEZ SOLANO, ALAN MAZZOCCO/SHUTTERSTOCK
Laguna de Atocha
02 Maze-like caverns filled with powdered white chalk form otherworldly landscapes at **Minas de Tiza**, 30 minutes from Tlaxcala City. Active in the 1960s and '70s, they remained abandoned until recent years.
03 In **Huamantla** learn about pulque at the **Museo del Pulque** in **Hacienda Soltepec** or how to make tortillas from scratch at **Hacienda Santa Bárbara**. In August, the town fills with color as ephemeral sawdust rugs adorn its streets.
Apizaco
Río Atoyac
Hacienda Santa Bárbara
Huamantla
Museo del Pulque
Tlaxcala
Texmelucan
Chiautzingo
Parque Nacional La Malintzi
Huejotzingo
01 A 40-minute drive from Puebla takes you to **Cacaxtla**, where you can observe well-preserved murals. In **Xochitécatl**, circular pyramids and fertility figurines provide insights into the ancient Olmeca-Xicalanca civilization.
04 Named after the Nahua woman who became Cortés' interpreter and lover, **La Malinche** is one of central Mexico's most impressive volcanoes. Its forested slopes and sweeping views make it a favorite for hikers.
Puebla
Tepeaca
Presa Manuel Ávila Camacho
Atlixco
0
0
20 km
10 miles
N

Lesser-Known Ruins

AROUND MEXICO CITY

01 Xochicalco
Meaning 'place of the house of flowers' in Náhuatl, Xochicalco is both scenic and extensive, with three ball courts, a temascal (sweat lodge), carved temples and circular altars.

02 Cacaxtla
A botched roof in the late 1980s may have cost Cacaxtla its place on UNESCO's Tentative List, but it's still worth a visit for its well-preserved murals.

03 Xochitécatl
Found near Cacaxtla, the ruins of Xochitécatl include a wide pyramid likely used for fertility rituals and a circular pyramid. Its museum has information about the site's link to fertility.

04 Great Pyramid of Cholula
Not nearly as visited as Teotihuacán, the Great Pyramid of Cholula is considered the largest pyramid in the world by volume and base width.

05 Tula
Famed for its majestic Atlantes – 4m-tall warrior sculptures that once supported the roof of the Temple of Tlahuiz-calpantecuhtli – Tula was a key Toltec site.

06 Chalcatzingo
Chalcatzingo is a pre-Olmec site featuring intricate stone carvings, including depictions of rain and fertility deities.

07 Malinalco
Malinalco is known for housing the Temple of the Eagle Warriors, a unique structure in all of Mesoamerica as it's carved directly into the rock of a mountain.

08 Tepozteco
El Tepozteco is a hill topped with a temple dedicated to the god of pulque and fertility. The ascent begins in the town center, following a steep trail surrounded by nature.

09 Tecoaque
Tecoaque, meaning 'place where the lords or gods were eaten,' played a key role during the Spanish conquest as Spanish captives were sacrificed and buried here.

10 Teotenango
Located near Toluca, Teotenango is a former Matlatzinca city with well-preserved walls, temples and a ball court.

01 ALEJANDROMEDINA/SHUTTERSTOCK, **02** LEV LEVIN/SHUTTERSTOCK, **03** LEV LEVIN/SHUTTERSTOCK, **04** LEONID ANDRONOV/SHUTTERSTOCK, **05** FRANCISCO TOLEDO LEON/SHUTTERSTOCK, **06** ABERU.GO/SHUTTERSTOCK, **07** ARLETTE LOPEZ/SHUTTERSTOCK, **08** PRISMAGA/SHUTTERSTOCK, **09** DANAE ABREU/SHUTTERSTOCK, **10** FJZEA/SHUTTERSTOCK

Pulque's Sacred Origins

THE DRINK CONSIDERED A 'GIFT FROM THE GODS'

In central Mexico, agave is used to make pulque, a milky, viscous drink with sacred origins. Once reserved for elders, priests or warriors before heading into battle, pulque is now widely consumed. The main difference between pulque and other agave-based spirits like tequila and mezcal is that it's fermented, not distilled.

Left Pulque for sale in a market **Centre** Pulque is made from the agave plant **Right** Pulque being served

ABERU.GO/SHUTTERSTOCK

Aztec Lore

The Aztecs worshipped the agave plant through Mayahuel, a deity seen as a generous mother with countless breasts to nourish all of humanity. According to legend, after creating humans, the gods worried they wouldn't find joy in their lives. Ehécatl – one of the many forms of the god Quetzalcóatl – decided to gift them a drink so they would sing and dance. He sought the help of Mayahuel, a virgin goddess guarded by her grandmother, Tzitzimitl, and convinced her to descend to Earth. Once there, the two hid, turning into a tree with two branches. When Tzitzimitl discovered her granddaughter missing, she summoned other goddesses to track them down. They found the tree, recognized which branch was Mayahuel's, and tore it apart. When they left, Ehécatl gathered what was left of Mayahuel and buried her. The agave plant is said to have taken root in that spot.

Ritual, Prohibition & Revival

Scientists believe pulque's origin goes as far back as 200 CE. To the Aztecs, pulque was only meant for the privileged and those at risk of perishing in battle soon. When the Spanish arrived, pulque morphed from a ritual beverage into a popular drink among the masses. As a major economic driver in central Mexico, it was widely produced. Eventually, the Spanish Crown banned it, alleging it was causing health and social issues – not to mention its connection to pagan faiths. Prohibition was lifted in the late 18th century and demand for it grew. Not everyone was a fan, though. When beer arrived in Mexico, rumor spread that pulque was unhygienic and low-brow. It remained that

ALEX BORDERLINE/SHUTTERSTOCK

ANGEL MALO/SHUTTERSTOCK

way for decades, sold only from cars and stalls along the highway. In recent years, it's been through a revival and *pulquerías* (pulque bars) started sprouting everywhere in central Mexico.

Pulque Today

Pulque is often enjoyed *curado* – mixed with fruits, nuts or other flavorings for a sweeter, more approachable taste. Those in the know say that it's better to enjoy it plain: the fresher, the better. It's made from lightly fermented agave sap, meaning it continues to ferment and spoils easily. One of the main reasons it's only found in central Mexico, close to where it's made, is that it doesn't travel well. *Curado* was born in an effort to avoid having to throw away pulque. Flavor was added to 'cure' pulque that was past its prime. Today, *pulquerías* will either have a selection of pre-prepared *curados* or make them on the spot, usually by the liter.

> To the Aztecs, pulque was only meant for the privileged and those at risk of perishing in battle soon. When the Spanish arrived, pulque morphed from a ritual beverage into a popular drink among the masses.

The 400 Rabbits

In Aztec mythology, the 400 rabbits, or *centzon totochtin*, symbolize the many effects of drinking. It was believed that drinking pulque meant being possessed by one of the 400 rabbits, explaining changes in behavior. These rabbits were considered Mayahuel's children, each with a unique personality.

The 400 rabbits were honored with a festival every 260 days. During this celebration, known as Ometochtli, the entire population was allowed to drink pulque, a practice that was frowned upon outside of this date. However, it was believed that anyone born on Tochtli (rabbit day) was destined for a life of excess.

Listings

BEST OF THE REST

Unique Eats

Cultivo $$

Transforming Puebla's culinary scene. Opened in 2022 in a restored manor, its 7- to 9-course tasting menu changes seasonally and features locally grown, sustainable products.

Acacia Cocina de Campo $$

This countryside restaurant is off the beaten path even by Mineral del Chico standards, but the drive through winding roads is entirely worth it. Traditional dishes are reinterpreted and paired with house cocktails.

Nonantzin $$

Market stall in Tepoztlán's new Mercado Municipal serving pre-Hispanic fare in the form of veggie patties made with flower petals, seeds and wild herbs. Selection of unique *mole* sauces that raises the flavor.

Barra Moby Dick $$

Mexican-style seafood is served fresh at this lunch counter eatery in Cholula. Asian and Peruvian influences converge in a few dishes. Buzzing at all hours.

Parcela $$

Meaning 'plot of land,' this spacious restaurant in Tepoztlán grows its own crops onsite. Large, communal tables offer great views of the Tepozteco and neighboring hills.

Evelia $

At Evelia in Cholula, traditional breakfast foods are elevated through unexpected ingredients. Menu highlights include the *quesadilla de chamorro* (beef hind shanks) and *tarta de huitlacoche* (corn mushroom tart).

Hijos del Hambre BBQ $$

When you need a break from local fare, this spot in Cholula serves great brisket and pulled pork. Their bread and BBQ sauce are homemade. Corn is served with cilantro mayo and fresh cheese from Chiapas.

Casareyna $$$

This opulent restaurant and hotel serves some of the best traditional dishes in Puebla. Its famous *chiles en nogada* come with a numbered card, letting you know exactly which one in their running tally you're about to enjoy.

Pulque, Mezcal & Wine

Museo del Pulque $

In Huamantla, this is the place to learn about pulque. On weekends, the backyard is where quesadilla dreams come true. Made-to-order *curado* or plain pulque pairs perfectly with the masa bites you order from the open kitchen.

Las Calaquitas $$

This rustic restaurant with adjoining *mezcalería* in Tepoztlán has a large selection of mezcal that will take you on a journey through Mexico with different varieties of agave. With a cantina-of-yore vibe, the *mezcalería* serves small bites.

Pulquería La Sed $

This small *pulquería* in Malinalco, next to the market, is the perfect spot to recover after ascending the 420-plus steps up to the Malinalco Archaeological Site. *Curados* are made fresh by the liter.

Pagana $$

This cozy wine bar in Cholula is so popular that it often spills onto the street. If you score an indoor table, order a cheese and charcuterie board and pair it with Mexican wine.

Bailongo $$

A fusion of art gallery, concept store, bar and cafe in Cholula. In the morning, they serve breakfast at communal indoor tables or streetside in the sun. Come nighttime, beers and mezcal take over the artsy scene.

Cultural Haunts

Museo Robert Brady

This eclectic house museum in Cuernavaca used to be the residence of an art collector, artist and designer who clearly took immense pride in his home. The property itself is fabulous and each room has a style of its own.

Museo Morelense de Arte Contemporáneo Juan Soriano

This museum in Cuernavaca specializes in modern and contemporary art. Its spacious gardens provide a serene space to relax while watching the ponds and art installations – and it's pet-friendly.

Museo Amparo

In Puebla, Museo Amparo has an impressive collection of pre-Hispanic art pieces. Its rooftop cafe offers stunning views of the cathedral and historic center and its shop is a great place to pick up high-quality home decor.

Markets & Cool Shops

Mercado de Artesanías de Metepec

Tree of life handicrafts have come to represent Metepec and there's no better place to purchase one than at this large outdoor market. Each shop is housed in a terracotta-tiled hut, making it seem like a picturesque village.

Casa de Innovación y Diseño Artesano Tina Valente

Traditional Mexican blouses and other clothing items are transformed into designer

JENNIFER FERNÁNDEZ SOLANO

Museo del Pulque

pieces in this shop close to Puebla's iconic Callejón de los Sapos.

Santa Fe Tepoztlán

Boho-chic clothing made from natural fibers coexists with statement-piece jewelry, Mexican crafts and artisanal products like honey and salsas in a store filled with good vibes in Tepoztlán.

Caska Casa de Diseño

Christmas is an all-year affair in Chignahuapan. With several branches in town, one consisting of three floors, Caska has scores of colorful baubles and other Christmas ornaments on display.

Lunaje

Concept store in Cuernavaca next to the **Mercado Comonfort** food court with Mexican design items at reasonable prices, from funky jewelry and denim jackets to fridge magnets and stationery.

Tianguis Orgánico Soltepec

In Huamantla, this farmers market pops up on weekends at **Hacienda Soltepec** bringing together more than 50 artisans from across Tlaxcala. Guides in English are there to explain artisanal techniques, and tastings are offered to customers.

VERACRUZ

HISTORIC | COASTAL | TROPICAL

RESEARCHED BY IAIN STEWART

- **Trip Builder** (p84)
- **Practicalities** (p85)
- **Along the Malecón** (p86)
- **Road-tripping the Coast** (p88)
- **Touring Coffee Country** (p90)
- **The Arrival of the Spanish** (p92)
- **Listings** (p94)

VERACRUZ
Trip Builder

Seldom visited, the intriguing state of Veracruz is the perfect place to escape the tourist crowds, with remote sandy bays dotted along a 720km coastline, rewarding ruins and low-key, culturally rich towns. A lot of coffee is grown here in the lush highlands.

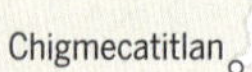

Naolinco

Explore the awesome ruins of **Quiahuiztlán** (pictured right; p89)
1½hr from Veracruz

Villa Rica

Swim in the pristine waters of **Playa La Mancha** (p89)
1hr from Veracruz

Xalapa

Cafe-hop in the highland town of **Coatepec** (p91)
30min from Xalapa

Coatepec

Xico

Enjoy the silence and natural beauty of **Xico** (p91)
1hr from Xalapa

Cardel

Experience night fever in Veracruz's **zócalo** (pictured left; p94)

Huatuxco

FROM LEFT: WITOLD SKRYPCZAK/GETTY IMAGES, MATT GUSH/SHUTTERSTOCK. PREVIOUS SPREAD: OOO.PHOTOGRAPHY/SHUTTERSTOCK

0 20 km
0 10 miles

Laguna Mandinga Grande

Practicalities

ARRIVING

Veracruz International Airport 9km from the *zócalo*. There's no bus connection to the center. Taxis charge M$280.

ADO Bus station is 3km south of Veracruz's city center; a taxi is M$60.

FIND YOUR WAY

Distances are short in Veracruz: it only takes two hours to get from the beach to the highlands.

MONEY

Eat at lunchtime when most restaurants service a good-value *menú del día* (set menu).

WHERE TO STAY

Area	Pros/Cons
Veracruz City	Widest selection of accommodations. Can be pricey and the city is spread out.
Xico	Tranquil, village-like environment. Choice is limited.
Coatepec	Fine selection of atmospheric hotels and guesthouses. Traffic is heavy.

GETTING AROUND

Bus There's a reliable, comfortable bus network between Veracruz City and all the main towns in the state including Xalapa and Papantla.

Car Renting a car allows you to explore the more remote ruins, highland coffee country and beach-hop up and down the coast. Not necessary in cities, however, where taxis are plentiful and walking is often the best option.

TOP: FANFO/SHUTTERSTOCK
BOTTOM: MARCO ORTIZ-MOF/SHUTTERSTOCK

EATING & DRINKING

Seafood Superb in Veracruz. Most beaches (including Playa La Mancha) have a shack rustling up amazing shrimp cocktails (pictured bottom left). Look out for chicken or pork cooked in *mole xiqueño* (spicy, rich sauce from Xico).

Coffee Huge crop in the highlands; savor the flavor.

Best coffee

Matita de Café (p94)

Must-try dish

Arroz a la tumbada (rice with seafood; pictured top left)

FEB–APR

Veracruz Carnaval is a huge city fiesta; Easter is celebrated throughout the state.

JUN–SEP

Peak holiday season for Mexicans; Xico's carnival is in July.

NOV–JAN

Dry season, with sunny days and cooler nights.

07 Along the MALECÓN

HISTORY | PORT | COASTLINE

Mexico's busiest port, bustling Veracruz City has a fine *malecón* (promenade) that takes in a succession of historic sites, piers, seafood shacks and cove beaches. During the day, enjoy arresting views across the bay, past giant cargo ships to the San Juan de Ulúa fort. In the evenings, a fiesta vibe prevails, with vendors selling snacks and souvenirs.

How to

Getting here The *malecón* begins in the heart of the city, just west of the *zócalo*.

When to go There's no good or bad time to explore, though shade is limited so it's best to avoid the heat of the day. It gets crowded (and very lively) on Saturday and holiday nights.

Refreshments Available en route at the Gran Café de la Parroquia.

Swimming Not recommended.

Veracruz's **malecón** extends for 15km, connecting the heart of the city with the offshoot town of Boca del Río. The first section, 2km or so, is the most interesting: a curious combo of the historic, naval and industrial.

Start at the **Mercado de Artesanías** and browse the kaleidoscope of souvenirs and handicrafts before an essential caffeine pit stop in the landmark **Gran Café de la Parroquia**. Here white-jacketed waiters serve the famous *lechero* coffee and prowling mariachis strut and strum the tables. From the cafe's terrace, you can gaze over the port where gargantuan cargo ships usually dominate the scene. You'll skirt the elegant **Faro**

Top right Lighthouse atop the Faro Carranza building **Bottom right** Mercado de Artesanías

ESTEBAN DAVID SAAVEDRA DEL RAYO/GETTY IMAGES

Monuments to Mexican History

Along the *malecón* are statues honoring Veracruz's status as gateway to the nation. Towards the western end is a statue dedicated to Spanish immigrants, while in front of the Faro Carranza is a depiction of Venustiano Carranza, an early President of Mexico. Next up is a statue of Alexander Von Humboldt, the German naturalist/explorer and expert on local flora and indigenous cultures.

Carranza building, topped with a lighthouse – the Mexican Constitution was drafted here – and have views of **San Juan de Ulúa** fortress, founded in 1535, over the port's waters.

Veering southwards, the *malecón* passes a series of piers used by commercial shipping companies, while offshore there are oil rigs. Just inland, the **Baluarte de Santiago** is the only surviving reminder of Veracruz's original walled fortifications.

Beaches The prom passes a succession of gray-sand beaches on its meandering way south, though these are certainly not of the tropical dream variety. Not surprisingly for such a large port, seawater quality is poor, so you may want to skip swimming.

ABALCAZAR/GETTY IMAGES

08 Road-tripping the COAST

ADVENTURE | BEACHES | RUINS

The wild coastline north of Veracruz City is speckled with lonely beaches, fishing ports and some terrific archaeological ruins. It's little-explored by travelers but if you're seeking an off-grid experience, it should be perfect.

ACCEPTPHOTO/SHUTTERSTOCK

Flying Men

According to a Totonac legend, the Gods told men: 'Dance, we will watch.' To appease their gods, the Totonacs created the bizarre yet mystical *voladores* tradition, flinging themselves off 30m-high wooden poles (without any safety equipment) and descending gracefully around them in a trance-like rotation. The ritual is performed several times per day at El Tajín.

Trip Notes

Getting around The best way to explore this coastline is with your own wheels, as some sites are not served by buses. **Tours Amphibian** runs good guided trips.

When to go High season (Jun–Sep) is when Mexican families hit the coast and hotels and beaches are busiest. Off-season things quieten down considerably.

Top tip **EcoGuías La Mancha** offers excellent tours of Playa La Mancha and has rustic cabins.

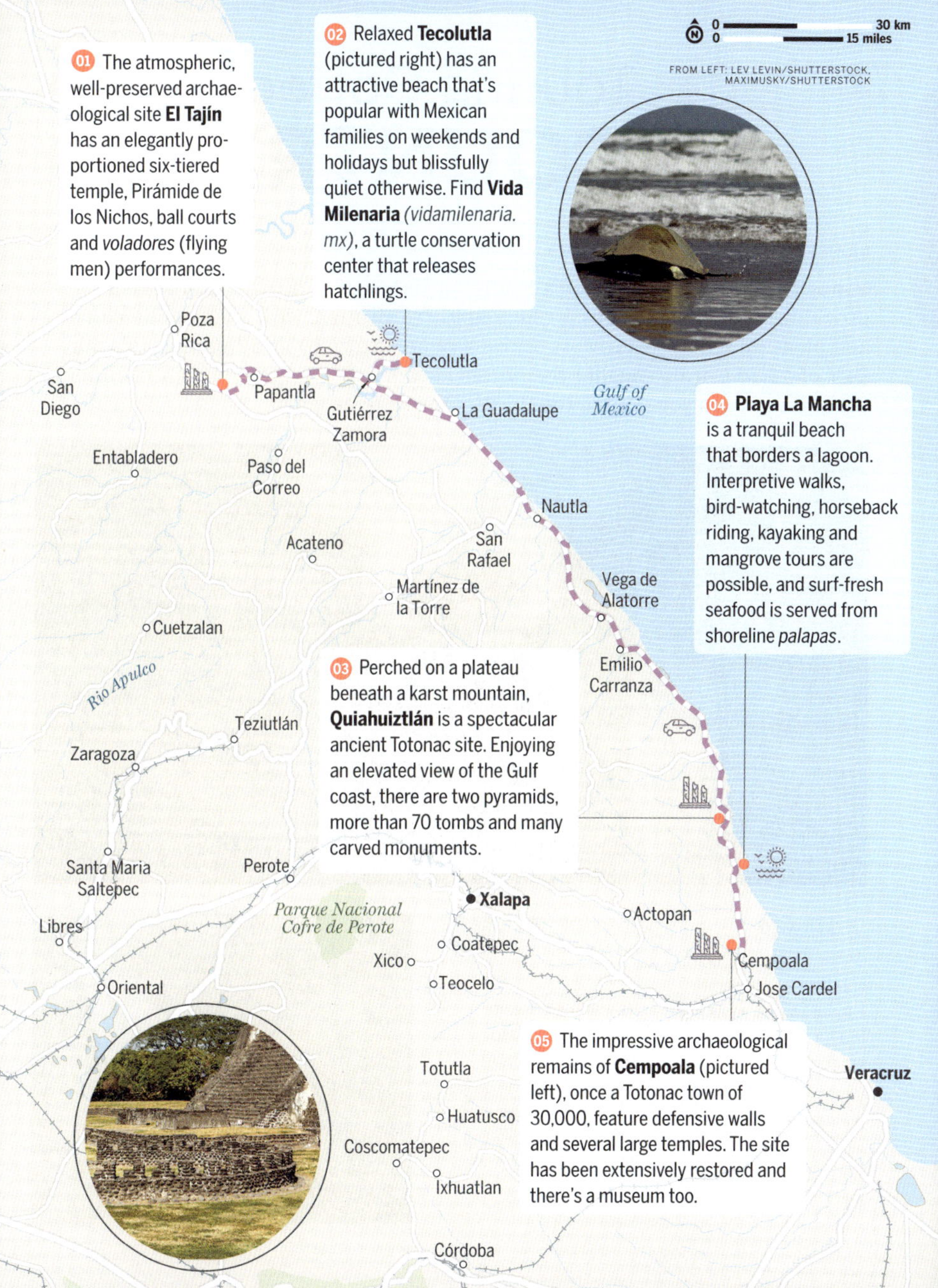
01 The atmospheric, well-preserved archaeological site **El Tajín** has an elegantly proportioned six-tiered temple, Pirámide de los Nichos, ball courts and *voladores* (flying men) performances.
02 Relaxed **Tecolutla** (pictured right) has an attractive beach that's popular with Mexican families on weekends and holidays but blissfully quiet otherwise. Find **Vida Milenaria** *(vidamilenaria.mx)*, a turtle conservation center that releases hatchlings.
0 30 km
0 15 miles
FROM LEFT: LEV LEVIN/SHUTTERSTOCK, MAXIMUSKY/SHUTTERSTOCK
Poza Rica
San Diego
Papantla
Tecolutla
Gutiérrez Zamora
La Guadalupe
Gulf of Mexico
04 **Playa La Mancha** is a tranquil beach that borders a lagoon. Interpretive walks, bird-watching, horseback riding, kayaking and mangrove tours are possible, and surf-fresh seafood is served from shoreline *palapas*.
Entabladero
Paso del Correo
Nautla
Acateno
San Rafael
Martínez de la Torre
Vega de Alatorre
Cuetzalan
Emilio Carranza
Rio Apulco
03 Perched on a plateau beneath a karst mountain, **Quiahuiztlán** is a spectacular ancient Totonac site. Enjoying an elevated view of the Gulf coast, there are two pyramids, more than 70 tombs and many carved monuments.
Teziutlán
Zaragoza
Santa Maria Saltepec
Perote
Xalapa
Parque Nacional Cofre de Perote
Actopan
Libres
Coatepec
Xico
Cempoala
Oriental
Teocelo
Jose Cardel
05 The impressive archaeological remains of **Cempoala** (pictured left), once a Totonac town of 30,000, feature defensive walls and several large temples. The site has been extensively restored and there's a museum too.
Totutla
Veracruz
Huatusco
Coscomatepec
Ixhuatlan
Córdoba

09 Touring Coffee COUNTRY

BEANS | FESTIVALS | HIGHLANDS

The foothills of the Sierra Madre form the coffee heartland of Mexico, providing perfect conditions for high-grade cultivation, with a temperate climate and plentiful forest cover. Most beans here are grown by small producers, with 94% of *fincas* (farms) smaller than three hectares. If you base yourself in either Coatepec or Xico you'll be in the thick of the caffeine action.

IVANMC_STOCK/SHUTTERSTOCK

How to

Getting here Coatepec is 14km from the state capital Xalapa, while Xico is a further 8km to the southwest.

When to go These highland regions see rain all year round, but it's wettest between April and October. Locals call the drizzle, which the area is famous for, *chipi chipi*.

Transport Buses to Coatepec and Xico regularly leave from Xalapa's Mercado de los Sauces. Xico is an easy and enjoyable day-trip from Coatepec.

LIGHT AND VISION/SHUTTERSTOCK

Top left Coffee harvesting in the high mountains **Bottom left** Cascada de Texolo

The captivating countryside around Coatepec and Xico takes in cloud forests, numerous waterfalls and verdant rolling hills planted with coffee bushes. Both towns are *pueblos mágicos* and rich in historic buildings, with cobbled lanes and colonial-era churches.

Coatepec Coffee was first planted here in 1808 and quickly brought great wealth to the area. Today, there are dozens of cafes, from traditional to third-wave like **Matita de Café**, several roasteries and specialist stores dedicated to the bean. There's nowhere else in Mexico more associated with coffee.

Xico Smaller and more tranquil than Coatepec, Xico is surrounded by coffee plantations too, though here the focus is a little more on the town's famous *mole xiqueño* (a rich salsa made with at least 20 ingredients including spices, nuts and two kinds of chili). Close by, the spectacular 80m **Cascada de Texolo** waterfall is definitely worth a visit.

Coffee fincas and tours Just outside Coatepec, **Museo El Café-tal Apan** has excellent information on the history of coffee in the Veracruz region, antique and modern coffee-making machinery, demonstrations and tastings. **Hacienda de Pacho Nuevo** is a beautiful historic estate where coffee is produced; it's a memorable setting for lunch and tours are informative. Meanwhile in Xico, the small coffee *finca* **Café Pepe** is a family-run affair that produces almost organic, shade-grown coffee, offers tours (call ahead) and sells delicious coffee and liquors.

Fiesta Time

Xico Hosts a huge annual **festival** (July 15–24) involving costumed dances and processions. Inside the town's main church, the Magdalena statue is dressed in a different elaborate outfit each day for a month around the fiesta. Expect gigantic floral arches and streets artistically decorated with colored sawdust.

Coatepec The **Feria Internacional del Café y la Orquídea** celebrates coffee and orchids (which flourish in the damp highland climate) during the first two weeks of May. There's also a large week-long celebration in late September with music, dance and art exhibitions in honor of San Jerónimo.

The Arrival of the Spanish

BLOOD AND THUNDER, DEFIANCE AND ALLIANCE

One of the most extraordinary episodes in the history of the Americas, a culture clash of seismic proportions with devastating consequences for the native Mexican population, began in coastal Veracruz in 1519. The outcome changed Mexico forever, bringing a new religion, ruling class and European culture.

Left Illustration of Hernán Cortés' Spanish flotilla of ships sailing to Mexico **Centre** Engraving of La Malinche **Right** Engraving of Hernán Cortés

MIKROMAN6/GETTY IMAGES

Driven by dreams of conquest and riches, on a mission from God under the sign of the cross, Hernán Cortés and his Spanish flotilla set sail from Cuba in 1519. After skirmishes in Cozumel and Tabasco (where they picked up an enslaved woman, later known as La Malinche) the Spanish docked on a beach (today located in Veracruz City).

Their arrival was not a surprise. Though his capital was 400km away in Tenochtitlán, the Aztec ruler Montezuma had been tracking the progress of Cortés along the Mexican coast and arranged for ambassadors to greet the Spanish (who numbered just 500 or so) with greetings and gifts, fresh water and supplies. By sounding cannon fire, and parading war horses (animals unknown in the American continent) and mastiff attack dogs, Cortés ensured the ambassadors returned to Montezuma's Tenochtitlán with an ominous message of military might.

Alliance with Totonacs

The first beach camp proved mosquito- and malaria-ridden so Cortés and his men trekked 40km north to the Totonac settlement of **Cempoala**. Here they were courted by the corpulent chief, Xicomecoatl, with whom they made an alliance against the Aztecs. Xicomecoatl then sent Cortés' entourage 30km further north to the city of **Quiahuiztlán** with 400 Cempoala-hired porters, where they were met by a population of 15,000 curious citizens.

With his ships already docked below Quiahuiztlán, Cortés was determined to cut ties with Diego Velázquez, his overseer in Cuba, and founded a town on the coast, declaring himself the legal *adelantado* (governor). Christened Villa Rica de la Vera Cruz, it consisted of little more

PHAS/GETTY IMAGES

THEPALMER/GETTY IMAGES

than a fort, chapel and some barracks, but small as it was, it was the first European-founded settlement in North America (aside from tiny Norse sites in northern Canada).

Allied with the Totonacs, Cortés then began preparations for the expedition to Tenochtitlán. Before the trip, he left a garrison in Veracruz and decided to sink his own ships to send a message to his own troops that no retreat was possible. The Spanish then returned to Cempoala, gathered resources and intelligence about the epic venture ahead, and took advice as to which route to follow. They departed on August 16, 1519, via Xalapa, Coatepec and Xico before ascending the Sierra Madre.

And make no mistake, Cortés' mission was not to foster trade links with Europe or diplomacy, but conquest and riches.

New Spain

Imagine the impact of this invasion force on those who encountered them: an army led by bearded men from the East with metal armor, guns and cannons, snorting horses and support troops of thousands of allied warriors.

And make no mistake, Cortés' mission was not to foster trade links with Europe or diplomacy, but conquest and riches. Religion also played an important part – Muslims had only been driven from Spain in 1492, during Cortés' childhood – and there was an element of crusading zeal evident in the Spanish desire to impose Christianity. And when the territory was subjugated, Cortés renamed it *La Nueva España* (the New Spain).

The Lead Actors

Hernán Cortés Born in Extremadura, Spain, 'the cradle of conquistadors,' Cortés had a thirst for adventure that propelled him to Mexico. Despite lacking military experience, his strategic ability and ruthlessness (descending to barbarity) proved decisive in the conquest.

La Malinche Sold into slavery, Doña Marina, or La Malinche, was a pivotal figure thanks to her linguistic skills and intelligence. Speaking both Maya and Nahuatl, she became Cortés' lover, mother of his *mestizo* son and key translator between the Spanish and Aztecs.

Both remain deeply divisive figures: Cortés is commonly seen as a rapacious colonizer, and Malinche is lambasted for betraying her people.

Listings

BEST OF THE REST

Parks, Plazas & Gardens

Veracruz's Zócalo

Beautiful city square framed by *portales* (arcades), the 17th-century Palacio Municipal and an 18th-century cathedral. On weekend evenings dancers groove to live bands.

Museo de la Orquídea

This orchid garden in Coatepec features over 5000 species, some so minuscule that they can only be properly appreciated with a magnifying glass. Take a guided tour.

Cerro de las Culebras

The walk takes you up cobbled steps to a lookout tower with a white statue of Christ. From the summit, there are magnificent views of Coatepec.

Craft Brews

Taproom de Cervecería Heroica

Right on the Veracruz *zócalo*, with an unmatched view of the weekend *danzón* action. Excellent locally brewed dark lagers and IPAs.

La Cervecería Del Puerto

Stocks artisan brews from Mexico and around the world, including ales and porters. Faces the Veracruz *malecón* and is LGBTIQ+ friendly.

Casa Bonilla

In business since 1939, this Coatepec bar-resto serves craft beers (including its own brews on tap), a whopping 350 different mezcals and fine seafood.

El Olonés

Eight beers on tap and fine tapas, just off Veracruz's *malecón*. Live music some weekend nights.

Espresso Bars

Impetus

Sip coffee prepared by award-winning baristas at this third-wave coffeehouse. Its cold-brew coffee (with giant ice cube) is perfect for Veracruz's sultry climate.

Matita de Café

Specialist Coatepec cafe, offering a full range of espresso options. They roast on site.

El Café de Avelino

Owner Avelino Hernández – known locally as the *poeta del café* (coffee poet) – brews minor miracles from his Coatepec micro-cafe using beans from Cosailton, Xico and Teocelo.

Bookstores & Souvenirs

Mar Adentro

Veracruz institution that's worth visiting for the lovely 18th-century building alone. A small section of books in English and many others, including antiquarian titles.

Plaza de las Artesanías

This covered market on Veracruz's *malecón* is packed with stalls selling Mexican crafts, clothing including Yucateca *guayaberas* (traditional shirts) and souvenirs.

Plaza Los Azulejos

Several decent souvenir shops selling colorful pottery, clothing, jewelry and other gifts. Just east of Coatepec's main plaza.

Quirky Museums

Museo del Danzante Xiqueño

Devoted to Xico's costumed dances that take pride of place during the town's celebrations dedicated to its patron saint. There's a superb array of masks and festival outfits.

Museo del Vestido de Santa María Magdalena

Go through Xico's main church to the courtyard behind to find this esoteric, niche display of St María Magdalena's past festival dresses – hundreds of them! – dating from 1910.

Museo Agustín Lara

Displays a range of local musician Agustín Lara's belongings, furniture and memorabilia in his old city residence, 4km south of the center.

Seafood by the Shore

Mariscos Villa Rica Mocambo $$$

Fish is the all-encompassing ingredient, from *camarones enchipotlados* (smoky chipotle shrimp) to stuffed sea bass, and the beachside location in Boca del Río is superb.

El Camarón Desvelado $$

The standout seafood restaurant in Tecolutla, serving platters of *arroz a la tumbada* (seafood rice with a tomato base), garlic shrimp and octopus in its own ink.

Restaurant Miriam $$

Family-run place just off Villa Rica beach, with delicious seafood dishes in what is essentially an extension of their living room. The *picantísimo* (spiciest) dishes are just that.

Fine Dining, Mexican Style

Namik $$$

Sleek, contemporary restaurant, helmed by chef Erik Guerrero, serving upscale gourmet food that's proudly Veracruzano. Tasting menu (M$960) available.

El Mesón Xiqueño $$

With a stunning courtyard setting in Xico, head here for the famous local *mole* (a rich sauce including seeds, many spices, nuts and dark chocolate) dishes, cooked to perfection.

JOSEPH SORRENTINO/SHUTTERSTOCK

Orchid, Museo de la Orquídea

Fussion $$$

In a venerable, highly atmospheric old timber house south of Veracruz's *zócalo*, Fussion delivers a winning contemporary take on Mexican cuisine.

Budget Eats & Treats

Tacos David $

Locals congregate around this beloved Veracruz taco spot that specializes in Yucateca-style *cochinita pibil* (slow-cooked pork) tacos served in a fragrant broth.

Mercado Hidalgo $

Head to this Veracruz market for cheap local cooking. **Tampico Mariscos** offers monster seafood cocktails *vuelve a la vida* ('come back to life' – a hangover remedy); **Los Michoacanos** serves fine meaty tacos.

Espacio Luciérnaga $

Homey, very welcoming vegetarian place offering healthy Mexican cuisine that's both delicious and nutritious. Family-run, 1km east of the main plaza.

YUCATÁN PENINSULA

BEACHES | TEMPLES | CENOTES

RESEARCHED BY REGIS ST LOUIS

- **Trip Builder** (p98)
- **Practicalities** (p100)
- **Undersea Adventures off Cozumel** (p102)
- **Mysteries of Chichén Itzá** (p104)
- **Beach-Hopping the Riviera Maya** (p106)
- **Swimming in Cenotes** (p108)
- **Wilderness Adventures in Calakmul** (p110)
- **Strolling Mérida's Historic Center** (p112)
- **Exploring Uxmal & the Ruta Puuc** (p114)
- **Maya Icons** (p116)
- **Maize & the Maya** (p118)
- **Return of the Jaguar** (p120)
- **Listings** (p122)

Learn about the Maya through evocative paintings in the **Palacio de Gobierno** (p113)

5min from Mérida

Wander past soaring temples dedicated to Maya gods at **Uxmal** (p114)

1¼hr from Mérida

Gaze across the rainforest from atop an ancient pyramid in **Calakmul** (p110; pictured right)

4hr from Campeche

YUCATÁN PENINSULA

Trip Builder

Only one destination can dazzle you with ancient Maya ruins, azure Caribbean waters and cobblestone-lined city centers in one fell swoop: the Yucatán Peninsula. Coral reefs and wildlife-filled jungles offer memorable adventures, though you'd be forgiven for focusing solely on those sun-kissed beaches.

CLOCKWISE FROM BOTTOM LEFT: ANGELA ARENAL/GETTY IMAGES, ARLETTE LOPEZ/SHUTTERSTOCK, SYLWIA K-SKA/SHUTTERSTOCK. PREVIOUS SPREAD: RICHIE CHAN/SHUTTERSTOCK

Practicalities

GEORGE WIRT/SHUTTERSTOCK

ARRIVING

Aeropuerto Internacional de Cancún The Yucatán's prime gateway. The airport has an ADO bus terminal and the **Tren Maya rail station** (pictured) is nearby: both connect to other Yucatán cities. ADO buses go downtown (M$140) and to the Zona Hotelera (M$140). Taxis cost US$60 to US$80.

Aeropuerto Internacional de Mérida A smaller airport, 7km southwest of Mérida's downtown. Hop on a Va y Ven Airport bus (M$45) to reach the **ADO terminal** in the historic center.

HOW MUCH FOR A

Street taco
M$30–40

Bag of churros
M$50

Margarita
M$120–200

WHEN TO GO

JAN–MAR
Slightly cooler temperatures and seaweed-free beaches draw holiday crowds.

APR–JUN
Seaweed covers Caribbean beaches; in mid-May, nesting sea turtles arrive.

JUL–SEP
Higher temperatures and more rain, plus the opportunity to swim with whale sharks.

OCT–DEC
Día de Muertos celebrations (November), plus Christmas celebrations – and feasting.

GETTING AROUND

Bus & colectivo It's easy to get between towns and cities on the Yucatán Peninsula, with an extensive network of buses. In some places (the Caribbean coast), *colectivos* (shared vans or taxis) provide fast, inexpensive transportation but are not ideal if you have sizable luggage.

Train The new Tren Maya (Maya Train) loops around the Yucatán Peninsula, linking major cities and Maya ruins (like Chichén Itzá and Calakmul) on three different routes.

Car Allows you to visit remote ruins and less developed areas in the interior and along the coast. Driving is challenging here: expect narrow roads, bad potholes, speed bumps and pricey car rentals and fuel.

TOP: GABRIELA CABALLERO/EYEEM/GETTY IMAGES
BOTTOM: LEON RAFAEL/GETTY IMAGES

EATING & DRINKING

The Yucatán is blessed with distinctive regional cuisine featuring ingredients not commonly used in other parts of Mexico, like *chaya* (a spinach-like leaf), sour oranges, toasted pumpkin seeds and *achiote* (annatto seeds that impart a red color and subtle nutty flavor). Highlights include *cochinita pibil* (marinated, slow-roasted pork often served on tacos; pictured top right), *papadzules* (sliced hard-boiled eggs wrapped in corn tortillas and topped with pumpkin seeds and tomato sauce; pictured bottom right) and *panuchos* (fried tortillas filled with beans and topped with chicken and veggies).

Best Yucatecan cooking
Museo de la Gastronomía Yucateca (p123)

Must-try mezcalita
La Guarida (p123)

CONNECT & FIND YOUR WAY

Wi-fi Most restaurants and cafes offer free wi-fi access. Purchase local SIM cards: Telcel has the best service in the Yucatán.

Navigation Most towns have a Plaza Principal at the center of town – and usually a tourism office nearby. Taxis rarely use meters; negotiate a fare before getting in.

WHERE TO STAY

Prices are high all along the Caribbean coast; save money by not staying right on the beach. Inland cities, including Mérida, are much better value.

Area	Pros/Cons
Cancún	Zona Hotelera has beautiful beachfront hotels, but can be very expensive and lacks local flavor.
Playa del Carmen	Options for all budgets, walking distance to beach. Bars in the area can be noisy.
Tulum	Walkable town center with shops and bars, but not very attractive and far from beach.
San Miguel de Cozumel	Good dining and shopping. You'll need a taxi or car rental to reach the beach.
Mérida	Historic center is a great base for exploring. Streets can be noisy.

SKIPPING SUNSCREEN

Most cenotes and aquatic reserves (including coral reefs) prohibit the use of sunscreen. Use a rash shirt or long-sleeve swimwear instead.

MONEY

Most restaurants and shops take credit cards but have pesos handy for the market and admission to cenotes (natural pools); many accept cash only. Save money by foregoing car rental (US$50 per day) and using public transportation.

10 Undersea Adventures off COZUMEL

CORAL | TOADFISH | SEA TURTLES

Let us be the first (of many) to tell you that the Mesoamerican Reef is the second-largest reef system in the world, stretching from the Yucatán down to Honduras. Not surprisingly, the diving here is world-class, particularly off the island of Cozumel. You can go for easy-going snorkeling trips right off the beach or head out on bigger adventures on multi-site excursions by boat.

How to

Getting here & around Ferries (Ultramar and Winjet) travel from Playa del Carmen hourly from 8am to 10pm.

When to go Cozumel is a year-round diving destination, though you'll find fewer crowds and ideal conditions in March and April.

Costs Four-hour snorkel trips cost M$1100; a two-tank dive costs M$2600.

Driving the island Book an old VW convertible with Rentadora Isis for a DIY island adventure.

Snorkeling the Reef

Lots of visitors to Cozumel rent snorkel gear and putter around the accessible sites just off the island and in front of beach clubs. **Buccanos**, **Skyreef** and **Playa Palancar** all have fine snorkeling right off the beach, as does **Anémona de Mar** *(anemonademarbeach.com)* inside the eco-reserve **Punta Sur**.

To see even more marine life, you'll want to book a boating excursion. Tour operators like **Cozumel Snorkel Center** *(cozumelsnorkelcenter.com)* offer frequent trips to lively snorkel spots on the south part of the island. You'll visit the translucent sea star bath at El Cielo, swim above massive, sponge-covered coral buttresses (and the occasional sea turtle and barracuda) at Colombia Gardens, and explore Palancar Shallows with its stunning underwater gardens of coral, sponges, fish, turtles, rays and eels.

BRENT DURAND/GETTY IMAGES

Deeper Explorations

Cozumel's dive sites offer fantastic year-round visibility (30m or more) and an eye-popping variety of marine life. A few standout spots include **Santa Rosa Wall**, a famous, plunging wall with overhangs and swim-throughs, and abundant coral and sponges. **El Cedral Pass** is a shallow drift dive that covers a vibrant reef teeming with marine life, including splendid toadfish, which are endemic to Cozumel. Cave lovers should book a dive to **Palancar Caves**, with fascinating subterranean caverns and canyons to explore. There are scores of dive operators on the island, including **ScubaTony** *(scubatony.com)*, **Aldora Divers** and **Miri Adventures** at **Casa Samay**.

Unusual & Amazing Dive Sites

Cave of the Sleeping Sharks North of the island, this site is a must-do for shark lovers. There are several caves where you can find 2m Caribbean reef sharks. Some are in a sleep-like state; others are wide awake. The season to see them is wintertime.

Eagle Ray Wall Also north of the island, local divers monitor eagle rays, which are best viewed in the summer. We have seen groups of up to 40 traveling together.

Recommended by Miranda Ríos González, *Cozumel scuba guide and owner of tour company Miri Adventures. @miri_adventures*

Above Divers over the Palancar reef, Cozumel

11 Mysteries of CHICHÉN ITZÁ

TEMPLES | CARVINGS | ASTRONOMY

The most famous of the Yucatán Maya sites, Chichén Itzá will impress even the most jaded visitor. Stretching across 10 sq km, the great city was once home to an estimated 50,000 people during its peak over 900 years ago. Today, the site is home to an astonishing array of ruins, including one peaceful region of temples, of which few visitors are aware.

How to

Getting here & around First-class ADO buses from Cancún, Tulum and other major towns drop you off right at the entrance.

When to go Chichén Itzá is always busy, but get there before opening time and you'll have a few hours before the majority of the tour buses arrive.

Cost Admission is M$648.

Noches de Kukulkán Wednesday through Sunday evenings, you can catch an impressive **sound and light show** *(nochesdekukulkan.com.mx; M$772)*.

Cenote Sagrado
El Castillo
Chichén Itzá
Cenote Xtoloc
El Caracol
Chichén Viejo
0 200 m
0 0.1 miles

Calendar in Stone

Chichén Itzá's greatest attraction is the soaring **El Castillo**. The structure is actually a massive Maya calendar. Each of El Castillo's nine levels is divided in two by a staircase, making 18 separate terraces that commemorate the eighteen 20-day months of the Maya Vague Year. The four stairways have 91 steps each; add the top platform and the total is 365, the number of days in the year. On each facade of the pyramid are 52 flat panels, which are reminders of the 52 years in the Maya calendar round.

Observatory

El Caracol is another one of Chichén Itzá's fascinating buildings. Masks of the Maya rain god Chaac adorn four external doors facing the cardinal points, while the windows in the observatory's dome are aligned with the appearance of certain stars at specific dates. From the dome, the priests may have decreed the times for rituals, celebrations and harvests.

RUI VALE SOUSA/SHUTTERSTOCK

Cenote Secrets

Around the year 1900, Edward Thompson, a Harvard professor and US consul to Yucatán, bought the hacienda that included Chichén Itzá and set to work dredging the Sacred Cenote. Gold and jade jewelry from all parts of Mexico and as far away as Colombia was recovered, along with other artifacts and a variety of human bones. It appears that all sorts of people – children and old people, the sick and the injured, and the young and healthy – were forcibly obliged to take an eternal swim in Chichén's Cenote Sagrado. Reach the cenote by walking about 400m north from the Plataforma de Venus.

Chichén Viejo

Don't tell anyone, but there's a part of Chichén Itzá that's delightfully free from the tourist crowds. **Chichén Viejo** features 25 little-seen structures set around two plazas. The catch: it's a long walk (1.5km) from the main site. It's also only open Fridays and Saturdays on guided tours (at 9am and noon) and limited to just 50 visitors. Go early to secure a spot; reserve when buying tickets at the main Chichén Itzá entrance.

Above El Caracol

Beach-Hopping the RIVIERA MAYA

SAND | SUN | SEA

White sand beaches, palm trees, turquoise waters: the Riviera Maya is the stuff of daydreams. Enchanting places to relax or frolic in the sea, idyllic shores dot the coast from Cancún to Tulum, but a handful of these photogenic spots stand out above all others. Start your Caribbean adventures by these three beaches, which are not well known but are still easy to reach from nearby towns.

How to

Getting here & around You need a car (or taxi) to reach Isla Blanca. For Playa del Carmen and Tulum, take a bus or train.

When to go Seaweed can mar beaches from April to September. November and March have pleasant weather and fewer crowds.

Bicycle power The best way to reach Punta Esmeralda or Playa Pescadores is by bicycle.

Virgin Shoreline

Despite the name, **Isla Blanca** is not an island but a peninsula, stretching north from Cancún for some 25km. At the end of the road (literally), it is barely more than a strip of sand, topped with sea scrub, and flanked by a shallow lagoon on one side and the Caribbean blue on the other. While busy with families on weekends, at other times, the place is nearly deserted. It is, possibly, your only opportunity for seaside solitude on the Yucután's entire Caribbean coast.

Blue Flag Beauty

Some 4km north of Playa del Carmen's bustling epicenter, **Punta Esmeralda** feels like an idyllic escape with soft white sand and crystalline waters. There's a small natural pool, which makes a fine spot for kids (or adults) to

Top right Laguna Bacalar
Bottom right Punta Esmeralda

ANNA EWA BIENIEK/SHUTTERSTOCK

Lagoon Life

To visit the region's most beautiful spot that's not on the coast, head south for some nature time at **Laguna Bacalar**. Known as the 'lagoon of seven colors,' the peninsula's largest lagoon has an astonishing color palette of blues and greens. The namesake town of **Bacalar** sits right on the water, and you can start your day with an early morning paddle while watching the sunrise over the lagoon. Later you can look for birds on the shoreline, go sailing or just relax on the shore. **Cocalitos** is a lovely spot for swimming and stretching out in a waterside hammock.

splash about. Hidden in the jungle is a tiny cenote and nearby marsh where you can spot reddish egrets and other birds early or late in the day.

Sands Near Maya Ruins

Sitting practically in the shadow of Tulum's ancient ruins, **Playa Pescadores** has a handful of beach-club restaurants where you can rent lounge chairs and sip cocktails while digging your heels in the sands. It's also a magical spot for long strolls along the shoreline. When you're ready for a bit more activity, boat captains lead trips out to the reef for short snorkeling excursions.

ARKADIJ SCHELL/SHUTTERSTOCK

13 Swimming in CENOTES

NATURE | DIVING | CAVES

A uniquely Yucatecan geological feature, cenotes (from the Maya word *d'zonot*) are sinkholes formed by the erosive effects of rainwater filtering down through the porous limestone. Thousands of cenotes dot the peninsula landscape. Some are set in stalactite-filled caverns, others are open and fringed with jungle-like greenery, but all have cool, crystalline waters that offer enchanting refreshment on hot days.

ACHINTHAMB/SHUTTERSTOCK

How to

Getting here & around It's handy to rent a car to reach the cenotes around the peninsula; the least crowded are well away from busy towns.

When to go There's no bad time to visit, as cenotes are open year-round. You'll find fewer crowds if you avoid the high season months of December and January.

How much? All cenotes are privately owned, with admission charges ranging from M$200 to upwards of M$1000.

SL-PHOTOGRAPHY/SHUTTERSTOCK

Top left Cenote Zaci **Bottom left** Cenote at Hacienda Mucuyché

Driving the Ruta de los Cenotes

Near the coastal town of Puerto Morelos, the Ruta de los Cenotes is a jungle-lined road (aka Hwy 307) passing over a dozen enchanting swimming spots. Rent a car and set out early for a day of exploring, stopping for swims and jungle adventures. A good place to start is **Siete Bocas**, which has *siete* (seven) different *bocas* (openings), allowing you to experience both cavern cenotes and open-air swimming spots.

Deeper Adventures

Some cenotes are so large that they're ideal for snorkeling or even scuba diving. Some 30 minutes' drive north of Tulum, the **Dos Ojos** ('two eyes') are openings into the gargantuan underground river feeding a series of spectacular cenotes. On sunny days, the waters take on a sapphire blue hue. You can explore on your own, but you'll get more out of a guided snorkeling excursion (arranged on-site). Certified divers can explore underwater caverns; book with reputable **La Calypso** in Tulum.

Off the Beaten Track

The inland city of Mérida lies within easy reach of countless hidden wonders. Amid the ruins of an 18th-century estate known as **Hacienda Mucuyché**, you can swim through a verdant vine-fringed canal and then visit two cavern cenotes. Or escape the crowds at little-known cenotes like **X'Batún** and **Dzonbakal** with their remote location (the dirt road there is rough, but a regular car can make it) and jungle-like setting.

Cenote Essentials

In an effort to protect the ecosystem and keep pollutants out of the water, sunscreens are banned at most cenotes. Signs will remind visitors to shower off those chemicals before entering. In open cenotes, wear a rash shirt to avoid getting sunburned. Bigger cenotes rent snorkel gear and life vests, but if you plan on visiting a few cenotes while you're here, it's worthwhile investing in your own snorkel mask so you can look for turtles and small fish. Another thing you may want is a pair of water shoes for safely walking the rocky surfaces that often encircle these water holes.

Wilderness Adventures in CALAKMUL

JUNGLE | WILDLIFE | TEMPLES

The jewel of the southern Yucatán is Calakmul, seat of the fearsome 'Snake Kingdom,' which was a Maya superpower throughout the Classic period. Set amid the lush forests of the Reserva de la Biosfera Calakmul, the ancient ruins are replete with temples and lofty pyramids. Calakmul is also the gateway for adventurous overland travel to little-visited ruins hidden deep in the jungle.

JON ORTIZ/SHUTTERSTOCK

How to

Getting here & around A car is essential here. Although you can get here by train (Calakmul station) or bus (Xpujil), you'll then have to book a tour to reach any of the ruins.

When to go Avoid the rainy season (May to October), when roads can be impassable and heat, humidity and mosquitos can be intense.

Wildlife Incredible, particularly when it comes to birds, with more than 350 avian species.

MAURIZIO PHOTO/SHUTTERSTOCK

Top left Calakmul **Bottom left** Cueva de los Murciélagos

Enter the Snake Kingdom

It's a 60km drive through the jungles of the **Reserva de la Biosfera Calakmul** to reach the magnificent ruins of **Calakmul**, the Snake Kingdom. Thousands of structures remain from the city's heyday (from 250 to 900 CE). Many are excavated and open for exploration and climbing, including three incredible pyramids that tower above the treetops. Wildlife also plays a starring role. Keep an eye out for ocellated turkeys, coatis, agoutis and spider monkeys.

Calakmul's Best Nature Show

The **Cueva de los Murciélagos** is better known as Volcán de los Murciélagos ('bat volcano'). This dry cenote is home to about two million bats, who emerge en masse at dusk. Thus, the volcano. It's an incredible sight, as the sky fills with bats within a matter of minutes.

Calling Indiana Jones

For a taste of old-fashioned thrills, local guides take adventurous travelers on rough roads to **Río Bec**, a remote site, deep in the forest southeast of Xpujil. Traveling by pick-up truck, ATV or motorbike, it takes more than an hour to cover the 15km, bouncing over ruts, sloshing through puddles and crashing through trees. Once you arrive, you can explore two main groups of ruins, with classic Río Bec architectural details deep in the jungle. You'll need a guide to visit Río Bec. Your best bet is English-speaking Ezequiel Cauich, also known as **Río Bec Explore** (*riobecexplore.com*).

Wildlife in the Biosphere

At El Ramonal Or, around Km 27, a 2km loop leads through howler monkey territory. At Km 20, there is a 2km out-and-back trail where you see plenty of birds, including toucans, orioles, trogons and woodpeckers, as well as mammals like monkeys, coatis and agoutis. If you're lucky, you might spot peccaries and deer, or even a puma or a jaguar. This trail is open to the public, but you need a guide because it is hard to follow.

Ezequiel Cauich, *a naturalist and archaeology guide, shares his favorite places to spot wildlife. @ezequielcauichcauich*

15 Strolling Mérida's HISTORIC CENTER

ARCHITECTURE | PLAZAS | MURALS

Take a walk into the past by exploring the centuries-old buildings and leafy squares of the historic center. The Yucatán's most vibrant city was founded in 1542, though its roots date back even earlier, when it was an ancient Maya settlement known as Ichcaanzihó.

ECSTK22/SHUTTERSTOCK

Trip Notes

Getting here & around It's a pleasant four-hour train ride from Cancún aboard the Tren Maya. Mérida airport has direct flights to North America and major cities in Mexico.

When to go The temperatures are more bearable from December to April, and there's a packed calendar of cultural events.

Yucatecan cooking Indulge in foods not found in other regions of Mexico, like *relleno negro* (a stew made of turkey and charred chilies).

Dancing at Plaza Santiago

Santiago is a popular neighborhood with a church, free activities at night and a famous market. On Tuesdays at 8:30pm, you can enjoy free music at the **plaza**. A local orchestra plays the old-time music of *danzón*, and it's a beautiful occasion to dance and meet locals.

Recommended by Andrea Mier y Teran, *director at Yucatán Today. @yucatantoday*

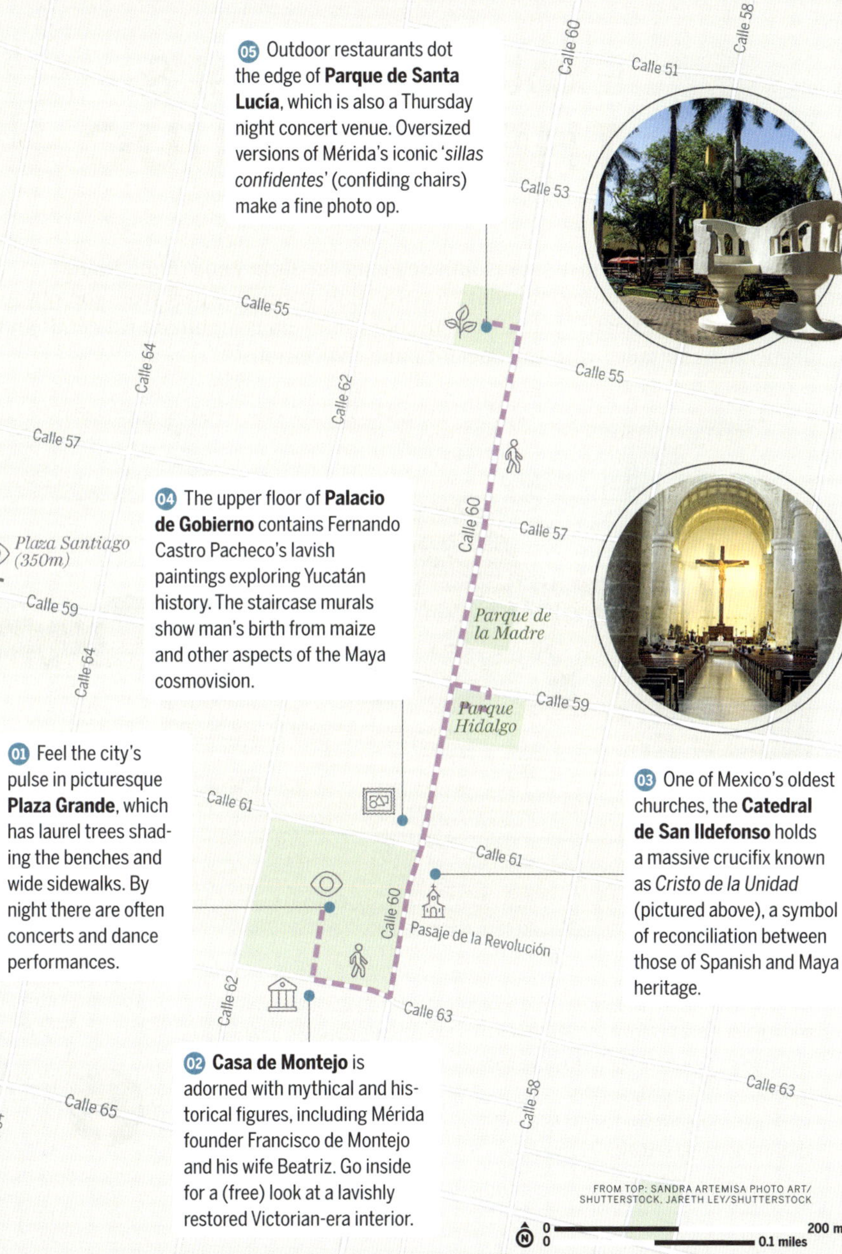

05 Outdoor restaurants dot the edge of **Parque de Santa Lucía**, which is also a Thursday night concert venue. Oversized versions of Mérida's iconic '*sillas confidentes*' (confiding chairs) make a fine photo op.

04 The upper floor of **Palacio de Gobierno** contains Fernando Castro Pacheco's lavish paintings exploring Yucatán history. The staircase murals show man's birth from maize and other aspects of the Maya cosmovision.

01 Feel the city's pulse in picturesque **Plaza Grande**, which has laurel trees shading the benches and wide sidewalks. By night there are often concerts and dance performances.

03 One of Mexico's oldest churches, the **Catedral de San Ildefonso** holds a massive crucifix known as *Cristo de la Unidad* (pictured above), a symbol of reconciliation between those of Spanish and Maya heritage.

02 **Casa de Montejo** is adorned with mythical and historical figures, including Mérida founder Francisco de Montejo and his wife Beatriz. Go inside for a (free) look at a lavishly restored Victorian-era interior.

FROM TOP: SANDRA ARTEMISA PHOTO ART/SHUTTERSTOCK, JARETH LEY/SHUTTERSTOCK

16 Exploring Uxmal & THE RUTA PUUC

GODS | MASKS | CAVERNS

Uxmal is the most important site along the Ruta Puuc (Puuc Route), a forested region of rolling hills dotted with Maya temples. Apart from the rewards of getting off the beaten track, the sites offer marvelous architectural detail and a deeper acquaintance with the ancient Puuc civilization.

ANTON_IVANOV/SHUTTERSTOCK

Trip Notes

Getting here & around Mérida (a 1¼ hour drive to Uxmal) is a handy gateway and a good place to rent a car, which you'll need to properly explore this region.

When to go Visit from March to November to avoid the high heat, humidity and downpours of the rainy season.

Stay in the jungle Near Santa Elena, you can overnight in eco-friendly bungalows in a forested setting at Nueva Altía.

The Sacred Ceiba

To the Maya, the ceiba tree (Yax'ché) symbolized a communication link between the three levels of the universe. The lower part of the trunk can appear swollen, which to the Maya was symbolic of a pregnant woman or even Mother Earth.

Recommended by Felipe A Fuentes, *Sotuta de Peón guide and historian. @haciendasotutadepeon*

01 First settled about 600 CE, **Uxmal** was influenced by highland Mexico in its architecture. Note the feathered serpent (Quetzalcóatl, or in Maya, Kukulcán) motif in the **Cuadrángulo de las Monjas**.

02 In the small peaceful village of **Santa Elena**, you can see unusual mummified infants and learn about syncretic burial traditions (Maya-Catholic) in the small **Museo de las Momias**.

03 **Kabah** is home to the impressive **Palacio de los Mascarones** (Palace of the Masks; pictured right). The facade is an amazing sight, covered in nearly 300 masks of Chaac, the rain god.

04 **Sayil** has some extraordinary sights, like the three-tiered 85m-long building of **El Palacio** (pictured left) adorned with friezes of 'diving gods' (look for the upturned legs) on the second story.

05 In addition to a fantastical mask-covered temple, **Labná** is known for a magnificent 6m-high arch (the finest in the Maya world) with reliefs decorating its upper facade in exuberant Puuc style.

FROM LEFT: BELIKOVA OKSANA/SHUTTERSTOCK, CK-TRAVELPHOTOS/SHUTTERSTOCK

Maya
ICONS

01 Maize
Corn is the building block of Maya civilization, in myriad foodstuffs and origin stories – indeed, the gods made people from maize.

02 Casa Maya
The traditional home has a high thatched roof and rounded, adobe walls (stays cool and is more resistant to hurricanes).

03 Ceiba
The most sacred of trees and three-part symbol of the universe: roots (underworld), trunk (human land) and branches (heavens).

04 Kukulkán
The feathered serpent is one of the most powerful of Maya deities, and his cult is deeply associated with Chichén Itzá.

05 Chac Mool
A reclining male figure holding a bowl in his lap, which may have been used for sacrificial offerings.

06 Cenote
In a land with few lakes and rivers, cenotes serve as vital water

sources and sacred entrances to the underworld.

07 Chaac
The Maya god of the rain is easily identified by his large hooked nose; Maya farmers made offerings in times of drought.

08 Pok-Ta-Pok
An ancient game where opposing teams tried to get a ball through a stone hoop without using hands or feet.

09 Ixchel
The goddess of the moon, associated with childbirth; in pre-Hispanic times, young women made a pilgrimage to her shrine on Cozumel.

10 Cacao
Beans to make chocolate were sacred to the Maya, and used in medicines, ceremonies and commerce.

01 MARCOS CASTILLO/SHUTTERSTOCK, **02** LEON RAFAEL/SHUTTERSTOCK, ©, **03** ARKADIJ SCHELL/SHUTTERSTOCK, **04** JIMMY LIPPI PINNA/SHUTTERSTOCK, **05** DARIO LO PRESTI/SHUTTERSTOCK, **06** TIAGO FIALHO/SHUTTERSTOCK, **07** BELIKOVA OKSANA/SHUTTERSTOCK, **08** NIK WALLER PRODUCTIONS/SHUTTERSTOCK, **09** ROSEMARIE MOSTELLE/SHUTTERSTOCK, **10** REBECAZ/SHUTTERSTOCK

Maize & the Maya

CORN PLAYS A STARRING ROLE IN THE YUCATÁN

The people of the Yucatán simply wouldn't be the same without maize. It was the building block of their society, and it fueled the growth of huge ancient cities like Chichén Itzá. Today, maize still plays an essential role in the contemporary Maya palate, with a wealth of corn-based dishes and even drinks.

Left Women making tortillas **Centre** Tamales **Right** Mural by Fernando Castro Pacheco depicting a Maya man emerging from an ear of corn as described in the *Popol Vuh*, the sacred book of the Maya. The mural is in the Palacio de Gobierno, Mérida

LEON RAFAEL/SHUTTERSTOCK

Seeds of Civilization

Although it might at first glance seem like an odd choice for a human building block, corn was one of the most important living things to the ancestral Maya. There are about 60 different varieties of corn, all cultivated from a wild grass known as teosinte, grown in southern Mexico over 8700 years ago. Corn grew well in the climate, was easily stored and could feed huge numbers of people. Byproducts could also be used: corncobs were burned for fuel or fed to livestock and the fibers of husks were used in basketry and craft-making.

The essential foodstuff could be prepared in numerous different ways, from porridge-like concoctions for breakfast to heartier dishes of corn flour mixed with meats and baked in underground ovens or even in alcoholic drinks like pox (pronounced 'posh'). The staple grain provided some 70% of the diet, and it was also used in medicine. Even today, corn plays a pivotal role in Yucatecan cooking, and it's still celebrated in big events, like Mérida's Pueblos del Maíz festival. Some of the year's most important gatherings have dishes featuring maize, like tamales, eaten during Día de Muertos, and *atole* (a corn-based beverage with cinnamon, vanilla and sugar), served around Christmas.

Corn also lies at the root of the Maya language. Despite the many variations among the 32 different Maya languages spoken today, the word for corn, *ixim*, is nearly identical to the ear in all of them.

SERGIO HAYASHI/SHUTTERSTOCK

REGIS ST LOUIS

Rituals & Legends

The supernatural was woven into Maya beliefs and everyday practices, and harvest time was no exception. This is perhaps not surprising given that corn was seen as a divine gift. Among the many gods the Maya worshipped was Hun Hunahpu, the god of maize and the father of the Hero Twins. According to tradition, he was decapitated every harvest time and returned to life at the start of the next planting season. The Maya would pray to the god for a fruitful season as well as a good life, since corn wasn't merely an agricultural product but also represented the cycle of human life and stood at the very essence of their existence.

The supernatural was woven into Maya beliefs and everyday practices, and harvest time was no exception.

Chaac, the god of rain, was another important deity, especially in parts of the Yucatán lacking in natural water sources (like Uxmal and the Puuc region). For a culture dependent on farming, too much or too little precipitation could mean the difference between life and death for entire communities. On temples throughout the peninsula, geometrical figureheads portray Chaac with a large trunk-like nose and an open mouth dotted with fangs. His name featured prominently at harvest rituals held before the planting season in March. The Maya made offerings to him at the Chichén Itzá's sacred cenote where he was said to reside. Still today, farmers on *milpas* (traditional plots) in the south of the Yucatán gather to conduct a special ritual in the springtime.

Humans from Corn

The gods first fashioned humans out of mud, but these beings were weak and simply dissolved in water. The second attempt, involving wood, succeeded on a superficial level, but these people had no hearts or minds and could not praise their creator, so they too were destroyed. In a final effort, the deities used white and yellow maize, mixed it with water and mashed it into a paste. Corn turned out to be the missing ingredient for creating a successful human being. This is the crux of the creation story according to the *Popol Vuh*, sometimes referred to as the Maya Bible.

Return of the Jaguar

DESPITE THREATS, JAGUARS STILL ROAM THE JUNGLES

Revered by the ancient Maya, the jaguar is making a surprising comeback in Mexico thanks to bold conservation initiatives. Local Maya communities play a vital role in the jaguar's return, and are taking part in wildlife monitoring and forest management, with sustainable industries helping to ensure the animal's long-term survival.

Left Jaguar **Centre** View of the Calakmul Biosphere Reserve **Right** Temple of the Jaguar, Chichén Itzá

PATRYK KOSMIDER/SHUTTERSTOCK

Brighter Days for the Jaguar

The world's third-largest feline once roamed a vast territory on two continents: stretching across much of North America all the way down to the southern reaches of Patagonia. Over the last two centuries, however, the jaguar's territory has shrunk to less than half of its initial domain. Deforestation, expanding cities and hunting have all led to precipitous declines of the native population.

Mexico contains less than 3% of the global jaguar population, but the outlook is no longer as bleak as it once was. Over the last two decades, a coalition of environmentalists, local communities and NGOs have been working hard to help bring the animal back from the edge of extinction. Back in 2005, the ecologist Dr Gerardo Ceballos founded the National Alliance for Jaguar Conservation (ANCJ). He and a team of 20 other scientists across the country made comprehensive studies of the jaguar and helped develop conservation strategies to stabilize the jaguar population.

Small communities were instrumental in the success of the project. In some areas, the government paid people not to deforest wildlife sanctuaries, reimbursed them for the loss of livestock caused by jaguar predation and provided them with electric fences to prevent future attacks on their properties. 'Local people have been critical,' Dr Ceballos told a reporter from Mongabay in 2021. 'When they have the funding and incentives to protect the forest, they become the most important ally.'

In 2018, the alliance took a census of the jaguar population. Dr Ceballos expected the results to show a small decline of jaguar numbers or at best a trend toward stabilization of the population. Instead, the results were much

GILLIAN HOLLIDAY/SHUTTERSTOCK

LUDOVIC FARINE/SHUTTERSTOCK

more impressive. Over an eight-year span, the population grew by 20% in Mexico, with some 4766 jaguars in the country – up from 4025 in 2010. It was a clear indication that the bold strategies were working.

The Power of Conservation

Environmentalists noted that the benefits weren't limited to the big cats. 'The jaguar is an umbrella species,' Morato told the *New York Times* in 2021. 'By protecting the jaguar, you are protecting everything else.'

In the Yucatán, that 'everything else' can mean an astonishing array of animal life. The Calakmul Biosphere Reserve (p111) is one of the most biodiverse regions on Earth, with 70,000 plant and animal species – including the highest concentration of jaguars in Mexico. In 2022, the Mexican government in partnership with ANCJ announced plans to expand the reserve, and in the last few years it has grown from 723,000 hectares to more than 1.5 million hectares. This makes Calakmul the largest protected intact tropical forest in the Americas outside of the Amazon basin.

> Calakmul is the largest protected intact tropical forest in the Americas outside of the Amazon basin.

In 2024, Mexico's federally run National Commission of Natural Protected Areas Mexico (CONANP) conducted a jaguar census across 460,000 hectares, and the results have been promising. The big cat population has remained stable or even increased slightly in some areas since the last completed census in 2018.

Jaguar of the Ancient World

For the ancient Maya royals, using the symbol of the jaguar was akin to conferring divinity. Rulers wrapped themselves in the spotted hide to show their inherent strength or sat on thrones carved in the shape of the roaring animal. During coronations in **Chichén Itzá**, Maya kings walked beneath a frieze of great cats carved on the aptly named **Temple of the Jaguar**. One fortified city was even named after the animal: **Ek' Balam**, meaning 'Jaguar Star.' There was also a mysterious element: some said looking at the jaguar's skin was like staring into the starry night sky.

Listings

BEST OF THE REST

Aquatic Adventures

Tsúuk Akumal Parque Natural

This small protected reserve south of Akumal is a prime spot for snorkeling with sea turtles. Book an excursion with **Marine Life Akumal** or **Akumal Dive Shop**.

Subaquatic Art Museum

The **Museo Subacuático de Arte** (MUSA) is an underwater sculpture garden with 500 works of art that also function as artificial reefs. Experience this otherworldly sight on a diving trip with **Solo Buceo** or **Scuba Cancún**.

Yum Balam Nature Reserve

From May to September, the reserve near **Isla Holbox** draws whale sharks who come to feed in these plankton-rich waters. Snorkel with these magnificent creatures on a tour offered by **VIP Holbox**.

Jungle Activities

Punta Laguna

An hour's drive from Tulum, take a guided forest hike in search of monkeys and go zip lining over a lagoon. Punta Laguna is run by a small Maya community.

Cobá Ruins

Dense greenery lines the dirt paths of Cobá, an impressive archaeological site 45 minutes from Tulum. Rent a bike on site and pedal past ancient temples and pyramids.

Jardín Botánico Dr Alfredo Barrera Marín

Near Puerto Morelos, this 65-hectare forest reserve has a fascinating array of plant species. Reliable place to spot coati (a raccoon-like creature) and spider monkeys.

Pro Seal

From Bacalar, join a one-of-a-kind guided bicycling tour out to Maya communities, with forest stops and wildlife-watching opportunities. Contact via WhatsApp: +52 983-1565413.

Idyllic Islands

Isla Mujeres

A 40-minute ferry ride from Cancún takes you to an island where the pace slows considerably, the sand is finer, and the waters are somehow even more turquoise.

Isla Contoy

Take a day trip from Cancún to spend the day at a gorgeous palm-fringed beach while keeping an eye out for 170 avian species.

Isla Holbox

Two hours north of Cancún, car-free Holbox draws an adventurous crowd to beachfront yoga, kayaking through wetlands, and sunset cocktails.

Biosphere Reserves

Sian Ka'an

Just south of Tulum, marine and shoreline ecosystems offer the chance to spy dolphins, sea turtles and birds. Various outfits run boat tours including Tours Sian Ka'an and Mexico Kan Tours.

Ría Lagartos

Head to the north coast for a boating trip to see Mexico's highest concentration of flamingos. Arrange an excursion through conservation-minded Río Lagartos Adventures.

Ría Celestún

From the Gulf Coast town of Celestún, enter a wildlife sanctuary of mangrove tunnels and lagoons, with huge flocks of flamingos (February to April). Book a low-impact visit with ecotourism pioneers Guardianes de los Manglares de Dzinitún. Contact via WhatsApp: +52 999-6454310.

Maya Museums

Museo Maya de Cancún

Cancún's Maya Museum contains a trove of archaeological artifacts: jade and obsidian jewelry, pottery and stone carvings. Includes admission to a small adjoining archaeological site, San Miguelito.

Gran Museo de Chichén Itzá

Opened in 2024, this beautifully designed museum displays sculptures, figurines, pottery, jewelry and other Chichén Itzá artifacts that delve into the Maya cosmovision, daily life and religion. It's 2.5km from the main entrance to the ruins.

Gran Museo del Mundo Maya

Mérida is home to Mexico's best museum dedicated to the Maya, with more than 1100 remarkably well-preserved artifacts, as well as exhibitions on Maya culture, past and present.

Parque del Jaguar

Tulum's newly created nature reserve is home to archaeological ruins, beaches, short walking trails and a new sunlit museum that sheds light on mythology, burial traditions, astronomy and the Maya calendar.

Yucatecan Cooking

Museo de la Gastronomía Yucateca $

This iconic courtyard restaurant in Mérida fires up first-rate traditional plates of Yucatecan favorites, including *cochinita pibil* (slow-cooked pork with spices).

STACYARTUROGI/SHUTTERSTOCK

Isla Contoy

Mercado Santiago $

The markets of Mérida are among the peninsula's best places for authentic cooking. Plaza Santiago's market is a local favorite for *panuchos* (fried tortillas stuffed with black beans and topped with delicacies).

El Atrio del Mayab $

Reason enough to visit historic Valladolid, this place has a lovely garden-fringed courtyard where you can indulge in *tikin xic* (fish cooked in banana leaves) and other Yucatecan classics.

Tropical Cocktails

La Guarida

In Tulum, La Guarida makes a great hideaway for an evening of cocktails in a multilevel space, and there's often live music or vinyl-spinning DJs.

Zenzi Beach

The seaside beach club and restaurant in Playa del Carmen is an enticing place to sip well-made drinks on the sand. Live music most nights.

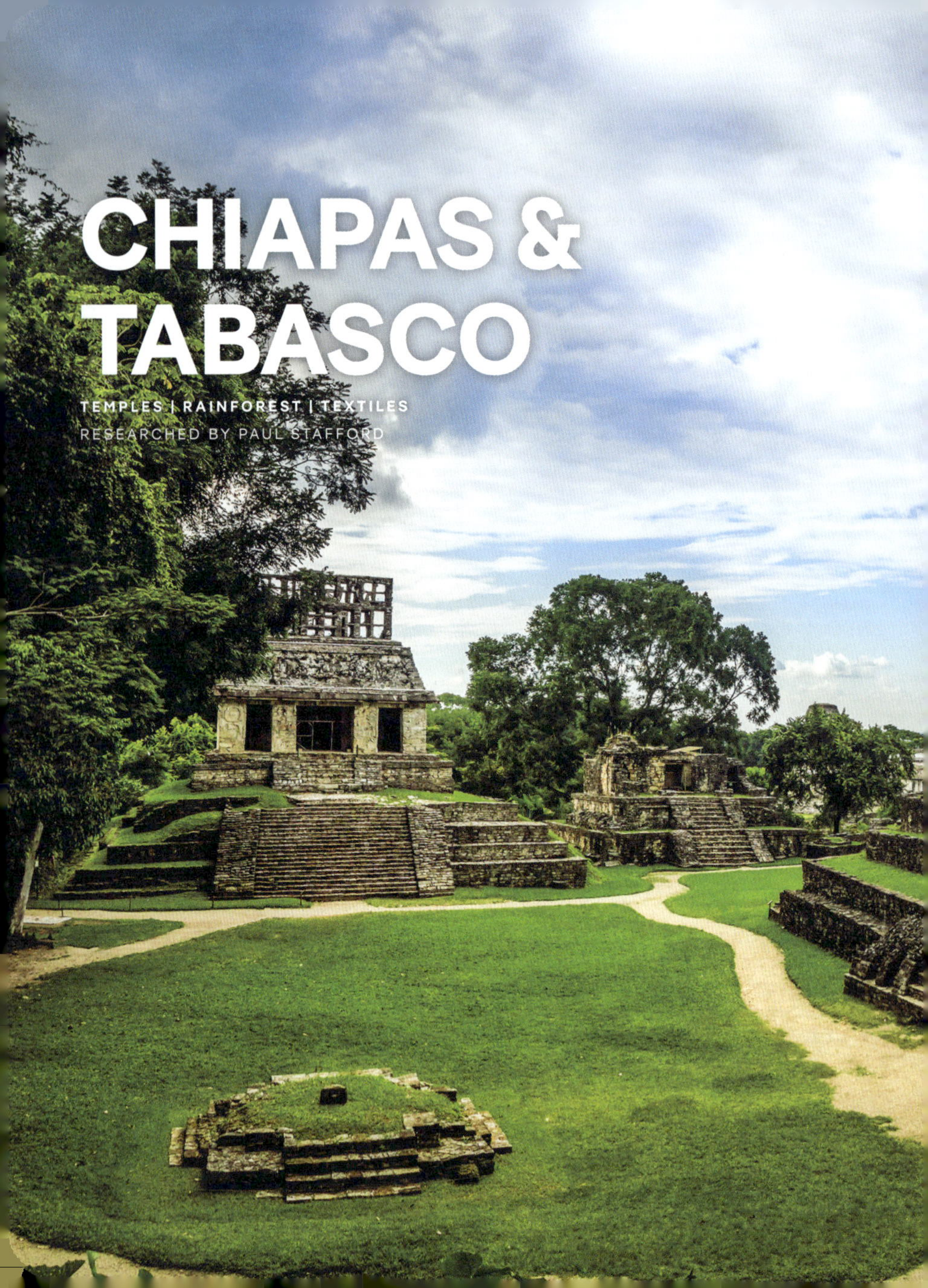

CHIAPAS & TABASCO

TEMPLES | RAINFOREST | TEXTILES

RESEARCHED BY PAUL STAFFORD

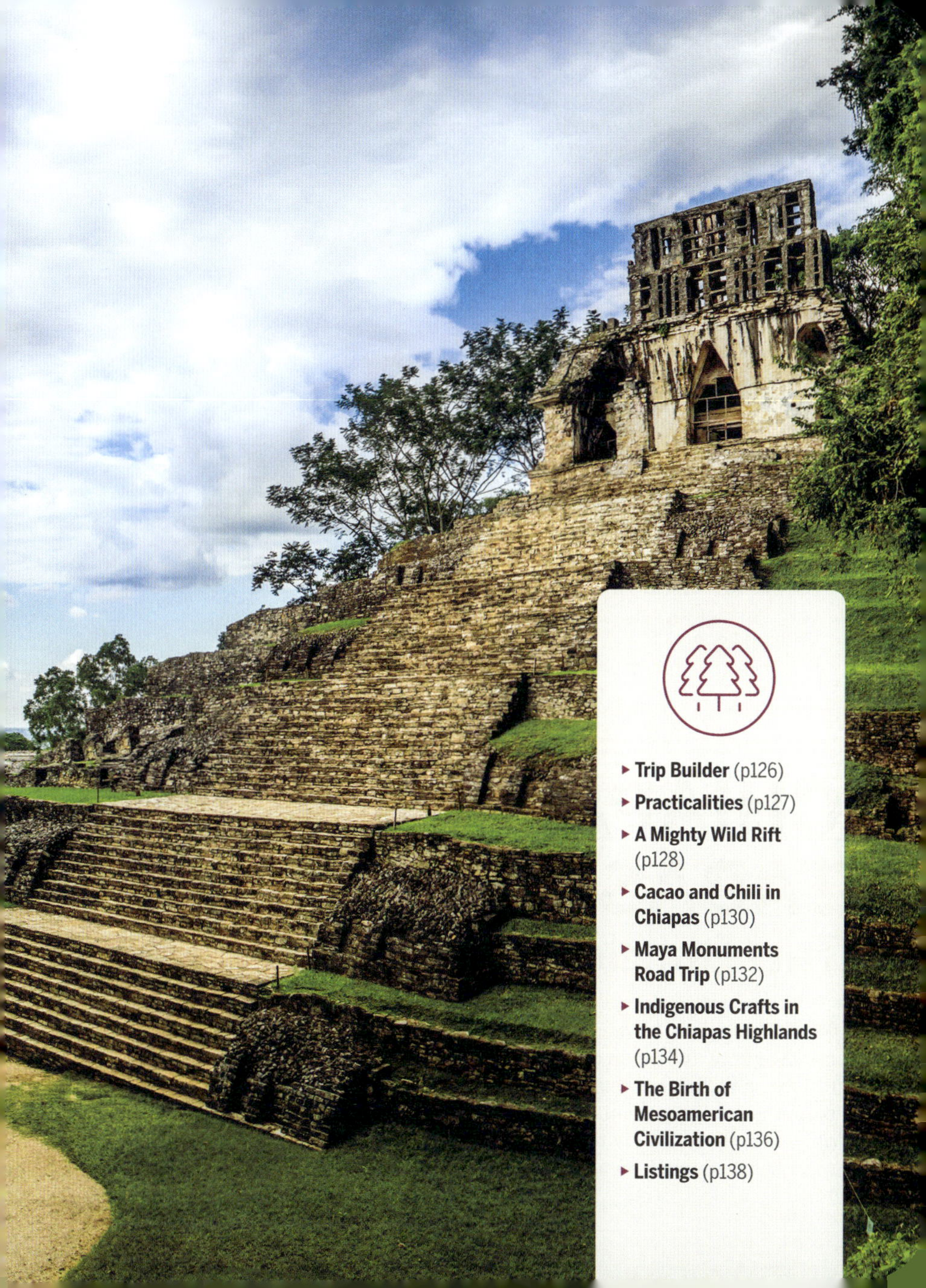

- **Trip Builder** (p126)
- **Practicalities** (p127)
- **A Mighty Wild Rift** (p128)
- **Cacao and Chili in Chiapas** (p130)
- **Maya Monuments Road Trip** (p132)
- **Indigenous Crafts in the Chiapas Highlands** (p134)
- **The Birth of Mesoamerican Civilization** (p136)
- **Listings** (p138)

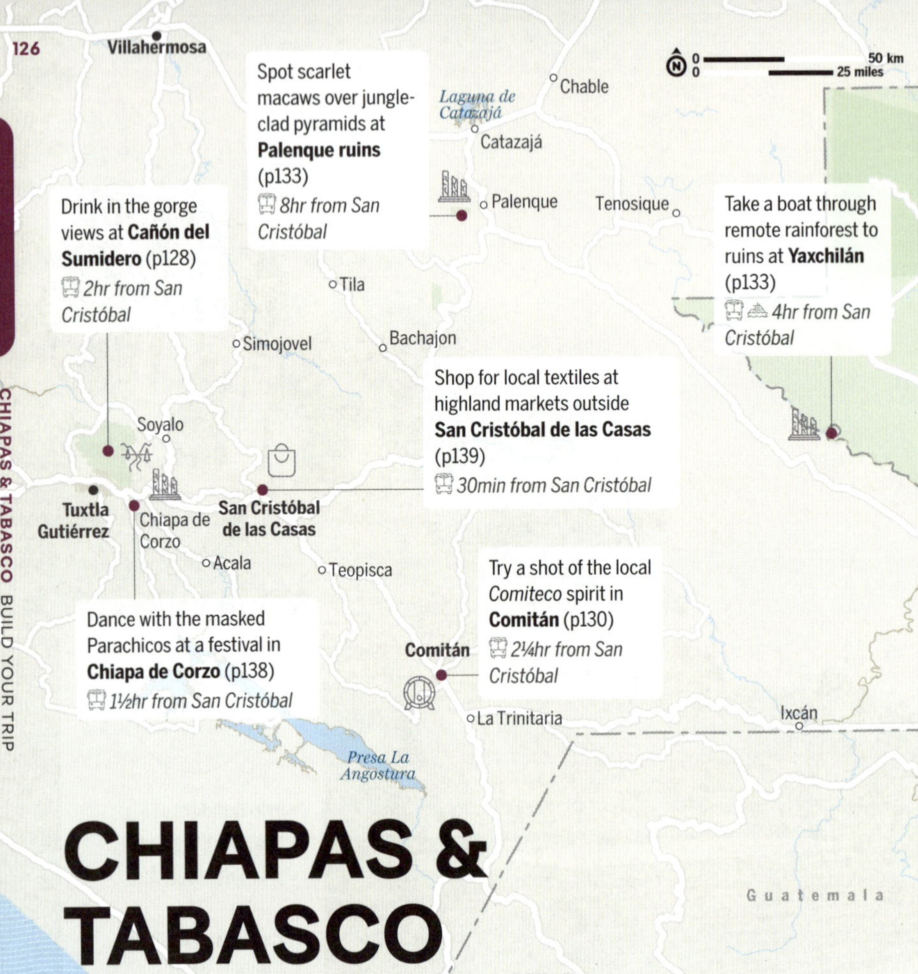

CHIAPAS & TABASCO
Trip Builder

Plunge into a waterfall pool, delve into a mighty gorge and connect with indigenous culture. Chiapas and Tabasco tempt with jungle adventure, pamper with unique cuisine and enthrall with otherworldly ruins. Then they give you somewhere to relax before doing it all again.

Practicalities

ARRIVING

Estación Palenque Trains arrive from the Yucatán.

Villahermosa International Airport and **Aeropuerto Ángel Albino Corzo** The closest airports are 12km away from Villahermosa and 31km from Tuxtla Gutiérrez.

FIND YOUR WAY

Guided tours to remote or primarily indigenous regions mean not worrying about local transport or falling foul of local customs.

MONEY

Cash rules in this region. ATMs are common in all bigger cities. Bring extra to cover you when visiting the remoter regions.

WHERE TO STAY

Neighborhood	Pros/Cons
San Cristóbal	Everything you'll need for a long-term stay. Expat scene is pushing up prices.
Palenque	Backpacker-friendly amenities. Can get very humid.
Comitán	Bargain accommodation in traditional highland mansions. Check security situation before staying.
Selva Lacandón	No-frills jungle escapes. Limited access to internet.

GETTING AROUND

Bus ADO buses provide a clean, reliable and regular way to move between the region's hubs.

Colectivo Legions of these small buses connect every single town, village and hamlet to the bigger cities.

Car Go at your own pace and to your own itinerary.

TOP: JROMERO04/SHUTTERSTOCK
BOTTOM: MARDOZ/SHUTTERSTOCK

EATING & DRINKING

Mole Originated in Chiapas, made with local ingredients like cacao and plantain (pictured top left: *mole* in powder form).

Chinculguajes Thick tortillas stuffed with beans, cilantro and chili.

Pozol Blends maize and cacao into an energizing drink (pictured bottom left) that has Olmec origins in Tabasco.

Best Coffee
Cafeología (p139)

Must-try Chinculguajes
Comitán (p130)

JAN–MAR
Dry, sunny days ideal for visiting Cañón del Sumidero.

APR–JUN
Semana Santa celebrations before the rainy season kicks in.

JUL–SEP
Tabasco and the rainforests see the highest levels of rain and humidity.

OCT–DEC
Cultural bounty at various festivals as the highlands cool.

17 A Mighty WILD RIFT

CANYONS | FESTIVALS | WILDLIFE

The wilderness north of Tuxtla Gutiérrez features one of North America's great canyons. Get above the Cañón del Sumidero and gaze out from gorge-rim viewpoints or scud over the silty Río Grijalva water, looking for crocodiles on a boat tour from Chiapa de Corzo. Visit in January and you can join in with Chiapa de Corzo's UNESCO World Heritage–listed festivities.

How to

Getting around *Colectivos* head to Chiapa de Corzo from San Cristóbal or Tuxtla. Rent a car or taxi to visit the rim.

When to go Chiapa de Corzo's Fiesta de Enero (p138) is a 12-day festival in the middle of January. The weather is ideal for touring the canyon then, too.

Boats A seat on a shared *lancha* (boat) costs around M$320 per person.

The Grandest Canyon of Chiapas

Cañón del Sumidero (Sumidero Canyon) reaches depths of up to 1000m. The vertiginous canyon walls frame the jade-green waters of the Río Grijalva below. Declared a national park in 1980, the Sumidero Canyon is only 25km in length, but sprawls across 54,000 acres of karst mountains and moss-covered rock formations.

The most popular way to visit is to take a *lancha* (motorboat) tour along the river. Boats depart regularly from the pier in Chiapa de Corzo (and less frequently from Embarcadero Cahuaré, 5km east of the Chiapas capital city, Tuxtla Gutiérrez). The two-hour tours visit a series of peculiar rock formations, including the Cueva de los Colores, a craggy cave naturally coated in a pastel-pink magnesium. Look out for wildlife such as crocodiles and huge flocks of cormorants.

MMANSON/SHUTTERSTOCK

Dance of the Parachicos

Chiapa de Corzo's streets are awash in colorful ticker tape during the **Fiesta Grande de Enero**, while the **Plaza de Armas** is filled with fairground rides, souvenir stalls and food vendors. The fiesta is best known for its Parachicos dancers, who don straw wigs, dazzling ponchos and lacquered wooden masks in sardonic mimicry of the Spanish. On January 21, the *combate naval* is a reenactment of the fateful battle that ensued when the Spanish ships arrived in town, celebrating the bravery of the native Chiapa people (Chiapanec) in the face of invasion, which ends in a mighty firework display.

Along the Rim

Driving into the national park (entry fee M$57) provides the most dramatic and staggering vistas of Sumidero. With six *miradores* (lookouts) perched on different sections of the canyon rim, you can easily hit them all on a short and sweet road trip from Tuxtla Gutiérrez or Chiapa de Corzo. **Los Chiapa** is the national park's visitor center, with all-encompassing views of the serpentine river canyon. Look out for hummingbirds in the gardens here. There is no public transportation to get to the viewpoints. Renting a car or taxi for the day is the best option.

Above Parachicos dancers

18 Cacao and Chili in CHIAPAS

COFFEE | TASTINGS | CHOCOLATE

Chiapas is a place of rolling highlands and teeming jungles, fringed by the Pacific Ocean to the south. Combined, this variety of ecosystems produces a wide array of ingredients for creative chefs to play with. But it's the combination of indigenous and European sensibilities that helps local gastronomy stand out. Here's a guide to what to eat and where to try it across the region.

How to

When to go There's never a bad time to try new foods. The dry season (November to May) is best for chocolate farm tours.

Getting here ADO buses connect to all the major towns and cities across the region. From there, *colectivos* and moto taxis connect to everywhere else.

Vegan diets Mexico isn't usually friendly to plant-based diets but in San Cristóbal de las Casas, you'll be spoilt for choice.

Eat & Drink Around Chiapas & Tabasco

Comitán's unique dishes Comitán de Domínguez is spearheading the rise of Chiapas as one of Mexico's unique food regions. Maize naturally features heavily in many of the city's bespoke dishes, such as *chinculguajes*, thick maize tortillas stuffed with beans, cilantro and chili. More substantial dishes include *hueso Comiteco* (aka *chamorro*) pork leg (with bone included), which is slow-cooked in a sweet and sour gravy. Comitán even has its own regional take on mezcal called *Comiteco*. It is concocted with agave Americana (aka maguey) and *piloncillo* (cooked sugarcane), giving it floral notes and a honeyed sweetness.

San Cristóbal's coffee culture In almost every corner of San Cristóbal de las Casas, the sweet aroma of coffee wafts through the

SANDOR MEJIAS B/SHUTTERSTOCK

air. Part of the third-wave coffee trend, San Cristóbal has an increasing repertoire of coffee shops and hipster cafes serving up some of Mexico's finest organic coffee. **Cafeología** even runs coffee tastings, where you can sample different beans.

Follow the Ruta del Cacao
Cacao has been harvested in Tabasco for thousands of years. These days, cacao production and small chocolate factories are legion along the **Ruta del Cacao**. A handful are open to the public. The most accessible is **Hacienda La Luz** *(haciendalaluz.mx; M$350; book in advance)* in Comalcalco. You will see its traditional methods of turning home-grown cacao beans into chocolate and, most importantly, be able to taste the end products.

From Earth to Plate

Rajas con queso Cheese was added to the Maya dish by Catholic nuns, but it's also possible to make it with vegan cheese made from almonds.

Tacos dorados I use a crispy tortilla and stuff it with spinach grown by Zapatista communal gardens in the surrounding hills. That's San Cristóbal's best street food.

Cacao Good food is peace. The spirit of cacao is to honor both Chiapas and the planet: it includes maize and cacao and gives you enough energy for the day.

PAUL STAFFORD

Gerardo Gonzalez Miranda, *head chef and owner of Art Librería in San Cristóbal, recommends authentic vegan eats.*

Above Tacos dorados

19 Maya Monuments ROAD TRIP

TEMPLES | WILDLIFE | HIKING

Once you reach the rainforests of eastern Chiapas, you encounter the remnants of once-mighty cities steeped in foliage. Wandering around these huge pyramids and palaces is a beguiling experience, particularly when the life of the surrounding wilderness is in full voice.

MADRUGADA VERDE/SHUTTERSTOCK

The True People

Palenque and Yaxchilán were once among the mightiest city-states in the Maya world. They occasionally found themselves at war with one another. The local Lacandones living in the surrounding forest call themselves *Hach Winik* (True People). They are believed to be direct descendants of the Yaxchilán and Palenque Maya.

Trip Notes

Getting around When visiting Bonampak and Yaxchilán, guided tours from Palenque often work out as better value than independent travel. Day tours start from M$1500 per person.

When to go Rainforests see rain throughout the year but trips in winter (November to February) avoid the worst heat and humidity.

Top tip Arrive in Palenque (pictured above) slightly before opening time to avoid crowds and watch the morning mist wrap around the tranquil pyramids.

FROM LEFT: PAUL STAFFORD, ALONZOKH/SHUTTERSTOCK

Indigenous Crafts in the CHIAPAS HIGHLANDS

01 Artisan Workshops
You can visit various artisan workshops and women's cooperatives found throughout the village of Zinacantán.

02 Huipiles
The outstanding indigenous artisans of the Chiapas highlands produce some of Mexico's highest quality *huipiles* (sleeveless tunics), weavings and blankets.

03 Hair Skirts
In Chamula village, the length of the fur of one's clothing determines class. The longer the fur, the higher one's social standing.

04 Fruit of the Loom
The old backstrap looms traditionally used to weave clothing are being phased out, with much of the embroidery now being machine stitched.

05 Flower Power
Zinacantán's love for flowers is reflected in the traditional wear. Its people, who are primarily Tzotzil, wear clothing with vibrant flower motifs.

06 Religious Fervor
Many villagers practice syncretic religious

07

08

10

traditions that are fusions of Catholic beliefs and pre-Hispanic elements at their colorful churches.

07 Market Day
Most of the highland villages have Sunday markets where textiles are bought and sold. They often take place in the plaza outside the main church.

08 Stitched into Memory
Zinacantán Women's Cooperative, Mujeres Sembrando la Vida, opened a school, called Yo'onik, that provides free weaving and embroidery classes to children.

09 Village Heads
Chamula's leaders are defined by their clothes, sporting sleeveless black tunics and white scarves on their heads.

10 Zapatista Territory
The Zapatistas (EZLN) have many autonomous villages in and around the highland villages that are known for their indigenous crafts.

01 RICUCCI MICHELE/SHUTTERSTOCK. **02** VERMONTALM/SHUTTERSTOCK. **03** JON G. FULLER/VWPICS/ALAMY. **04** SL-PHOTOGRAPHY/SHUTTERSTOCK. **05** SL-PHOTOGRAPHY/SHUTTERSTOCK. **06** RUBI RODRIGUEZ MARTINEZ/SHUTTERSTOCK. **07** RUBI RODRIGUEZ MARTINEZ/SHUTTERSTOCK. **08** ALDO PAVAN/GETTY IMAGES. **09** RICUCCI MICHELE/SHUTTERSTOCK. **10** JORGE ISAAC MC/SHUTTERSTOCK

The Birth of Meso-american Civilization

INSPIRATION AND INFLUENCES FROM THE OLMEC

If you thought that the Maya were mysterious, the civilization that preceded them by about 1500 years is even more fascinating. Emerging around 1300 BCE, the Olmec rose to become Mesoamerica's first major civilization, inspiring many beliefs and practices central to subsequent civilizations for centuries to come, including the Maya and the Aztecs.

Left Colossal Olmec basalt head, Parque Museo La Venta **Centre** Olmec stone altar, Parque Museo La Venta **Right** Monument, Parque Museo La Venta

PAUL STAFFORD

The Maya, Aztecs, Toltecs and Zapotecs are the great pre-Hispanic civilizations responsible for building Mexico's most impressive landmarks. But while each group had distinct customs, languages and architectural styles, there are plenty of common themes that bind these Mesoamerican cultures together: towering pyramids, a panoply of deities – in which animals, vegetables and human forms are often combined – and the practice of human sacrifice.

Rubber People

Go back far enough and all of these inspirations can be traced to a single group: the Olmec. The name loosely translates to 'People from the Region of Rubber' in the Nahuatl language. They were Mesoamerica's first complex major civilization, rising to prominence along the humid Gulf of Mexico in the modern-day states of Tabasco and Veracruz about 3300 years ago.

The height of their power was from 1200 to 500 BCE, many centuries before the Maya started to flourish and a full two millennia before the Aztecs emerged on the scene. But very little remains of the Olmec settlements. There is also no written record about them, which means what we do know comes from the artifacts discovered at sites in the flat, northern plains of Tabasco and Veracruz states.

Influence Etched in Stone

The Olmec penchant for carving beautiful sculptures out of basalt – in particular of colossal warrior heads – is an important indicator that they were an advanced society. The same applies to their stone stelae (carved stone slabs), earthen mounds and pyramids that would become

BARNA TANKO/SHUTTERSTOCK

LEV LEVIN/SHUTTERSTOCK

ubiquitous in all Mesoamerican societies. These relics tell us that the Olmec were likely settled and had the resources to sustain artisans, religious leaders, shamans and other members of society who were not directly engaged in hunting and farming.

One of the most striking aspects of all Mesoamerican cultures is the religion. Animals and plants were anthropomorphized into a plethora of deities by the Olmec. This is the first known instance of such a practice in Mesoamerica. Archaeological discoveries, particularly of carved stelae at various sites, suggest that the plumed serpent, maize god, and were-jaguar (like a werewolf, but even cooler) – all of which appear in some form in later cultures – were all widely worshipped across the Olmec world.

It's currently not possible to say what exactly brought an untimely end to such an established culture, but around 400 BCE, the Olmec suddenly disappeared.

Other elements of daily life most likely pioneered by the Olmec include the carving of jade into figurines, the development of ceramics and the cultivation of cacao, which would later go on to benefit the entire world as the principal building block in chocolate. It's currently not possible to say what exactly brought an untimely end to such an established culture, but around 400 BCE, the Olmec suddenly disappeared, even though their cultural, architectural and scientific advances would remain decisive factors in the region's development right up until the European world crashed into it two millennia later.

Where to See Olmec Heritage

Most Olmec cities are sadly long gone. **Parque Museo La Venta** *(tabasco.gob.mx/parque-museo-venta; M$60)*, Villahermosa's standout attraction, is a purpose-built park for displaying some of the finest Olmec basalt sculptures, most notably the colossal heads. The sculptures were discovered 130km further west, at the original site of La Venta (close to the border with Veracruz). La Venta was the Olmec capital city during the civilization's height. Archaeologists relocated the sculptures to Tabasco's state capital for safekeeping in the 1940s when oil exploration threatened to damage the original site. Many more colossal Olmec heads can be found in the permanent collection of Museo de Antropología in Xalapa, Veracruz.

Listings

BEST OF THE REST

Cultural Festivals & Events

Fiesta de Enero

Chiapa de Corzo celebrates the Fiesta de Enero, a 12-day festival in the middle of January with regional food, music and the famous Parachico masked dance.

Feria de Tabasco

Tabasco's biggest party of the year takes place in May. The Feria de Tabasco, held in the state capital Villahermosa, entertains with cattle shows, food fairs and traditional dances.

Feria de Chiapas

The Chiapas Fair overtakes Tuxtla Gutiérrez in the first two weeks of December. This coincides with the Guadalupana, where, in the days leading up to the Día de Guadalupe on December 12, you'll likely see runners along highways carrying flaming torches, running in relay all the way from Mexico City.

Local Flavors

Mercado Municipal $

San Cristóbal de las Casas' main food market is the best place to sample authentic Chiapan food, including *sopa de pan*, broth concocted with bread, boiled eggs, plantain and green beans.

Camino Secreto $$

Cheery, inexpensive Comitán spot for local dishes such as *hueso comiteco* – pork leg on the bone in a sweet and sour gravy. If you're lucky, your meal will be soundtracked with live marimba music.

Art Librería $$

Homemade vegan dishes based on traditional Chiapas recipes, using organic ingredients grown on Zapatista farmsteads. The guacamole is exceptional.

La Cevichería Tabasco $$$

Nowhere does a better ceviche in town, with mighty portions. Ask your waiter for menu recommendations. Great seafood tacos.

Water World

Misol-Ha

The landscape south of Palenque is awash with waterfalls and cascades. The elegant Misol-Ha (which means 'waterfall' in Mayan) plunges 35m from an overhanging semicircular cliff into a shimmering pool.

Agua Azul

The most popular waterfall near Palenque, where the Río Xanil thunders down multiple tiers of stepped limestone in a symphony of white and aquamarine water (outside of rainy season).

Reserva Ecológica Villa Luz

Rivers run milky white in the forests south of *pueblo mágico* Tapijulapa in Tabasco, owing to naturally released hydrogen sulfide. These rivers culminate in a series of beautiful cascades south of the town.

El Chiflón

Lauded as the finest falls in Chiapas, Cascadas El Chiflón are a series of frothy cerulean cascades tumbling 120m off an escarpment into swirling cobalt blue pools. South of Comitán.

Parque Nacional Lagunas de Montebello

Hugging the Mexico–Guatemala border is Parque Nacional Lagunas de Montebello, some 60km southeast of Comitán, featuring 59 small lakes of varied hues. **Lago Pojoj**, where you can rent kayaks, is the highlight.

Coffee Time in San Cristóbal

Cafeología

This slick coffee house runs coffee experiences where you can taste different beans and pair them with baked goods.

Tulan Chulel

Great little shop selling cocoa, coffee and handicrafts. Everything comes from the autonomous Zapatista zone.

Café la Selva

An institution in San Cristóbal. It was one of the first coffee shops here and it continues to serve 100% organic coffee from the Lacandón Jungle.

Overlooked Ruins

Zona Arqueológica de Tenam Puente

The main attraction is the expansive Acropolis, which clings to a steep hillside in tiers, occasionally flattening into plazas and ball courts (of which the site has three) before steps continue up to yet another level.

Zona Arqueológica Chinkultic

Magnificent view of the surrounding lakes and forests of Lagos de Montebello from the Acrópolis, a partially restored temple. It'll likely be only you, the birds and the susurration of insects during your visit.

Zona Arqueológica Comalcalco

Not in the usual rainforest demesnes of the Maya, Comalcalco was an outlier. The Maya built their large temples using brick. These were then covered in an unusual type of stucco made by charring oyster shells to extract the lime from them, then mixed with sand and water.

PAUL STAFFORD

Zona Arqueológica de Tenam Puente

Hand-picked Handicrafts in San Cristóbal

Sna Jolobil

Women's weaving cooperative Sna Jolobil exhibits and sells some of the very best *huipiles*, rugs and blouses in town.

Kuxul Pok'

Founded by Alberto Lopez Gomez, whose work has been shown at New York Fashion Week. Upper end of the price scale.

Folklora

This locally owned design store sells original blankets, shawls and handicrafts produced by more than 20 Maya communities.

El Camino de los Altos

A collaboration between French textile designers and 160 women from indigenous communities.

Centro de Textiles del Mundo Maya

Showcases over 500 examples of handwoven textiles from throughout Mexico and Central America.

OAXACA

ART | WILDLIFE | ECOTOURISM

RESEARCHED BY LIZA PRADO

- **Trip Builder** (p142)
- **Practicalities** (p144)
- **Art of Oaxaca City** (p146)
- **Oaxaca's Sea Turtles** (p148)
- **Zapotec County Hiking** (p150)
- **Oaxacan Artesanía** (p152)
- **Día de Muertos** (p154)
- **Listings** (p156)

OAXACA
Trip Builder

With a culture rooted in artistic creativity and indigenous traditions plus a landscape of astonishing beauty and biodiversity, Oaxaca is a traveler's wonderland. Revel in its many offerings, from world-class museums and bustling markets to mountain-high hikes and turtle tourism.

Reserva de la Biosfera Tehuacán-Cuicatlán

Tejupan

Visit the **Museo Textil de Oaxaca**, one of many outstanding museums (p146)
5min from Oaxaca's Zócalo

Fill up on fantastic folk art at **Mercado de Artesanías** (p147)
5min from Oaxaca's Zócalo

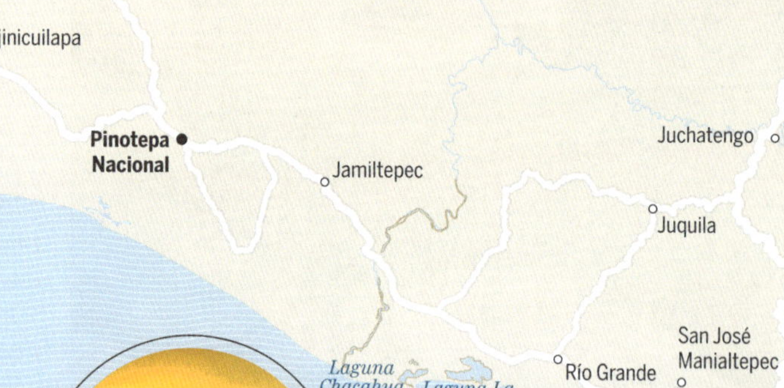

Release (and cheer on) baby sea turtles at **Playa Bacocho** (p149)
10min from Puerto Escondido bus station

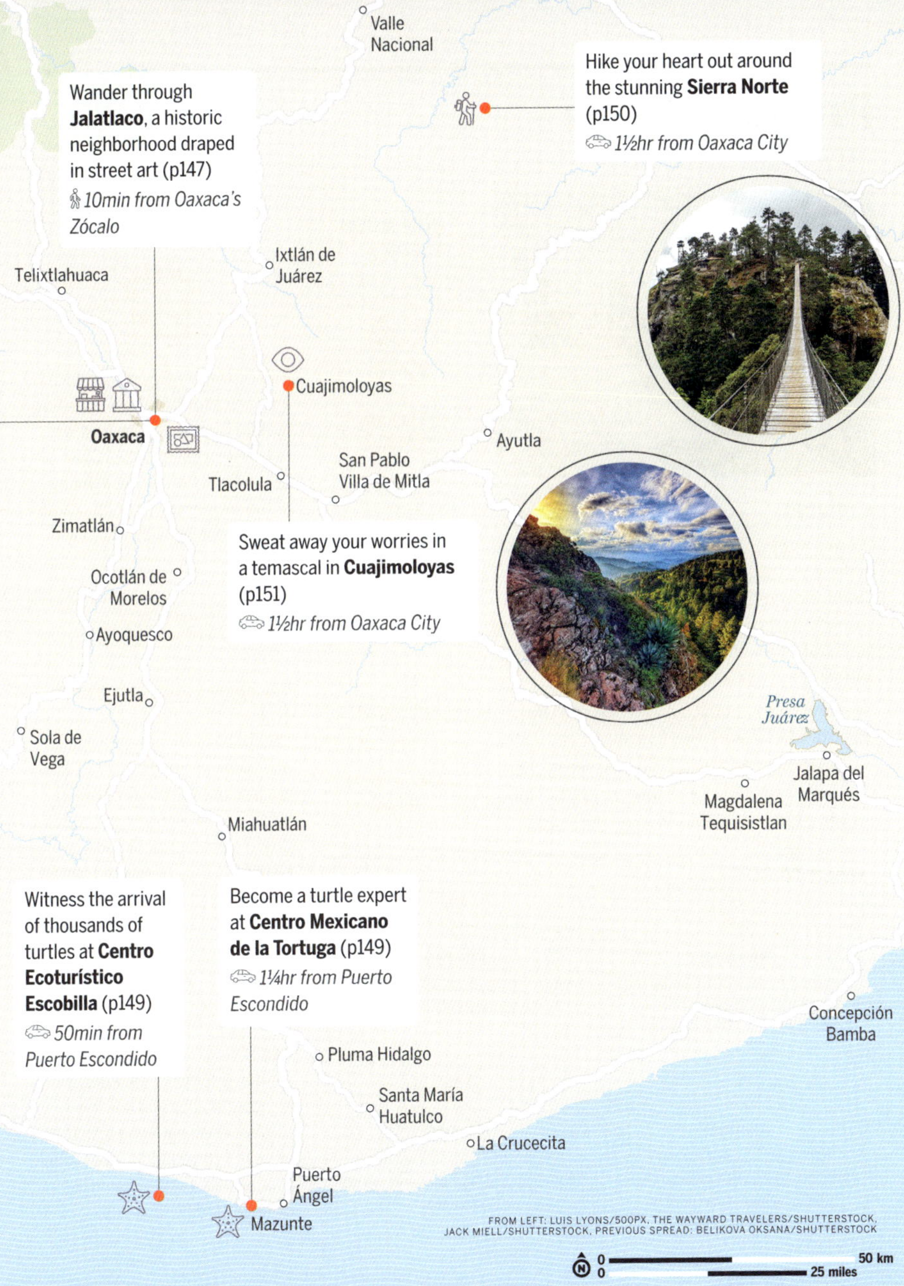

FROM LEFT: LUIS LYONS/500PX, THE WAYWARD TRAVELERS/SHUTTERSTOCK, JACK MIELL/SHUTTERSTOCK, PREVIOUS SPREAD: BELIKOVA OKSANA/SHUTTERSTOCK

Practicalities

SANTIAGO CASTILLO CHOMEL/SHUTTERSTOCK

ARRIVING

Oaxaca International Airport The main gateway to the state (pictured). Shared shuttles to downtown Oaxaca City, including the bus station, cost M$120 (taxis M$465). Whichever you choose, purchase a ticket from the kiosk near the arrivals entrance.

Huatulco International Airport Located on the coast; receives direct flights from the US and Canada.

Puerto Escondido Airport Domestic flights only. From either, take shared shuttles to nearby cities or taxis to smaller destinations along the coast.

HOW MUCH FOR A

Tlayuda M$100

Mole negro M$180

Mezcal shot M$50

WHEN TO GO

JAN–MAR
Temperate, dry months perfect for sightseeing and hiking. Ideal for whale-watching.

APR–JUN
Warmer days mean the rainy season and big surf.

JUL–SEP
Rain persists but doesn't dampen epic state-wide festivals like Guelaguetza (p156).

OCT–DEC
Dry, sunny days bring Día de Muertos (p154) plus Christmas festivities.

GETTING AROUND

Bus Oaxaca's efficient, comfortable and affordable first-class bus system is generally the best way to travel on main routes. Older second-class buses serve many of the smaller towns on the same roads, stopping along the way.

Colectivos (shared transport) Typically the quickest and cheapest way to navigate cities and their surrounding areas; they are also used to travel between smaller coastal towns. In Oaxaca City, expect four-door sedans; elsewhere they're covered pickup trucks.

Car Driving is the most convenient way to reach the Pueblos Mancomunados and coastal towns, especially if you plan to explore the surrounding areas. Ditch your wheels, though, when you're in congested Oaxaca City.

TOP: ERNESTO CHI/SHUTTERSTOCK
BOTTOM: LU YANG/SHUTTERSTOCK

EATING & DRINKING

Oaxaca ranks among Mexico's top foodie cities – no small feat in a country known for its creative cuisine. Signature Oaxacan eats include the renowned *mole* (complex chili sauce) dishes, *salsa de queso* (cheese bathed in a spicy tomato sauce), *tlayudas* (large grilled tortillas filled with cheese, refried beans and topped with optional beef or Mexican sausage; pictured top right) and *garnachas istmeñas* (fried tortillas topped with shredded beef and pickled cabbage). For drinks, there's mezcal, Oaxaca's quintessential agave spirit, mountain-grown coffee and *tejate* (a corn and cocoa beverage; pictured bottom right).

Best cocktails
Esencia Oaxaca Bar (p157)

Must-try mole
Levadura de Olla (p157)

CONNECT & FIND YOUR WAY

Oaxaca City has reliable wi-fi as do its surrounding communities. The coast is another thing, with spotty wi-fi even in larger towns. That may change as Starlink, a satellite-based internet service, is more widely adopted. In mountain villages, some cabin hotels offer wi-fi for a fee, otherwise don't count on it or even cell service. Be sure to download maps!

WHERE TO STAY

Oaxaca's accommodations are as varied as its landscapes, with price points to match. From adobe cabins to modern boutique hotels, you're sure to find a comfortable spot.

Place	Pros/Cons
Oaxaca City, Centro Histórico	Central to sights, restaurants and bars. Variety of price points. Traffic and late-night buzz.
Oaxaca City, Xochimilco	Artsy, historic neighborhood. Quiet. Several blocks from the action.
Puerto Escondido	Surf hub and vibrant night-life. Spread out; taxi or *colectivo* needed between neighborhoods.
Mazunte	Boho, low-rise beach town. At times, crowded with more foreigners than locals.
Cuajimoloyas	Mountaintop Zapotec village. Endless views. Spotty wi-fi and cell service.

RIDESHARE

The rideshare app DiDi makes getting around Oaxaca City and Bahías de Huatulco easy and more affordable than a taxi.

MONEY

Beyond Oaxaca's cities, cash rules and ATMs can be scarce (and often run out of money). If headed to the mountains or small coastal towns, bring enough pesos to get you through your stay.

20 ART OF Oaxaca City

MUSEUMS | MURALS | FOLK ART

Oaxaca City is a wonderland of art. The historic downtown, already an architectural gem, is replete with first-rate museums and galleries, while murals and provocative street art bring the walls to life. And that's not even mentioning the markets, shops and street vendors selling folk art, much of it rooted in indigenous tradition. For art lovers, Oaxaca City is where it's at.

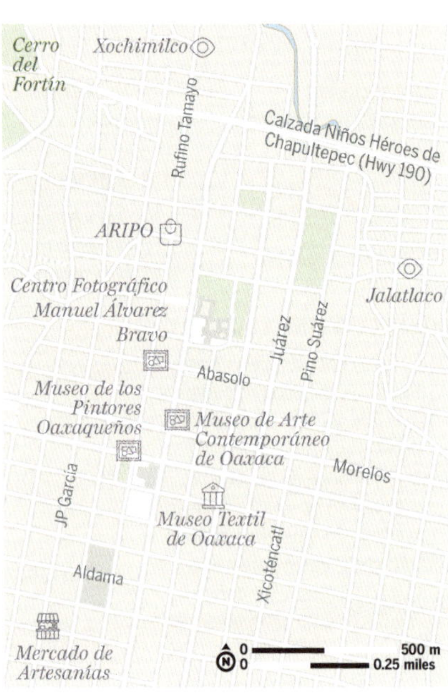

How to

Getting here & around Access is easy: the airport is 6km south, and the long-distance bus station is downtown. The historic center is walkable, especially with the **Andador Turístico**, a pedestrian-only corridor, running through.

When to go November is optimal for a visit, with dry, temperate weather plus Día de Muertos festivities. Book early.

Shaky ground Earthquakes are common. If you hear a seismic alert, stay calm and move to an open space.

Museums galore Oaxaca City is peppered with art museums, all located within blocks of one another. Most are free or donation-based, making it easy to spend a morning or two museum-hopping. If you're interested in a particular art form, you'll find it here: photography at **Centro Fotográfico Manuel Álvarez Bravo** (*cfmab.com.mx*), painting at **Museo de los Pintores Oaxaqueños** (*sic.cultura.gob.mx*), and even textile art at **Museo Textil de Oaxaca** (*museotextildeoaxaca.org*). For contemporary art, don't miss **Museo de Arte Contemporáneo de Oaxaca**, the only museum on the Andador Turístico.

Art everywhere Walking through Oaxaca's historic center is like being in an outdoor gallery. From vibrant murals to linocut prints pasted onto walls, the works provide a window into

PAUL VOWLES/SHUTTERSTOCK

Oaxacan culture and society. For the highest concentration of street art, beeline for the cobblestoned barrios of **Jalatlaco** and **Xochimilco**, historic neighborhoods that double as artistic hubs.

Folk art central Surrounded by villages that produce some of the state's finest folk art, Oaxaca City has become an artisanal hub. From polished *barro negro* (black pottery) and *alebrijes* (colorful wood creatures) to handwoven Zapotec rugs and basketry, you're sure to see stunning pieces in Oaxaca City. Spend a day leisurely window-shopping on the **Andador Turístico**. Or one-stop-shop at either **ARIPO**, a collection of high-end folk art boutiques, or the **Mercado de Artesanías**, a bustling artisanal goods market.

Oaxaca's Political Art

Meandering through downtown Oaxaca, you'll inevitably see large-scale linocut prints wheat-pasted onto public walls or sold as prints in galleries and open-air markets. Often politically charged, the art form began in support of a series of mass protests in 2006, when a teachers' strike in Oaxaca City turned violent. Against this backdrop, 12 art collectives took hold in the city, using their graphic stencils as a form of political protest against issues like social injustice, gentrification and environmental degradation. To learn more and meet the artists, join the **Pasaporte Gráfico** *(facebook.com/pasaportegrafico)*, a three-hour tour of these collectives' workshops and galleries.

Above Museo Textil de Oaxaca

Oaxaca's Sea TURTLES

WILDLIFE | CONSERVATION | EDUCATIONAL

With nearly 600km of pristine coastline, Oaxaca is a haven for sea turtles. Each year olive ridley, leatherback, hawksbill and green turtles arrive by the millions to nest on Oaxaca's beaches, sometimes en masse. Conservation initiatives, including hatchling releases and nesting tours, help protect these endangered creatures and can be an unforgettable part of any trip to the region.

DOUGLAS BRANDON/GETTY IMAGES

How to

Getting around Traveling Oaxaca's coast is easy in *pasajeros* (shared pickup trucks), *colectivos* (shared taxis) and taxis. Flag them down along the main coastal highway and in bigger towns. Driving a rental car is convenient but doesn't come cheap!

When to go Sea turtles are seen year-round in Oaxaca. To witness an *arribada*, come between July and February.

How much Turtle experiences cost M$200 per person, and double if you need a ride.

DANNY LEHMAN/GETTY IMAGES

Top left Olive ridley turtle, Playa Escobilla **Bottom left** Baby sea turtles, Mazunte

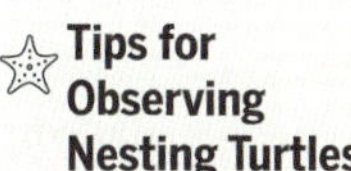

Arrivals by the thousands The 15km-long beach sanctuary of **Playa Escobilla** is one of the few places in the world where *arribadas* occur, an astonishing phenomenon when tens of thousands of olive ridley turtles come ashore together. Waves deposit turtles onto the beach like giant stones with flippers that pull themselves across the beach to lay their eggs. Come around the new moon, especially from July to February, to see the most turtles. Only guided visits are permitted here, offered by the locally run **Centro Ecoturístico Escobilla** *(facebook.com/ecoturismo.escobilla)*.

Release into the wild On the western edge of Puerto Escondido, **Playa Bacocho** is a ribbon of golden sand popular with beachgoers. Come sunset, it's the go-to spot for baby turtle releases. Run year-round by **Vivemar** *(vivemar.com.mx)*, a local NGO, excursions see participants receive a short educational talk before being handed a tiny hatchling in a *jicara* (dried fruit gourd). Participants line the beach, releasing the squirming creatures onto the wet sand, watching them scurry to the sea for the first time. Cheering is encouraged.

Deep dive Learn all about Mexico's turtles at the **Centro Mexicano de la Tortuga** (M$44 per person), a turtle research, rehabilitation and educational center in Mazunte. A winding path leads past habitats for land and freshwater turtles, plus wide tanks filled with swimming sea turtles. Signage and QR codes provide loads of educational info in Spanish and English.

LIZA PRADO

Tips for Observing Nesting Turtles

When encountering a turtle emerging from the ocean, give it some space. Your presence can encourage it to leave before laying eggs.

Avoid looking a nesting turtle in the eye as it can bother them; observe the turtle from behind, at a safe distance.

Do not use flashlights or take flash photography around sea turtles; they are drawn to white light and can be distracted by it. Instead, use a red-hued light.

Do not touch sea turtles. Human hands often have creams, bug repellents and sunscreen, which can be potentially harmful.

Recommended by Mireya Viadiu Ilarraza, *environmental education coordinator, Centro Mexicano de la Tortuga. @CONANP_mx*

22 Zapotec County HIKING

OUTDOORSY | ECOTOURISM | WORKSHOPS

Revel in the culture and beauty of the Sierra Norte by hiking between the Pueblos Mancomunados, a group of eight mountain villages devoted to sustainable tourism. Together, they offer wilderness escapes, traditional workshops and insight into day-to-day life in Zapotec country.

WU SWEE ONG/GETTY IMAGES

Trip Notes

Getting here & around **Expediciones Sierra Norte** arranges door-to-door service to the Pueblos Mancomunados (pictured); they also book drivers between villages, as regular public transportation is almost nil.

When to go The dry season (November to April) means ample sun and minimal mud – optimal conditions for hiking and driving.

Packing list Pack layers, a jacket and a winter hat. The high altitude brings temperate days and cold nights year-round.

Cash economy Bring cash!

Travel Planning

The Pueblos Mancomunados manage their ecotourism efforts through their own Oaxaca City–based tourism agency, **Expediciones Sierra Norte** *(sierranorte.org.mx)*. Staffers customize itineraries for each client, arranging guided hikes, activities, accommodations, meals and transportation. Trips can usually be pulled together with a day's notice; book earlier if you need English-speaking guides.

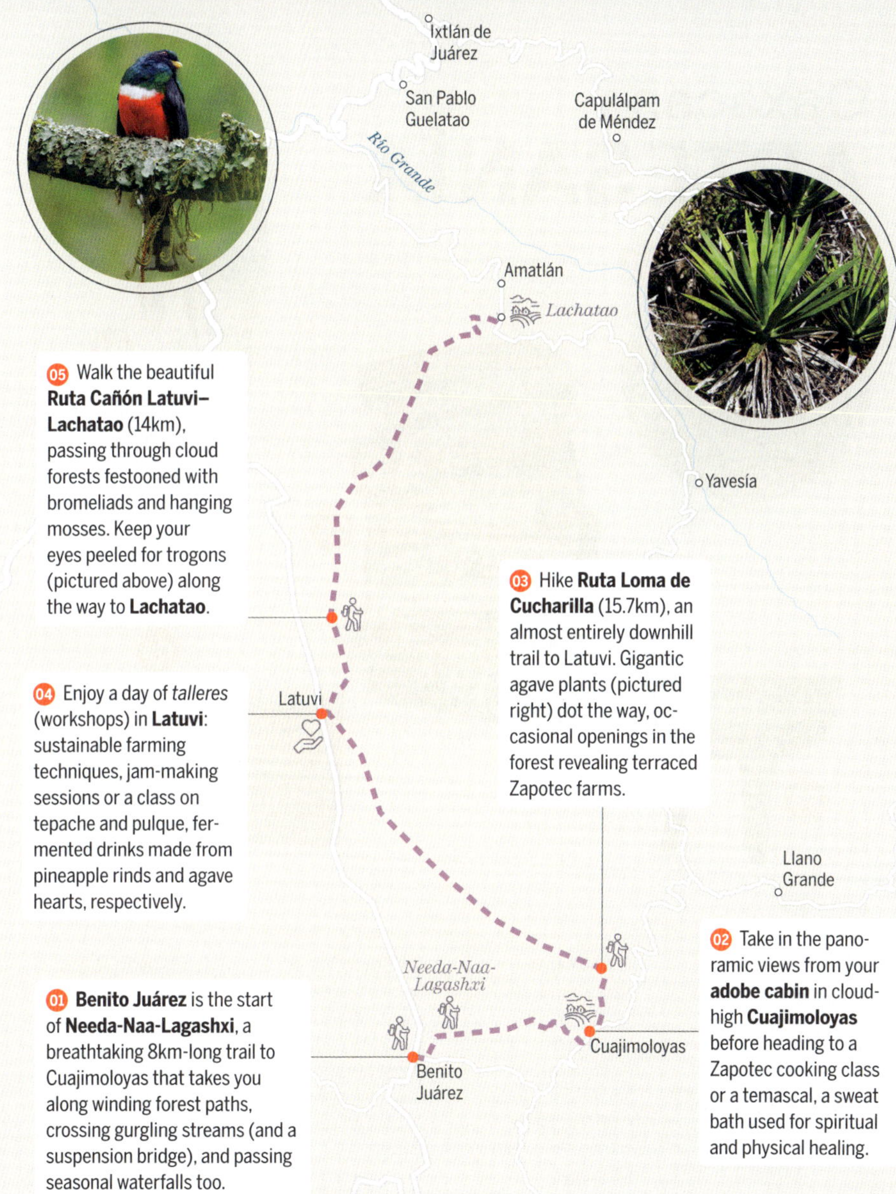

05 Walk the beautiful **Ruta Cañón Latuvi–Lachatao** (14km), passing through cloud forests festooned with bromeliads and hanging mosses. Keep your eyes peeled for trogons (pictured above) along the way to **Lachatao**.

04 Enjoy a day of *talleres* (workshops) in **Latuvi**: sustainable farming techniques, jam-making sessions or a class on tepache and pulque, fermented drinks made from pineapple rinds and agave hearts, respectively.

03 Hike **Ruta Loma de Cucharilla** (15.7km), an almost entirely downhill trail to Latuvi. Gigantic agave plants (pictured right) dot the way, occasional openings in the forest revealing terraced Zapotec farms.

02 Take in the panoramic views from your **adobe cabin** in cloud-high **Cuajimoloyas** before heading to a Zapotec cooking class or a temascal, a sweat bath used for spiritual and physical healing.

01 **Benito Juárez** is the start of **Needa-Naa-Lagashxi**, a breathtaking 8km-long trail to Cuajimoloyas that takes you along winding forest paths, crossing gurgling streams (and a suspension bridge), and passing seasonal waterfalls too.

Oaxacan ARTESANÍA

01 Barro Negro
Barro negro is hand-molded using ancestral techniques, including using pit kilns that turn the clay black from the smoke and heat.

02 Alebrijes
These whimsical zoomorphic sculptures, popularized by Oaxacan artist Manuel Jiménez Ramírez in the 1960s, often incorporate Zapotec symbolism and mythology.

03 Barro Verde
Oaxaca's signature jade green pottery hails from Santa María Atzompa, whose artisans have been making the verdant art since the 1500s.

04 Woven Rugs
Oaxaca's best rugs come from the weaving village of Teotitlán del Valle, using wool from local sheep and natural dyes.

05 Tapestries
These are woven on hand-operated looms

and typically integrate traditional motifs inspired by local culture and landscapes.

06 Huipiles
These traditional women's blouses are worn in many indigenous communities, each incorporating patterns and cultural symbolism representative of the place.

07 Basketry
Oaxacan basketry is an age-old art, using natural fibers like palm leaves, reed and river cane to create functional items.

08 Corn Husk Figures
Today associated with holiday ornaments and Día de Muertos decorations, corn husk figures are rooted in indigenous harvest fests.

09 Jicaras
Whether intricately carved or painted, Oaxacan gourd art reflects a deep connection to the natural world.

01 ROGER1979/SHUTTERSTOCK, **02** VIVA MEXICO/SHUTTERSTOCK, ©, **03** FOTOSDEALMA/SHUTTERSTOCK, **04** YANKOVSKAIMAGES/SHUTTERSTOCK, **05** PHOTOSTOCK BY LEONARDO EM/SHUTTERSTOCK, **06** BILL PERRY/SHUTTERSTOCK, **07** FOTOSDEALMA/SHUTTERSTOCK, **08** BODEGA PHOTOGRAPHY/SHUTTERSTOCK, **09** ARIADNA126/GETTY IMAGES

Día de Muertos

REMEMBERING THE DEPARTED

Few festivals reveal more about Mexicans than Día de Muertos (Day of the Dead), the remembrance of departed loved ones. Complex and deeply heartful, it weaves together mourning and remembrance with the celebration of life. It is filled with family, food and music, where all are welcome and none are forgotten.

Left *Ofrenda* **Centre** Día de Muertos celebrations **Right** *Pan de muerto*

CAVAN-IMAGES/SHUTTERSTOCK

Origins

Día de Muertos dates back over a thousand years, to the Toltecs and Aztecs, who believed the spirits of their dead returned to their communities once a year. Originally celebrated in August, Spanish colonizers assimilated the holiday through their favored tactic of cultural *mestizaje* (mixing), by moving it to coincide with the Catholic holidays of All Saints' Day (November 1) and All Souls' Day (November 2), days of prayer and remembrance.

Today, while preparations often begin in mid- to late October, November 1 and 2 remain the official Día de Muertos celebration days. November 1 focuses on children who have died and is called Día de los Inocentes (Day of the Innocent Ones); November 2 is centered on adults and is referred to as Día de los Difuntos (Day of the Departed).

Common Threads

The uniqueness of Mexico's Día de Muertos has earned it a UNESCO designation of 'Intangible Cultural Heritage of Humanity.' Each region of Mexico, however, celebrates it a little differently, integrating local foods, music, imagery and customs. Nonetheless, these common threads run throughout.

Ofrendas

Beginning in mid-October, many Mexicans set up *ofrendas* (altars) in their homes and businesses for loved ones who have passed. The centerpiece of the Día de Muertos festivities, *ofrendas* range from simple displays or elaborate multi-level affairs but all share the same elements: photos of the deceased, food and drink they enjoyed in life, and

KOBBY DAGAN/SHUTTERSTOCK

ALEXML2020/SHUTTERSTOCK

small items they loved (say, a certain doll, book, or domino set). Candles, flowers and religious symbols are common; some families even erect an arch made of bright-orange *cempasúchil* (marigolds) as a symbolic gate for the spirits to enter. And no *ofrenda* is complete without *pan de muerto*, a spongey, round loaf with bone-shaped decorations representing the cycle of life and death.

Cemetery Vigils

Día de Muertos is a time when Mexicans go to their cemeteries to clean the graves of their loved ones and decorate them with flowers and candles. The energy is often both festive and reflective, with families bringing folding chairs and blankets to settle in for a day and even a night of food, drinks and storytelling. Groups of musicians often wind through cemeteries stopping at gravesites to play favorite tunes of the deceased. In central and southern Mexico, especially, cemeteries are decked out in marigolds and hundreds of flickering candles.

City-wide Celebrations

Though Día de Muertos is traditionally a family-oriented celebration, larger-scale celebrations are becoming increasingly popular throughout Mexico, from cemetery processions and *mega-ofrendas* (massive altars) displayed in main squares to carnival-like fairs with food vendors and neon-lit rides. Festivities often stretch out over a full week, with city-wide parades taking over downtown streets. In many places, people paint their faces to mimic the holiday's most famous skeleton character – *La Catrina*, a high society representation of Death, created by Mexican satirical cartoonist José Guadalupe Posada and immortalized by master muralist Diego Rivera.

Día de Muertos in Oaxaca

With a strong indigenous presence, Oaxaca hosts some of Mexico's most vibrant Día de Muertos celebrations. Throughout the state, you'll encounter elaborate *ofrendas* and candlelit cemeteries, with copal incense enveloping towns and nonstop firecrackers. In Oaxaca City, the festivities kick off with a week of *comparsas*, traditional parades with brass bands, giant puppets and dancers in traditional dress and skeleton paint. Meanwhile, San Agustín Etla hosts *muerteadas*, lively theatrical-like productions with a storyline, costumed characters and battling bands. In Mitla, an ancient Zapotec burial site, the Tierra de los Muertos festival integrates stage performances into its remembrance celebrations.

Listings

BEST OF THE REST

Ancient Cities & Sites

Zona Arqueológica de Monte Albán

The ancient Zapotec city of Monte Albán is one of Mexico's most impressive ruins. Located 10km from Oaxaca City.

Zona Arqueológica de Mitla

Located in the same-named town, Mitla was a Zapotec religious hub and burial site for nobility; it is best known for its exquisite geometric stonework and ornate architecture.

El Tule

Stop at El Tule near Oaxaca City, home to a massive 2000-year-old **Montezuma cypress tree**. Towering over the main plaza, the 14m-wide tree is said to be the world's widest.

Art & Culture

Valle de Zimatlán Folk Art

Tour the villages of Valle de Zimatlán, known for their artisan workshops in *barro negro* (black pottery) and *alebrijes* (whimsical wood sculptures). Book with **Las Bugambilias Tours** in nearby Oaxaca City.

Vida Nueva

In the weaving village of Teotitlán del Valle, this renowned women's coop offers demos in weaving and sells one-of-a-kind handmade goods. Offers workshops in natural dyeing techniques.

Tianguis de Domingo

Head to Tlacolula on Sundays to experience Oaxaca's oldest open-air market filled with Zapotec villagers buying and selling handmade crafts and tantalizing street eats.

Centro de las Artes de San Agustín (CASA)

A 19th-century textile factory turned arts complex in San Agustín Etla, CASA has superb modern art exhibits, concerts and occasional dance performances. Workshops in the visual arts, too.

Unmissable Festivals

Guelaguetza

An extravaganza of indigenous dance, music and food. Held every July in Oaxaca City and its surrounding towns.

Velas Muxe

In November, Juchitán hosts the festive Velas Muxe, a celebration of all things *muxe,* a third gender in Zapotec culture. Expect parades, dancing and an annual 'crowning-of-the-queen' ceremony.

La Gran Fiesta del Mezcal

Head to mezcal country in July for a vibrant multi-day celebration held in Matatlán.

Natural Wonders & Wildlife

Hierve El Agua

Rising 50m above the valley, these stunning clifftop springs near Mitla offer panoramic views while trails reveal petrified mineral deposits that give the appearance of frozen waterfalls.

Laguna de Manialtepec

Tour the spectacularly biodiverse Laguna de Manialtepec known for its birdlife and bioluminescent waters. Just west of Puerto Escondido, go with Lalo Ecotours or lagoon-side La Puesta del Sol.

Sociedad Cooperativa Turística Nueva Punta Escondida

Spinner and bottlenose dolphins can be seen year-round in Puerto Escondido's waters. Take an early-morning boat tour with the local coop, leaving from Playa Principal daily.

Huatulco Salvaje

Check out humpback whales (November to March), go birding or release baby turtles with Huatulco Salvaje, a group of certified guides that lead fascinating eco-tours in Bahías de Huatulco.

Gnarly Waves

Mexican Pipeline

Puerto Escondido's Mexican Pipeline is one of the best beach breaks in the world, with massive hollow waves standing up to 6m high on the northern end of **Playa Zicatela**. Expert surfers only!

Barra de la Cruz

A Chontol village, **Barra de la Cruz** is a renowned surfing spot known for its long and fast right-hand point break. Spring and summer bring international surf competitions.

Cocktails & Coffee

Esencia Oaxaca Bar

This intimate and off-the-beaten-track cocktail bar in Oaxaca City features in-house spirits and regional botanicals artfully mixed into delicious (and photo-worthy) drinks. Reservations required.

Prana Cocktail Bar

A Puerto Escondido hot spot, this beachfront bar is all about classic cocktails infused with local flavors. Expect a laid-back vibe, live music and big surf views.

Boulenc

Longtime Oaxaca City fave, this French bakery/cafe features organic coffee from the state's western highlands. Their robust coffee pairs oh-so-perfectly with Boulenc's buttery-good almond croissants.

Cafetería Origen Mágico

This mountaintop cafe serves up strong, flavorful cups of arabica coffee with panoramic views. Located in Pluma Hidalgo near the central plaza.

All About Mezcal

Mezcaloteca

In the heart of downtown Oaxaca City, this *mezcalería* offers educational tastings with knowledgeable servers. Expect meticulously selected mezcal, *sotol* and *destilados de agave* (mezcal-like spirits). Reservations required.

Gracias a Díos

One of Matatlán's artisanal *palenques* (mezcal distilleries), with tours sharing background on cultivation techniques, distilling methods and the history of their family-run business; tastings included. Drop-ins welcome.

From Markets to Michelin Stars

Pasillo del Humo $$

Enjoy grilled meats in the smoky east corridor of Mercado 20 de Noviembre, a quintessential Oaxaca City experience. Follow it with a frothy *tejate*, a toasted corn and cocoa beverage.

Levadura de Olla $$

Michelin-starred chef Thalía Barrios García serves ceremonial dishes, exquisite *moles* and savory tamales in an inviting downtown Oaxaca City locale.

Almú $$

Homestyle Oaxacan eats are prepared over wood-burning grills at this sustainable farm for copal trees in San Martín Tilcajete, in the heart of Valle de Zimatlán. Cash only.

CENTRAL PACIFIC COAST

BEACHES | SURFING | SEAFOOD

RESEARCHED BY BRENDAN SAINSBURY

- **Trip Builder** (p160)
- **Practicalities** (p161)
- **Artistic Ingenuity** (p162)
- **See Acapulco's Cliff Divers** (p164)
- **Surf's Up in Troncones** (p166)
- **Soporific San Blas** (p168)
- **Tropical Style in Old Mazatlán** (p170)
- **Puerto Vallarta from the Water** (p172)
- **Zihuatanejo Coastal Hop** (p174)
- **Acapulco & the Manila Galleon** (p176)
- **Listings** (p178)

Admire the tropical neo-classical architecture of **Old Mazatlán** (p170)
6hr from Puerto Vallarta

Contemplate the delicious tranquility of **San Blas'** colonial ruins (p168)
4hr from Puerto Vallarta

Go whale watching in the **Bahía de Banderas** (p172)
20min from Puerto Vallarta

Choose your favorite parcel of sand on the beaches of **Zihuatanejo** (p174)
5½hr from Acapulco

Experience the high drama of a *clavadista* performance in **Acapulco** (p164)
5½hr from Zihuatanejo

CENTRAL PACIFIC COAST
Trip Builder

Manicured resorts and wild surfer beaches, glitzy modern cities and handsomely disheveled ruins, fresh-off-the-boat seafood and experimental indigenous crafts – the Central Pacific Coast offers way more than a stereotypical jet-skis-and-margaritas beach vacation.

PREVIOUS SPREAD: FERRANTRAITE/GETTY IMAGES

Practicalities

ARRIVING

Aeropuerto Internacional Gustavo Díaz Ordaz Puerto Vallarta's international airport is the hub and gateway to the Jalisco and Nayarit coast. There are additional airports in Mazatlán, Acapulco and **Ixtapa-Zihuatanejo**.

FIND YOUR WAY

There are few direct flights between the four main coastal resorts. You generally have to connect via Mexico City.

MONEY

Always carry a little cash. Some of the smaller restaurants and taco carts still don't accept credit cards.

WHERE TO STAY

Area	Pros/Cons
Puerto Vallarta	Hotels and beachside resorts galore. Busy and expensive in peak season.
Mazatlán	Historic buildings in charming old town. Zona Dorada's large hotels are further away.
Acapulco	Big beachfront hotels and fancy boutiques in Diamante. Some closures after recent hurricanes.
Zihuatanejo	Boutique properties with views. Lack of decent budget places.

GETTING AROUND

Bus Safe, air-conditioned buses connect most major towns and cities.

Car Some surfing breaks are remote; get off the beaten track with a car. Otherwise, you can get by with public transportation and taxis.

Water taxi Wallet-friendly water taxis connect Puerto Vallarta to outlying southern beaches.

TOP: MARCOS CASTILLO/SHUTTERSTOCK
BOTTOM: PAMELA MACNAUGHTAN/SHUTTERSTOCK

EATING & DRINKING

Taco carts offer the best Mexican street food at economical prices. For the full Pacific Coast eating immersion, we hope you like fish: *huachinango* (red snapper) is the default dish, invariably served whole, with the head, tail and fins still attached.

Best coffee
Cuattro Casa de Café (p178)

Must-try fish dish
Huachinango a la talla in Los Buzos (p178)

FEB
Perfect beach weather; the Carnaval reigns in Mazatlán.

JUN & JUL
Surf's up and prices are down at Pacific Mexico's prime surfing destinations.

NOV & DEC
Puerto Vallarta celebrates sportfishing and gourmet food, and ushers in the whale-watching season in December.

23 Artistic INGENUITY

ART | SCULPTURE | SHOPPING

You can't spell 'Vallarta' without 'art.' The city is dripping in it. Get ready to have your head swiveled by a vast array of murals, galleries, community art projects and public sculpture with exhibits covering everything from Mexican folk art to the avant-garde. Take a day's vacation from the beach and seek out your inner Frida Kahlo.

How to

Getting here & around Puerto Vallarta is well connected by airplane and bus to the rest of Mexico. Once in town, the central gallery district is highly walkable.

When to go Visit during the Art Walk season, which runs from late October to mid-May.

Looking, not buying Most items in the galleries are for sale but staff are generally not pushy. You're under no obligation to buy.

Unmissable Galleries

Puerto Vallarta's Zona Centro district is teeming with plush private galleries. **Galería Colectika** *(peyotepeople.com)* is considered home to the great masters of Mexican folk art. The Huichol beadwork pieces are mostly one of a kind and sit alongside fine Huichol yarn art pieces, metalwork from Chiapas and ceramics from Oaxaca.

Near Galería Colectika, **Galería Omar Alonso** *(galeriaomaralonso.com)*, Vallarta's first contemporary art gallery, has branched out into photography and abstract art. Across the street, **Galerie des Artistes** *(galeriedesartistes.mx)* is home to an eclectic collection, running the gamut from bronze sculpture by Mexican masters to abstract pieces by emerging artists. Close by, **Manmade México** champions modern design and showcases works by artists who approach traditional folk art with modern techniques.

Galería Corsica *(galeria corsica.mx)* is arguably the most cutting-edge of PV's potpourri of galleries, presenting bold abstract canvases and sculptures in and around an Andalucian-style patio.

ALESSANDROV/SHUTTERSTOCK

Art Walks

From late October to mid-May, 18 participating downtown Vallarta galleries take part in the Wednesday evening **ArtWalk** *(puertovallartaartwalk.com)* when they stay open later than usual and offer beverages and lay on music, with their owners happy to chat. Some are part of the Vallarta Art District, with a particularly dense cluster of galleries along Calles Vicario, Sánchez, Juárez and Domínguez in the *centro histórico,* while others are independent. Pick up Vallarta ArtWalk and Art District brochures at tourist info kiosks around town to assist you in your artistic quest. The Zona Romántica has its own separate art walk, the Paseo del Arte.

Street Sculpture

Street sculpture helps define Puerto Vallarta. Two of the most representative symbols – the *Caballito de Mar* and **Los Arcos** – are artistically hewn from stone and bronze. Plenty more surrealistic statues line the Malecón. The most outlandish is a toss-up between *The Subtle Stone-Eater* and the bow-shaped *Millennia* sculpture that incorporates Frankish emperor, Charlemagne, and pre-Columbian sage, Nezahualcoyotl. Beyond the Malecón, there's plenty more to ponder. Look out for an intimate study of Liz Taylor and Richard Burton called *The Lovers* on Calle Zaragoza.

Above Los Arcos

24 See Acapulco's CLIFF DIVERS

DRAMA | PERFORMANCE | SPORT

The cliff divers of La Quebrada – Acapulco's most famous tourist attraction – have been performing daredevil dives off the cliffs since the 1920s, though it wasn't until 1934 that the so-called *clavadistas* became an organized spectacle. Full of skill, drama, bravery and precision, the daily shows are a sight to behold, especially at sunset.

How to

Getting here & around Most visitors arrive in Acapulco by air or bus. La Quebrada is a 1km uphill walk from the main square (*zócalo*).

When to go The spectacle is performed five times a day year-round.

Tipping Divers will pose for photos with you and happily accept tips for their brave endeavors.

Dinner Book dinner at **La Perla** in Hotel Mirador and you can watch the show for free.

Clifftop Stage

The **Clavadista Show** *(clavadistaslaquebrada.com; adult/child M$100/50)* takes place in a narrow gulch called La Quebrada, close to downtown, overlooked by sheer 40m-high cliffs. These days the divers are all consummate professionals: in over 90 years of performances, there have been no casualties.

As an audience gathers on the viewing platform below the cliff, a team of seven lithe young divers jumps down into the churning waves before valiantly free-climbing the vertical cliff opposite (an impressive feat in itself). In the evenings, torches are lit at the clifftop shrine to the Virgin, asking her for protection, before the show takes place. Most dive from the lower (25m) platform – first a solo diver, then a pair simultaneously, then three divers leaping gracefully in sync. The final diver dives from the very top (35m).

DENNIS MACDONALD/SHUTTERSTOCK

Paseo Amor Eterno

A 2km stretch of Avenida Adolfo López Mateos between La Quebrada and Playa La Angosta is lined with 57 sail-shaped panels that chronicle famous personalities that have been connected with Acapulco over the years, from the obvious – Frank Sinatra, Liz Taylor and Johnny Weissmuller (who once owned the Hotel Flamingos) – to the more unexpected: George Harrison, Sly Stallone and Queen Elizabeth II. The panels make up a unique outdoor museum overlooking the ocean known as the **Paseo Amor Eterno**. Halfway along sits the dramatic **Sinfonía del Mar**, an open-air amphitheater grafted into the hillside that hosts symphony concerts, rock bands and dance troupes.

Timing it Right

The trick is the timing: they have to get it right and meet the incoming wave, otherwise there is not enough water in the churning cove to cushion their fall, and you find the audience holding their collective breaths as they watch the divers make their way out of the roiling sea without getting dashed against the rocks. The spectacle lasts for around 20 minutes. Show times are 1pm, 7pm, 8pm, 9pm and 10pm. The last show features the final diver holding two flaming torches as he dives into the darkness (they turn off the floodlights for that one).

Above Cliff diver, La Quebrada, Acapulco

25 Surf's Up in TRONCONES

BEACHES | SPORT | FOOD

A world-class, year-round surfing destination, Troncones in Guerrero has managed to stay relatively low-key and avoid the unbridled development of Acapulco or Mazatlán. Notwithstanding, the long beachfront road that connects the village proper with the traditional fishing community of La Majahua has edged its way into the deluxe price range in recent years, sporting boutique hotels, fusion restaurants, expat homes and sunrise yoga.

GLASS AND NATURE/SHUTTERSTOCK

How to

Getting here & around **Ixtapa-Zihuatanejo** is the nearest international airport. Troncones is 40 minutes away by taxi.

When to go November to March has the best weather, along with consistent but not monstrous waves.

Find more waves Head 25 minutes north to La Saladita, a smaller more laidback version of Troncones.

Go kayaking For a day off surfing, kayaking trips can be organized on the local Boca de Lagunillas estuary with Troncones-based operator **Costa Nativa** *(costanativa.com.mx)*.

CSP/SHUTTERSTOCK

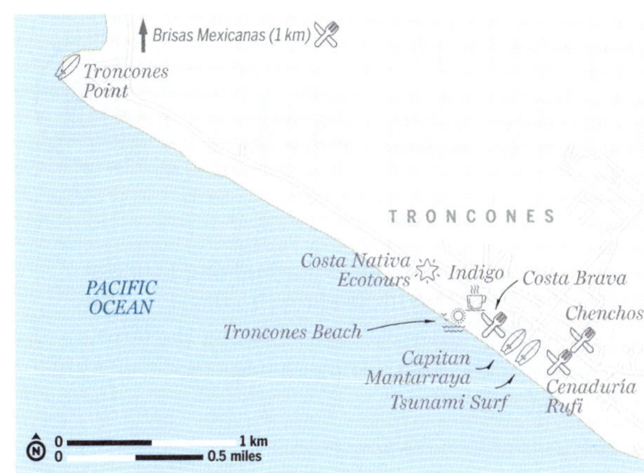

Perfect Waves

Troncones' superb year-round surf means you don't have to waste energy finding the perfect wave. The miles-long, crowd-free **beach** between the village of Troncones and Troncones Point is punctuated by sandbars that create several consistent left- and right-hander beach breaks, ideal for short, intense rides for intermediate and expert surfers, particularly shortboarders. Get the scoop from local surfers about rocky areas and watch out for rocks in summer.

Point Break

You may hear local and visiting long boarders rave about **Troncones Point**, one of the finest left-hander point breaks in Mexico. When it's small, the takeoff is right over the rocks (complete with sea urchins), and it offers a steep drop and fast wall over a shallow reef. When it's big, it's beautiful and beefy, and rolls halfway across the bay, with occasional barrels.

Rental & Lessons

If you haven't surfed before, or if you want a local expert to show you the best hot spots, team up with the guys from **Tsunami Surf** *(tsunamisurftroncones.com; lessons US$50)*, Troncones' original surf school with over 20 years' experience. Swing by the office on the main street in the village to rent a surfboard or SUP, or to sign up for surfing lessons and boat trips to the best breaks. Another popular local surfing instructor is **Capitan Mantarraya** *(tronconestours.com)*, who offers group and private surf lessons, as well as other outings on the ocean including snorkeling, sailing and paddleboarding.

Top left Beach, Troncones **Bottom left** Surfing, Troncones

Après-Surfing Spots

Cenaduría Rufi With chequered tables under a corrugated shelter, locally run Rufi delivers no-nonsense Mexican standards including chicken *mole*.

Chenchos Family-run restaurant specializing in fine homestyle Mexican cooking; expect shrimp enchiladas *con salsa verde* and *chiles rellenos*.

Costa Brava Keeping it real amid the gringo-izing of Troncones, this likable open-air restaurant does a solid selection of seafood.

Brisas Mexicanas Surf-side *marisquería* (seafood restaurant) serving catch of the day (*al ajillo* or breaded) and *aguachile*.

Indigo Quintessential beach-town cafe delivering wall-to-wall deliciousness, from breakfast pancakes to dinner steaks.

26 Soporific SAN BLAS

HISTORY I RUINS I BOAT TOUR

While you might not guess it today, the fishing village of San Blas was once an important Spanish port. From the late 16th century to the early 19th century, it served as the main base for Spanish explorations along the Pacific Coast as far north as Alaska, and elements of its history-shaping past can still be glimpsed in some delightfully overgrown ruins.

ABEL GONZALEZ/GETTY IMAGES

How to

Getting here & around San Blas is linked by bus to Puerto Vallarta and Mazatlán. You can walk to the historical sights from the bus terminal.

When to go If you're interested in birds, visit in January for San Blas' International Festival of Migratory Birds.

See crocodiles If you don't see any on the Trovara boat trip, drop by the **Cocodrilario Kiekari** where you can view captive crocs rehabilitating.

ADRIANA MARGARITA LARIOS ARELLANO/SHUTTERSTOCK

Top left San Blas **Bottom left** Crocodile, San Blas

Hilltop Remains

For an hour or two of satisfying solitude mixed with haunting history, head up the hill just east of San Blas' town center for a remembrance of things past.

Nestled among ancient trees and thick foliage sits the semi-ruined **Templo de la Virgen del Rosario** *(entry M$20 incl fort)* built in 1768 in honor of the patron saint of sailors, before it was partially destroyed in a fire less than 20 years later. Among the roofless remains you can still pick out the grand nave with its subtly decorated pillars and a shell-shaped baptismal font lying on the ground like a fallen meteorite. Further up the hill, the rectangular **La Contaduría fort** is of a similar provenance. It survived intact until 1811 when rebel priest José María Mercado died defending it during the Independence War. A giant gold-hued bust of the man stands overlooking the ocean.

A Fine Place to Stay

Back in town, proceed along Avenida Juárez to the attractive plaza and the remodeled **Casa de la Cultura** a couple of blocks west, which hosts temporary art exhibitions. There are some characterful ruins out back. Another block west, the revived San Blas pier has a sculpture trail and a striking new port building with food concessions. Consider staying over in the **Hotel Hacienda Flamingos**, the finest and oldest hotel in Nayarit state, housed in a beautifully furnished 1883 mansion with an intimate patio.

La Tovara Boat Tours

Aside from the history, one of San Blas' most popular activities is a boat trip to the freshwater swimming hole of **La Tovara National Park** *(latovara.com; tours from M$200)* where you can spot crocodiles. The three-hour trips depart frequently between 9:30am and 2:30pm and go up the San Cristóbal estuary to the spring, passing through mangrove-fringed wetlands where you can see iguanas, terrapins and wading birds. Go early in the morning to maximize wildlife sightings, and bring bug repellent. The swimming hole is enclosed, so you needn't fear becoming a croc's meal. Boats leave from the *embarcadero* at San Blas' eastern edge.

Tropical Style in OLD MAZATLÁN

ARCHITECTURE I THEATER I HISTORY

Thought you were in Mazatlán on a beach vacation? Think again. Welcome to the only city on the Pacific coast with an intact *centro histórico*. Dating mostly from the 19th century, plenty of outside influences have left their mark on this urban pastiche – including French, Italian, German and Spanish – forming a unique Mazatlán-forged style known locally as 'tropical neoclassical.'

Catedral de la Inmaculada Concepción
Old Mazatlán
Plaza República
Teatro Ángela Peralta
Playa Olas Altas
Plazuela Machado
Av Alemán
Av Barragán
Centenario
PACIFIC OCEAN
Calz Camarena
Isla El Crestón
Faro
0 500 m
0 0.25 miles

How to

Getting here & around Mazatlán has an international airport and buses to Puerto Vallarta. The central zone is traffic-light and easy to walk around.

When to go Come in February for the city's world-renowned carnival.

Taxis For the classic Mazatlán experience, hail a Pulmonia taxi (unique reconfigured VW Beetle) in Plazuela Machado and get it to drive you around Zona Centro's highlights.

Eating The *centro histórico* has truly exquisite places to enjoy breakfast.

Old Town Nexus

The city's oldest square, **Plazuela Machado** is a relatively small and intimate space. It dates from 1837 and retains most of its original two-story neoclassical buildings, the bulk of which have been reborn as bars, hotels and restaurants. Lean palms surround a wrought-iron bandstand (El Kiosko) with an umbrella-shaped roof that acts as a gathering spot for musicians, festivals and the annual carnival.

A Night at the Theater

Half a block south of Plazuela Machado, Mazaltan's historic **Teatro Ángela Peralta** is named after internationally acclaimed soprano Ángela Peralta, the so-called 'Mexican Nightingale,' who died during a yellow fever epidemic at the hotel next door in 1883. Built between 1869 and 1874, its relatively austere neoclassical façade hides an

MEHDI33300/SHUTTERSTOCK

opulent three-level interior restored to its former splendor in the 1990s. Known as the Rubio until 1940, it presents music, musicals, dance and – of course – opera.

Twin-Spired Gothic Cathedral

The city's twin-towered 19th-century **cathedral** is a Gothic Revival creation with pointed arches and a gold-tiled octagonal dome. It was constructed piecemeal between 1856 and 1899, and its surprisingly bright interior has gilt ceiling roses and enormous French chandeliers supported by monochrome blocks of stone. The church was designated a minor basilica by Pope Pius XII in 1941 and is famous for its majestic 19th-century organ. The facing **Plaza República**, while devoid of any notable architecture, is ringed by an impressive collection of ornate wrought-iron benches and shoe-shining chairs.

Olas Altas Beach

In Old Mazatlán, crescent-shaped **Playa Olas Altas** is where tourism first flourished in the 1920s. Buffeted by heavy surf, it's popular with bodyboarders but isn't safe for swimming. Several notable statues provide photo ops: Mexican actor and singer Pedro Infante atop a motorbike, singer Fernando Valadés tinkling on the ivories above the waves and, on the landward sidewalk, a life-sized recreation of The Beatles crossing the road in their famous *Abbey Road* album cover. From the beach, you can see Mazatlán's famous **Faro** (lighthouse) perched atop a giant crag at the jaws of the marina, like a displaced Rock of Gibraltar.

Above *Centro histórico*, Mazatlán

28 Puerto Vallarta from THE WATER

WILDLIFE | WATER SPORTS | SWIMMING

When it comes to comprehensive water activities on the Central Pacific Coast, Puerto Vallarta reigns supreme. There may be better individual spots to snorkel, kayak and whale-watch, but nowhere else is the quality and accessibility so concentrated and well-coordinated. Grab an oar, wetsuit and underwater mask and embrace the sea in all its salty, choppy, tempestuous glory.

How to

Getting here & around The majority of tourists fly into Puerto Vallarta. The water adventures are dotted around town, with many departing from the large marina near the airport.

When to go The best time for whale watching is early December to late March.

Boat taxis Access to beaches south of town is provided by boats that leave throughout the day from the pier on **Playa de los Muertos**.

Whale Watching

Imagine you're gazing at the ocean from the boat, trying to discern whether that ripple might be a giant fin. Then suddenly, a huge dark shape vaults out of the waves in a whirlwind of spray, twisting in the air and giving you a terrific glimpse of its torso and fins before crashing down with an almighty splash. Between December and March, Vallarta is squarely on the annual migration route of humpback whales, who come to the **Bahía de Banderas** to breed. **Ocean Friendly Tours** *(oceanfriendly.com)* is the best of the operators, offering three- to five-hour tours, with bilingual marine scientists leading each excursion and an eco-friendly ethic. Occasionally you'll get lucky, and spot whales from water taxis bound for southern beaches.

Snorkeling & Diving

Stand-up paddleboarding aside, which you can practice off various beaches with

ALBEERTO LOPEEZ/SHUTTERSTOCK

Xiutla Riders *(xriderspv.com)*. Puerto Vallarta is one of Mexico's best destinations for scuba divers, with abundant wrecks, caves, reefs galore and marine life – from clownfish to dolphins, whales and sea turtles – and excellent visibility of up to 30m, best in summer. Highly professional **Vallarta Undersea** *(vallartaundersea.com)* offers certification courses, plus diving excursions in **Los Arcos National Marine Park** and off **Islas Marietas**, among other dive sites. Los Arcos, and beaches such as **Majahuitas** and **Quimixto** are terrific snorkeling destinations. Reach them under your own steam or with the likes of **Vallarta Adventures** *(vallarta-adventures.com)*.

Best Beaches for...

Swimming The picturesque turquoise shallows of **Playa Palmares**, 6km south of the Zona Centro, are favored by locals for swimming as the beach is far from rivers ensuring clear water year-round.

Kitesurfing Breezy **Playa Flamingos**, just north of Nuevo Nayarit, is a prime kitesurfing and windsurfing spot.

SUPs **Playa de Camarones**, Zona Centro's main strip, is narrow but sandy with calm waters that are ideal for balancing on your paddleboard, especially in the morning.

Snorkeling Palm-fringed **Playa de Quimixto** is backed by a small fishing village, and there's good snorkeling at the rocky outcrops that bookend the beach.

Above Los Arcos de Mismaloya

29 Zihuatanejo COASTAL HOP

BEACH WALKS | SNORKELING | SEAFOOD

The best way to uncover the nuances of Zihuatanejo's complex personality is to walk its shoreline from the modern pier in the north to Playa Las Gatas in the south. On the way, the soles of your feet will caress paving stones, sand, asphalt and rocks.

BRESTER IRINA/SHUTTERSTOCK

Walking the Beaches

A variety of paths link Zihua's beaches. **Playa Municipal** and **La Madera** are joined by the paved Paseo del Pescador. A short stretch of road connects Madera with **Playa La Ropa** (pictured), while **Playa Las Gatas** is accessible by a short esplanade followed by 500m-long coastal path. Be prepared to rock-hop!

Trip Notes

Getting here & around By air from Mexico City or by bus from Acapulco. At the end of the walk, get a boat (M$100) back to the *muelle* (dock).

When to go Zihua is refreshingly cooler during 'winter' (Dec–Mar).

Coffee break Stop at **Cafecito** opposite the municipal beach to watch Zihua life drifting by.

Fishing Book sportfishing trips with **Triángulo del Sol** close to the *muelle*.

Mangos
Cocos
Plaza Kyoto
Ortiz
Canal Agua de Correa
Camino a Playa La Ropa
Álvarez
Adelita
López Mateos
Laguna de Las Salinas
Marina
Álvarez
Paseo del Pescador
La Noria
Pier
Contramar Andador
Carretera Escénica
Bahía de Zihuatanejo
Rocks
01 The modern **muelle** is ideal to watch the comings and goings of fishing boats from the nearby beach: fishers roll their craft over logs to propel them into the sea.
02 The **municipal beach** is chockablock with small single-motor fishing boats that head out at night and return in the morning to sell their catch on the aptly named Paseo de Pescador.
03 Bookended and sheltered by rocks, **Playa Madera** is known for its shallow, swimmable water and candlelit bistros whose tables abut the sand.
04 Some of the best hotels and restaurants are dotted along **Playa La Ropa**, Zihua's widest and finest beach. Its long stretch of white sand provides fine swimming, waterskiing and paddleboarding conditions.
05 Despite no direct road access, **Playa Las Gatas** has an unbroken line of *palapa* restaurants greeting boat-throngs of people at weekends. The narrow beach is beloved by families for its shallow calm waters.
ALYSTA/SHUTTERSTOCK
0 400 m
0 0.2 miles

Acapulco & the Manila Galleon

INTERCONTINENTAL TRADE ROUTE ACROSS THE PACIFIC

For 250 years between 1565 and 1815, Spanish ships plied the open waters of the Pacific between Acapulco and Manila laden with silver for the Philippines and silk, spices and other luxury goods for New Spain. The precarious globe-spanning trade route became known as the Manila Galleon or *La Nao de China*.

Left Artifacts, Museo Histórico de Acapulco **Right** View of the Port of Acapulco c 1745 by George Anson

NIKITICH VIKTORIYA/SHUTTERSTOCK

Early Pioneers

The Philippines had first been explored by Europeans in 1521 on the Magellan exhibition, which ultimately went on to circumnavigate the globe. Magellan had been sent west by the Spanish king, Charles I, to find a new trade route to the Spice Islands (in present-day Indonesia) that avoided unnecessary confrontations with the Portuguese. It was a goal he accomplished by the skin of his teeth when he landed on Homonhon Island in March 1521, thus logging the first successful crossing of the Pacific. Notwithstanding, due to volatile ocean currents and weather patterns that necessitated sailing at higher latitudes when heading east, it took another 41 years for Spanish navigators to plot a return route back to America.

The first successful eastern voyage across the Pacific was completed in 1565, the year the Philippines were colonized by Spanish conquistador Miguel López de Legazpi. Two ships made the journey, including the galleon *San Pedro* guided by skilled navigator Andrés de Urdaneta, which arrived in Acapulco in October 1565 after a 129-day voyage. It was the first recognized outing for the Manila Galleon.

Silver for Silks

Thereafter, one or two galleons a year set sail in either direction from Acapulco and Manila, establishing a trade network that linked Asia and America with markets in Europe and ushered in a history-shaping era of globalization and cultural interchange.

Manila Bay developed into a meeting place for Spanish galleons and Chinese junks that would swap goods and

CREATOR:GEORGE ANSON, PUBLIC DOMAIN, VIA WIKIMEDIA COMMONS

services in a month-long trading frenzy. The Spanish brought pots of South American silver and supplies of corn, tobacco, potatoes and chocolate, along with olive oil, wine and armaments from Europe. The Asian traders brought Chinese silk and porcelain, Indian spices and Persian carpets.

The Role of Acapulco

In Acapulco, the booty was offloaded and stored in quayside warehouses. A month-long trade fair then ensued, with merchants from Peru, the Caribbean and Europe arriving to barter and bid. Most of the goods were transported by land via Mexico City to the Caribbean port of Veracruz from where the annual treasure fleet flotillas would ship them on to Spain.

To protect the valuable goods, Acapulco was increasingly fortified in the 17th century. In 1617, the sturdy Fuerte de San Diego was completed and by the end of the century the bastion was defended with 42 cannons and a system of warning beacons that stretched along the Mexican coast.

The galleons were equally well built, mostly in Manila. In the space of 250 years, only four of them were successfully captured by pirates, most famously the *Santa Ana,* which was raided by British privateer Thomas Cavendish off the coast of Baja California in 1587 and looted of US$122,000 worth of silver.

End of an Era

After 250 lucrative years of trade, the Nao declined in importance in the early 19th century when Spain became embroiled in the Peninsula War and various American colonies, including Mexico, successfully fought for independence. It was abolished by royal decree in 1813 and the last ship, the *San Fernando*, sailed into Acapulco Bay in 1815.

Fuerte de San Diego

Acapulco's majestic pentagonal fortress was founded in 1617 and rebuilt in 1776 after an earthquake toppled the original. The large muscular structure you see today is the intact remains of the 18th-century reboot and is home to the intelligently curated **Museo Histórico de Acapulco** *(mediateca.inah.gob.mx; entry M$75)* dedicated to Acapulco's crucial role in the Pacific Trade Route. Mercifully air-conditioned rooms follow a logical trajectory with printed displays backed up by superbly crafted model ships, and archaeological remains found in the nearby bay. The mandatory walk around the ramparts reveals aging cannons poking through the crenelated turrets.

Listings

BEST OF THE REST

Cheap Tacos

El Puerco de Oro $

A superb breakfast *taquería* in Puerto Vallarta's Versalles district. The stand-out is the flagship pork belly tacos on heirloom blue corn tortillas with salsa verde.

Taquería Playa Sur $

Come evening, the breezy dining area of this Mazatlán *taquería* becomes fragrant with smoke from the grill as hungry customers vie for the default beef tacos.

Pancho's Takos $

Drawing a regular crowd, this humble *taquería* near Los Muertos beach is a solid contender for Puerto Vallarta's best *tacos al pastor*.

Seafood by the Beach

Los Buzos $$

One of many *palapas* on Acapulco's Playa Tamarindos, 'The Divers' serves locally caught fish including super-fresh *huachinango a la talla* (red snapper in a spicy sauce).

Tacos Los Abuelos $

Grilled octopus tacos stand out at this seafront spot on boat-in-only Yelapa Beach, an hour south of Puerto Vallarta. All the mains come with a Colosseum-sized salad.

El Muchacho Alegre $$

A seafood institution overlooking the city's Playa Norte, this place combines live *banda* music with terrific seafood, including *aguachile*.

Breakfast & Coffee

Espresso 45 $

Early birds catch more than superb coffee at this spartan-decorated joint in Puerto Vallarta's Versalles quarter, a leading light among a good half-dozen local cafes. The avocado on toast is as good as *huevos rancheros*.

Nueva Zelanda Café $$

Step back in time at this long-standing Ixtapa institution, where you can order a banana split or soursop smoothie with your shrimp taco and chicken fajitas. Good for breakfast.

Cuattro Casa de Café $

Save your biggest Zihuatanejo caffeine urges for cycle-themed Cuattro, which produces an eye-popping selection of cakes and pastries served in a salubrious interior with a patio and mezzanine.

Looney Bean $$

Terrific beachside coffee shop overlooking Mazatlán's Playa Olas Altas serving strong coffee, fruity juices, creamy smoothies and flavor-loaded Mexican or American breakfasts.

Shopping for Mexican Crafts

Casa Etnika

Family-run shop in Old Mazatlán offering quality gifts made by Mexican artisans, from Huichol beadwork, psychedelic weavings and papier-mâché skeletons to copper-wire and wool jewelry, and fair-trade coffee.

Mundo de Azulejos

Puerto Vallarta institution that has been making dazzlingly colored Talavera tiles and ceramics for decades, anything from sinks to whimsical tiles to hang around the house.

Manyana

Sayulita-born concept store selling contemporary ceramics, stylish linen wear, funky glasses, copper lamps, Molluskhemp T-shirts and surfer garb.

El Jumil

Devils, angels, jaguars and other fantastic creatures peer down at you from El Jumil on Zihuatanejo's Paseo del Pescador. The striking masks are well-known traditional handicrafts in Guerrero state.

 Dreamy Beaches

Playa Icacos

Acapulco's most southerly segment of sand is dotted with kiosks encouraging you to soar above the sea, attached to a parachute and propelled by speedboat, or be dragged along the surf by banana boat.

Playa de las Ánimas

A long, spectacularly located beach south of Puerto Vallarta, lapped by teal waters and overlooked by a fishing village with assorted *palapa* restaurants. Good for water sports.

Playa Sayulita

Just north of Puerto Vallarta, this charismatic strip of sand is busy but chilled, with a carefree surfer vibe and vendors selling everything from candy to massages.

Playa Norte

Golden sands stretch north from Old Mazatlán for several kilometers through the Zona Dorada. Look for wandering *bandas sinaloenses* with their distinctive sousaphone players.

 Museums to Ponder

Museo Naval

This well-structured institution on Puerto Vallarta's Malecón delves into maritime history, from waterways, to the Maya, to trade with the Philippines under the Spanish.

Observatorio 1873

Relatively new tourist complex atop Mazatlán's Vigia hill that sports a restored astronomical observatory and an extraordinarily detailed museum about whales and dolphins.

MEHDI33300/SHUTTERSTOCK

The beach in Mazatlán

Museo Arqueológico de la Costa Grande

Fanning out around a central courtyard, this Zihuatanejo establishment displays jewelry, stone tools, rock carvings and ceramics with Olmec, Teotihuacán, Tarascan and Mexica elements from key archaeological sites.

 Pacific Surf Spots

La Saladita

Half an hour's drive north of Troncones, Playa La Saladita lures longboarders to the Wave Machine (aka Ubliam, or reverse Malibu) – a beautiful, slow-breaking left-hand point break.

Sayulita

The beach break at Playa Sayulita's south end, and its long, mellow waves, provide excellent learning conditions for rookie surfers.

Punta de Mita

Southeast along the coast from Punta de Mita, **Burros** is a long and mellow right-hander point break with occasional lefts. Great for aficionados, rough for beginners.

WESTERN CENTRAL HIGHLANDS

NATURE | CULTURE | ART

RESEARCHED BY ANNA KAMINSKI

- **Trip Builder** (p182)
- **Practicalities** (p183)
- **Tequila Tasting in Tequila** (p184)
- **Millions of Marvelous Monarchs** (p186)
- **Trekking in Volcán Nevado de Colima** (p188)
- **Exploring Guadalajara's Centro** (p190)
- **Folk Art of the Western Central Highlands** (p192)
- **Listings** (p194)

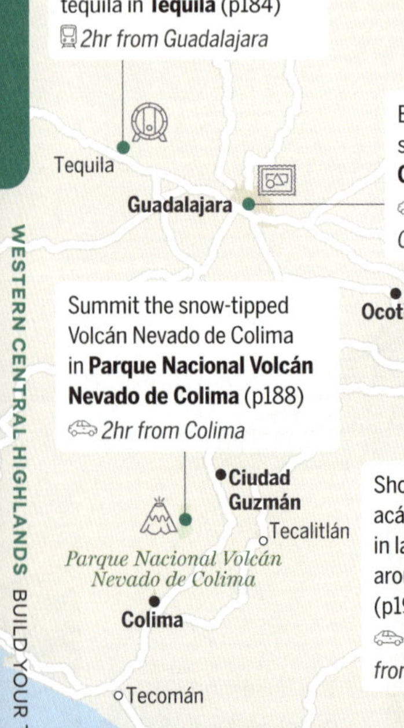

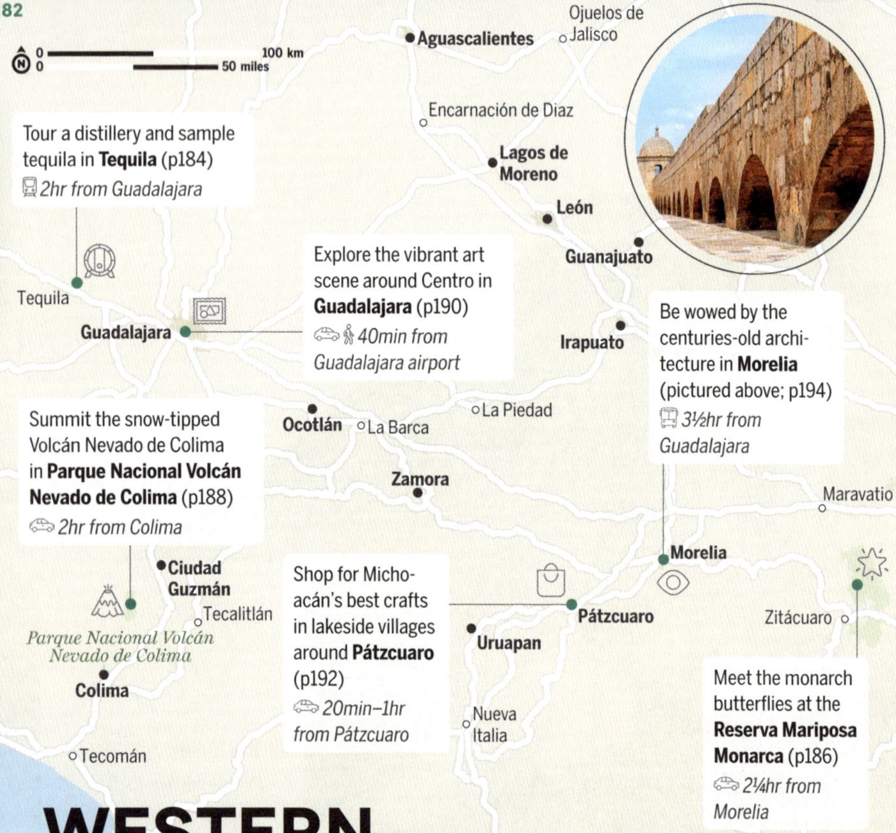

0 100 km
0 50 miles
Aguascalientes
Ojuelos de Jalisco
Encarnación de Diaz
Lagos de Moreno
León
Guanajuato
Tequila
Guadalajara
Irapuato
Ocotlán
La Barca
La Piedad
Zamora
Maravatio
Morelia
Ciudad Guzmán
Tecalitlán
Pátzcuaro
Zitácuaro
Uruapan
Parque Nacional Volcán Nevado de Colima
Colima
Nueva Italia
Tecomán
Tour a distillery and sample tequila in **Tequila** (p184)
2hr from Guadalajara
Explore the vibrant art scene around Centro in **Guadalajara** (p190)
40min from Guadalajara airport
Be wowed by the centuries-old architecture in **Morelia** (pictured above; p194)
3½hr from Guadalajara
Summit the snow-tipped Volcán Nevado de Colima in **Parque Nacional Volcán Nevado de Colima** (p188)
2hr from Colima
Shop for Michoacán's best crafts in lakeside villages around **Pátzcuaro** (p192)
20min–1hr from Pátzcuaro
Meet the monarch butterflies at the **Reserva Mariposa Monarca** (p186)
2¼hr from Morelia

WESTERN CENTRAL HIGHLANDS

Trip Builder

If any one region captures Mexico's natural beauty, cultural complexity and urban buzz, it's the Western Central Highlands. From volcanoes, a marvelous butterfly migration, traces of pre-Hispanic civilizations and centuries-old craft traditions to superb dining in bigger cities, it truly has it all.

JORCH R ORRANTIA/SHUTTERSTOCK
PREVIOUS SPREAD: RUBI RODRIGUEZ MARTINEZ/SHUTTERSTOCK

Practicalities

ARRIVING

Aeropuerto Internacional Miguel Hidalgo Guadalajara's airport, 18km south of downtown, has direct flights across Mexico, the US, Colombia and Spain. Airport buses drop passengers off in Centro. Airport taxis cost M$300 to M$400.

CONNECT

In Guadalajara and larger towns, wi-fi is ubiquitous in hotels and restaurants. There's little wi-fi in remoter locations.

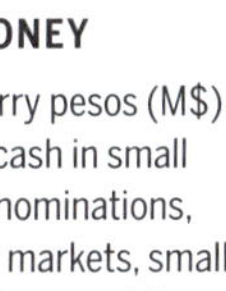

MONEY

Carry pesos (M$) in cash in small denominations, for markets, small villages, public transportation, tipping and paying at some restaurants.

WHERE TO STAY

Area	Pros/Cons
Guadalajara	Museums, market, historic architecture. Superb dining and nightlife. Noisy.
Morelia	Historic architecture, art, great restaurants, characterful hotels, proximity to butterfly reserve.
Pátzcuaro	Excellent craft shopping, historic hotels, close to craft villages; limited amenities.
Colima	Good restaurants, proximity to volcanoes; few attractions, limited accommodations.

GETTING AROUND

Car A car is useful for reaching more remote places, such as the villages around Pátzcuaro, the *pueblo mágico* (magical village) of Tapalpa and the Reserva Mariposa Monarca, and allows for maximum flexibility.

Bus & Train Major cities and towns are well connected by national bus lines. Jalisco's only train line is a private one, linking Guadalajara to Tequila.

TOP: CAROLINA ARROYO/SHUTTERSTOCK
BOTTOM: NATA_VKUSIDEY/GETTY IMAGES

EATING & DRINKING

Guadalajara specialties to look out for include *birria* (a spicy goat stew), *carne en su jugo* ('meat in its juice,' a type of beef soup) and, above all, the ubiquitous *torta ahogada* (pictured top left), a chili-sauce-soaked *carnitas* (fried pork) sandwich. Tequila is, incidentally, home to tequila (pictured bottom left) production.

Best Restaurant
Alcalde, Guadalajara (p190)

Best Tequila Distillery
Casa Sauza, Tequila (p185)

JAN & FEB
Monarch butterfly season in Michoacán's mountains; peak time for volcano ascents.

MAR & APR
Festival time in Guadalajara and Morelia.

JUN–AUG
Wet, sultry weather; mariachis and *charros* (cowboys) descend on Guadalajara.

OCT–DEC
Warm, dry weather, Día de Muertos celebrations in November.

30 Tequila Tasting in TEQUILA

DRINK | CULTURE | HISTORY

Surrounded by seas of blue agave, the *pueblo mágico* and UNESCO World Heritage Site of Tequila, with its cobbled streets and brightly painted houses, is the heartland of the namesake spirit most closely associated with Mexico. The tequila barrel-shaped shuttles disgorging bachelor(ette) parties aside, it's an attractive town, and its distilleries offering tours of their facilities are a must.

How to

Getting here & around Most distilleries are centrally located and reachable on foot. Tequila is connected to Guadalajara by frequent buses as well as the private Jose Cuervo train that runs tequila tours.

When to go There is no tequila off-season; tours are offered year-round.

Tours & tastings Half a dozen distilleries offer a variety of tours (in Spanish and English), from basic tastings to visiting private cellars. Book in advance.

A Brief History of Tequila

Agave-based pulque is a pre-Hispanic drink, but tequila was first created in the mid-16th century using European distillation techniques. In 1795, when the Cuervo family first bottled the drink, it was called 'mezcal de tequila.' Mexico gave tequila an appellation of origin in 1974, which decreed the drink must be made from at least 51% blue Weber agave, grown in Jalisco, plus parts of Nayarit, Michoacán, Tamaulipas and Guanajuato.

Know Your Tequilas

Blanco tequila is the clear, young variety that most drinkers are familiar with; it spends 15 days in stainless-steel tanks and is commonly used for mixing cocktails. *Reposado* (rested) is golden-colored tequila that has spent from two months to a year in oak barrels. Darker, barrel-aged tequila that's been in the barrel for over a year is known as *añejo*

MEL GONZALEZ/SHUTTERSTOCK

Must-visit Distilleries

La Rojeña Oldest tequila distillery in the Americas, with antique equipment; extended tours include food pairings and private cellar visits.

Casa Sauza Impressive manicured grounds with Italianate fountains and Venetian mosaic. Plant your own agave during the extended tour.

Hacienda La Cofradía Hillside distillery where you can stay in a giant tequila barrel; taste raw agave and multiple tequilas on a tour.

La Fortaleza Contemporary distillery with a viewpoint overlooking agave fields. Tours include ample tastings and Baja-style taco lunches.

Tequila Cascahuín El Arenal distillery where you'll see the entire process, from *piña* harvesting to bottling and labeling.

(aged) and has complex flavors, while *joven* (young) is a mix of *blanco* with either *reposado* or *añejo*.

Tequila Tours

There are several ways of visiting tequila distilleries. You can day-trip from Guadalajara on the upmarket **Jose Cuervo Express** *(mundo cuervo.com)*, with tastings onboard, or take the **Herradura Express** *(herradura.com)* to the La Herradura distillery in Amatitlán, which attracts true tequila connoisseurs. Alternatively, put yourself in the hands of the **Experience Agave** *(experienceagave.com)* team to visit Tequila's lesser-known, more intimate distilleries – either on a day trip or four-day immersion – with hotel transfers included.

Above La Rojeña distillery

31 Millions of Marvelous MONARCHS

NATURE | WILDLIFE | SCENERY

The Spanish thought it was a plague. Locals believed that it was the souls of the dead taking flight. Whatever you believe, a visit to the 563-sq-km **Reserva Mariposa Monarca** is an unparalleled experience. Every fall, monarch butterflies make their 4500km, five-week journey from northeastern Canada and the United States to the hilltop fir forests in Michoacán and Mexico state.

ATOSAN/SHUTTERSTOCK

How to

Getting here & around The easiest way to visit is by day tour with **Yei! Tours** from Morelia. Self-driving from Morelia takes 2½ hours each way. Alternatively, overnight in Zitácuaro or in Angangueo and take a taxi to the reserve.

When to go Butterfly season is from November to March; butterflies are most populous in January and February.

Before you go Before visiting the sanctuary, track the monarch migration via **Journey North** *(journeynorth.org)*.

JUAN PABLO HINOJOSA/SHUTTERSTOCK

JUAN PABLO HINOJOSA/SHUTTERSTOCK

Top left Reserva Mariposa Monarca **Bottom left & right** Monarch butterflies

A Butterfly's Life

While the typical monarch life cycle is two to six weeks, those that make the journey south enter the 'reproductive diapause' phase, which extends their lifespan to around seven months. Butterflies remain in Mexico from November to March, when they finally mate. Then the females lay eggs on local milkweed plants – the sole food source for their caterpillars. This offspring of overwintering monarchs then makes the journey in reverse.

Meeting the Monarchs

Seeing entire trees covered in a dense carpet of butterflies, then watching thousands upon thousands unfurl their wings in the morning to dry them, turning the landscape a fiery orange, is enough to make your jaw drop in wonder. When they take to the air, the susurrations of myriad wings are surprisingly loud and eerie; and when they cover the ground in the afternoons, forced down by rising humidity, it's as if the forest floor is aflame.

Butterflies in Peril

In December 2024, the United States Fish and Wildlife Service designated the monarch butterfly a threatened species under the Endangered Species Act. Illegal logging in their crucial mountain habitat and the destruction of milkweed – the butterflies' sole food source – by agricultural interests has made overwintering populations at Reserva Mariposa Monarca erratic. In 2024, monarchs occupied an area of just 0.9ha – a staggering 59% drop from the 2022–23 overwintering season. Monarchwatch.org gives tips on protecting the butterflies.

Visiting the Sanctuary

The sanctuary has four publicly accessible parts: two in Michoacán (El Rosario and Sierra Chincua), accessible from Angangueo, and two in México state (Cerro Pelón and Piedra Herrada), reached from Zitácuaro. El Rosario receives up to 10,000 visitors per day, with a 3km ascent (on foot or horseback) to reach the butterflies; Sierra Chincua offers a less strenuous hike. Cerro Pelón involves a steep ascent (1½ to two hours) through cathedral-like firs, while Piedra Herrada is inundated with day trippers from Mexico City on weekends. However you visit, you must pay the daily admission fee and be accompanied by a mandatory guide.

32 TREKKING IN Volcán Nevado de Colima

HIKING | ADVENTURE | SCENERY

With the Volcán Nevado de Colima and Volcán de Fuego looming dramatically 30km north of Colima, Parque Nacional Volcán Nevado de Colima acts as an irresistible lure for mountaineers looking to take advantage of dry winter days. Choose between hiking in the foothills of the still-active Volcán de Fuego (3860m) and summiting the larger, long-dormant Volcán Nevado de Colima (4330m).

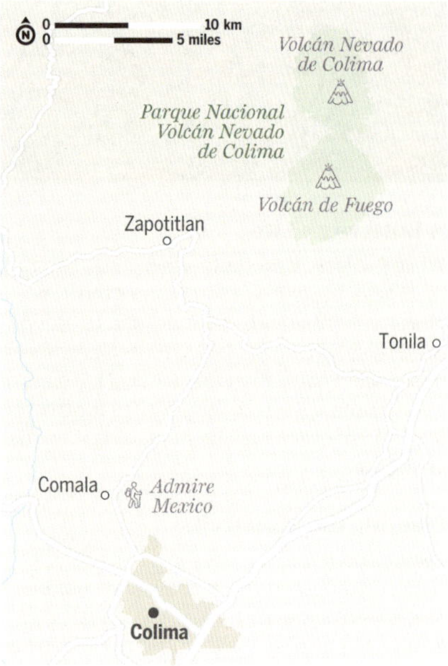

0 10 km
0 5 miles
Volcán Nevado de Colima
Parque Nacional Volcán Nevado de Colima
Volcán de Fuego
Zapotitlan
Tonila
Comala
Admire Mexico
Colima

How to

Getting here & around There is no public transport to the park, so it's easiest to access the Parque Nacional Volcán Nevado de Colima, 135km north of Colima, via a guided tour with Comala-based **Admire Mexico**.

When to go December through May is best for climbing, when weather is driest.

Essential info To visit the park independently, you need a high-clearance 4WD and to be completely self-sufficient.

A Fiery Giant

Volcán de Fuego is North America's most active volcano. It has erupted dozens of times in the past four centuries, with a big eruption every 70 years, and its cone is wreathed in a halo of smoke. Recent large eruptions in 2015 and 2017 showered ash on Ciudad Guzmán, 23km to the northeast. While its peak is off-limits, there's a rewarding hike in the exclusion zone within 10km of the summit. **Admire Mexico** *(admiremexicotours.com)* offers an engaging and moderately strenuous day trip into the Volcán de Fuego foothills; during the hike, you pass through coffee, avocado and sugarcane plantations, with excellent views of the smoking cone en route.

To the Snow-Tipped Summit

Summiting **Volcán Nevado de Colima**, aka Zapotepetl, is

JROMERO04/SHUTTERSTOCK

a more challenging endeavor. During the 12-hour guided excursion with Admire Mexico, you start at 5:30am to summit and return before sunset. Setting off from the La Joya/Puerto Las Cruces trailhead (3500m) and ranger station where you pay the entry fee (M$80), the breathless 9km trek to the summit takes three to four hours, involving a steady climb through pine forest to some radio antennae, then some flattish sections near the top, and a final steep scramble. A good level of physical fitness is essential. Spectacular views en route take in both Fuego's plumes of smoke and glimpses of the Pacific Ocean beyond.

Nevado de Colima Solo

Solo ascents are recommended for fit and experienced hikers only. Since temperatures from December to February dip below 0°C (32°F) and it may snow, you need crampons and an ice ax. To get here by public transportation, take a bus from Colima to Ciudad Guzmán (1½ hours), and then another to El Fresnito (30 minutes), and then hike 20km up the rough service road to La Joya (six to eight hours). Bring camping gear, a warm sleeping bag, food and water, camp at La Joya, summit the volcano, then descend to El Fresnito. To reach La Joya by car, you need a high-clearance 4WD.

Above Hiking, Volcán Nevado de Colima

33 Exploring Guadalajara's CENTRO

HISTORY | ART | FOOD

Mexico's second-largest city, Guadalajara is the birthplace of *charreadas* (rodeos), mariachi music and wide-brimmed sombreros – images traditionally associated with the country. Though founded in 1532, it's a young, forward-looking city, with a wealth of excellent museums, folk art–filled neighborhoods, and a cutting-edge dining scene.

Trip Notes

Getting here & around Guadalajara's historic center is best explored on foot. There are excellent bus connections across the Western Central Highlands, plus the private Jose Cuervo trains to Tequila.

When to go October to December is warm, dry and festival-filled; January to May means lower hotel prices.

Walking tours Guadalajart_MX (Instagram) runs small-group tours of Guadalajara's thriving art scene, while **Jalisco Trip Tours** *(jaliscotrip.com)* offers walking tours of Tonalá and Tlaquepaque.

Guadalajara's Best Meals

Alcalde Food-as-art plates of reimagined traditional Jalisco dishes, in a stunning setting.

Bruna Playful takes on generations-old recipes, creative desserts and remarkable mixology concoctions.

Pig's Pearls Devour your superlative lamb, maple sirloin or *pastor*-style pork burger on the industrial-chic terrace.

Tomate Taquería A bustling, sit-down *taquería* locally renowned for its tacos *al pastor*.

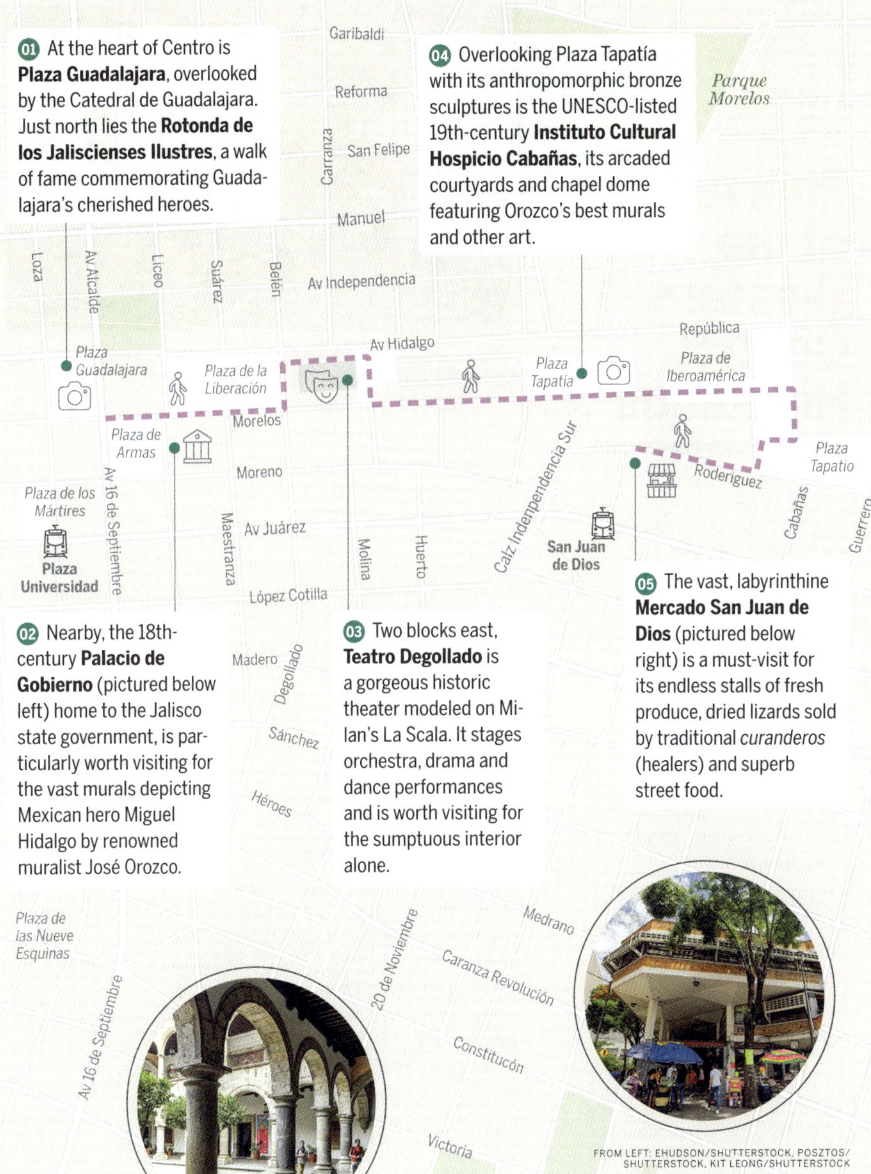

01 At the heart of Centro is **Plaza Guadalajara**, overlooked by the Catedral de Guadalajara. Just north lies the **Rotonda de los Jaliscienses Ilustres**, a walk of fame commemorating Guadalajara's cherished heroes.

02 Nearby, the 18th-century **Palacio de Gobierno** (pictured below left) home to the Jalisco state government, is particularly worth visiting for the vast murals depicting Mexican hero Miguel Hidalgo by renowned muralist José Orozco.

03 Two blocks east, **Teatro Degollado** is a gorgeous historic theater modeled on Milan's La Scala. It stages orchestra, drama and dance performances and is worth visiting for the sumptuous interior alone.

04 Overlooking Plaza Tapatía with its anthropomorphic bronze sculptures is the UNESCO-listed 19th-century **Instituto Cultural Hospicio Cabañas**, its arcaded courtyards and chapel dome featuring Orozco's best murals and other art.

05 The vast, labyrinthine **Mercado San Juan de Dios** (pictured below right) is a must-visit for its endless stalls of fresh produce, dried lizards sold by traditional *curanderos* (healers) and superb street food.

FROM LEFT: EHUDSON/SHUTTERSTOCK, POSZTOS/SHUTTERSTOCK, KIT LEONG/SHUTTERSTOCK

Folk Art of the Western Central Highlands

CENTURIES-OLD MICHOACÁN CRAFT TRADITIONS ARE FACING MODERN CHALLENGES

In the 1540s, the first bishop of Michoacán turned a number of indigenous settlements around the town of Pátzcuaro into Christianized *pueblos hospitales*, organized according to principles from *Utopia* by Thomas More, and each specializing in a particular craft. Their present-day inhabitants continue to practice their centuries-old trades.

Left Mercado de Artesanías **Centre** Handmade toys, Pátzcuaro **Right** Pottery for sale, Tzintzuntzan

OSCAR GARCES/SHUTTERSTOCK

Age-Old Craftsmanship

Come to Pátzcuaro's **Mercado de Artesanías** and you'll see artisans from the lakeside villages of Tzintzuntzan, Ihuatzio, Tócuaro, Santa Clara del Cobre and other lakeside towns plying their wares: ceramics, painstakingly carved masks, copper vessels, animal figures made from reeds. Simultaneously, at the Friday flea market, you may spot Purépecha women bartering fruit and dried fish for medicinal herbs and clothing, as part of an age-old tradition that predates the arrival of the Spanish. The Purépecha, whose empire was centered on Pátzcuaro and Tzintzuntzan, were sophisticated craftspeople who specialized in ceramics as well as metallurgy and textiles; in fact, superior arms crafted by the Purépecha kept the Aztecs at bay. Today, as was the case 500 years ago, Pátzcuaro remains the main trading hub for artisans residing in lakeside *pueblos*.

Enter Bishop Quiroga

The Purépecha were unprepared for the 1522 arrival of the Spanish conquistadors. Though the Purépecha emperor converted to Christianity, that did not spare his subjects from the mass slaughter and torture inflicted by Nuño de Guzmán, a particularly brutal conquistador who reigned over the Pátzcuaro region from 1529 to 1534, until his brutality became too much even for the Spanish Crown, and he was recalled to Spain and imprisoned. In 1538, Guzmán was replaced by Vasco de Quiroga – a judge and bishop who became determined to prevent the Purépecha from being slaughtered and to set up a utopia

LUISMRIVAS80/SHUTTERSTOCK

OSCAR GARCES/SHUTTERSTOCK

based on Christian teachings and economic self-sufficiency. Having witnessed the wealth of locally produced crafts and the existing informal bartering system, Quiroga sought to facilitate the craft trade (and the conversion of the indigenous people to Christianity) by encouraging them to settle in so-called *pueblos hospitales*, where he duly built missions and workshops, and imported new craft techniques and experts from Spain to enable each *pueblo* to focus on a single craft.

Craft Towns of the Pátzcuaro Region

South of Pátzcuaro, copper is the soul of Santa Clara de Cobre, where the production of copper cauldrons plus church bells, kitchenware and other copper crafts employs more than 80% of residents. In lakeside Tzintzuntzan, the centuries-old tradition of *alfarería* (pottery making) is thriving, with individual artisans decorating their vessels with animal and fish motifs, as well as pre-Hispanic geometric designs. In Sanabria, between Tzintzuntzan and Pátzcuaro, tablecloths, napkins and shawls, embroidered by the local women's cooperative, depict pastoral and fishing scenes, Día de Muertos processions and more.

West of Pátzcuaro, Tócuaro specializes in carving intricate wooden masks with fierce human and animal visages, used in rituals and traditional dances. In Capula, half the town creates *punteado* ceramics, with the dots painted using hairs from squirrels' tails, differing from *piñas* – appliqued ceramics in the shape of pine cones – from San José de la Gracia. Ceramic *diablitos* – devil masks and figurines – hail from the mountain town of Ocumicho, and are in great demand for Día de Muertos celebrations, while the musically inclined head for Paracho to purchase exquisite handmade guitars.

Traditional Crafts in Danger

Over the past two decades, the craft economy around Lago de Pátzcuaro has been struggling. Drug trade–related cartel violence in parts of Michoacán has made tourists reluctant to visit Pátzcuaro, even though the town and its environs are safe to visit. Young people have been leaving the villages in search of more lucrative jobs in the city rather than learning traditional trades. Bargain-seeking tourists have taken advantage of artisans' need for cash by offering them rock-bottom prices for their wares. To support local artisans, don't bargain on the price when buying a quality piece from the artisan directly, or else purchase from galleries committed to paying artisans a *precio justo* (fair price).

Listings

BEST OF THE REST

Quintessential Mexican Pastimes

Arena Coliseo

Watch masked wrestlers, depicting characters from timeless stories of good and evil, theatrically duking it out in the ring using high-flying maneuvers during a rowdy *lucha libre* match.

El Parián de Tlaquepaque

Be serenaded by mariachis – street troubadours whose folk songs are deeply rooted in the daily struggles of ordinary Mexicans.

Campo Charro Jalisco

Watch riders on horseback dazzle the crowd with various skill-testing competitions, including spinning their horse in a circle, plus *escaramuzas* (female stunt riders performing bold equestrian maneuvers at a gallop).

Pueblos Mágicos

Tapalpa

A favorite with Guadalajara weekend visitors, Tapalpa is a labyrinth of whitewashed walls and cobbled lanes, wrapped around two impressive 16th-century churches. Enjoy the scenic drive and hike to a waterfall.

Comala

A short ride from Colima, this delightful *pueblo mágico* resembles an Andalusian white village and is renowned for its *tuba* (fermented palm-tree sap drink) and hand-carved wooden masks.

Ancient Ruins

Zona Arqueológica Guachimontones

Some 40km west of Guadalajara, there's a stepped pyramid, built in nearly perfect concentric circles, where the Teuchitlán people worshipped Ehecatl, the wind god, between 300 BCE and 350 CE.

Zona Arqueológica Tingambato

The beautiful ruins of a ceremonial site, which predates the Purépechan empire and which thrived from about 450 to 900 CE.

Historic Architecture

Biblioteca Pública de la Universidad Michoacana

Morelia's breathtaking university library is inside a mural-covered 17th-century chapel. Antique manuscripts include seven incunabula (books printed before 1500 CE in Europe).

Catedral de Morelia

The twin towers of what's arguably Mexico's most beautiful cathedral – a mix of Herreresque bases and multicolumned neoclassical tops – soar above Morelia's plaza. Gorgeous nighttime illumination.

Craft Shopping

Casa de las Artesanías

Arguably Morelia's most comprehensive range of Michoacán crafts concentrated in one cooperative marketplace, designed to benefit indigenous craftspeople.

Casa de los Once Patios

The patios of this former 18th-century nunnery in Pátzcuaro host workshops, specializing in woodwork, lacquerwork, blanket weaving and other local craft traditions, where you can watch local artisans at work.

Del Corazón de la Tierra

A shop in Tlaquepaque, Guadalajara, showcasing indigenous art from Michoacán and further afield.

Creative Cuisine

Matrice $$

This lovely garden restaurant in Pátzcuaro does remarkable things with vegetables, and the surprise tasting menu and the desserts are incredible. Book ahead.

Tata $$

Superb *cocina de autor* (signature cuisine) of chef Fermín Ambás in Morelia. Think rabbit tartare or tuna with tortilla crust, paired with 190 different mezcals.

Lu Cocina Michoacana $$

Atápakua de milpa (squash-flower soup), trout with coconut and other food-as-art dishes by chef Lucero Soto Arriaga in Morelia.

¡Ah Qué Nanishe! $$

This Oaxacan restaurant in Colima excels at the rich, chocolatey *mole negro* as well as *chiles rellenos* (stuffed chilies). Half-orders available.

Allium $$$

This minimalist restaurant in Guadalajara does amazing things with Jalisco ingredients; try the fish with smoked *jitomate* or the *huitlacoche* risotto. Book ahead.

Marvelous Museums

Museo de Artes e Industrias Populares

Excellent introduction to Michoacán's handicrafts, from copper vessels from Santa Clara del Cobre and guitars from Paracho to traditional masks from Tócuaro.

Museo Regional Michoacano

Inside an 18th-century baroque palace, this museum in Morelia showcases Michoacán's history, from a reconstructed open tomb from El Opeño to a carved stone coyote from Ihuatzio.

MUSA Museo de las Artes

This 1917-built Renaissance-style building in Guadalajara is particularly renowned for its powerful murals by José Clemente Orozco.

Zona Arqueológica Guachimontones

Special Stays

Hotel de la Soledad $$$

Built in 1735 and retaining many of its original architectural features, this inn in Morelia is a palm-fringed showstopper, its individually styled rooms combining period furnishings and mod cons.

Hotel Boutique Hacienda del Gobernador $$$

Carved bedsteads in opulent rooms and well-tended grounds define this centuries-old hacienda, the former home of Colima's 19th-century governor.

Tastiest Tacos

Tacos Los de Asadita $

A full array of *tortas* and quesadillas is available, but the star of this spot in Pátzcuaro is the *taco asado* (flank steak), with or without chorizo.

Callejon del Hambre $

These tongue, tripe, *al pastor* and chorizo tacos, with extra beans and an array of salsas, are a guaranteed hangover cure in Tequila.

Tacos Fish La Paz $

For prawn, fish, crab and octopus tacos, this simple place in Guadalajara can't be beat. Ceviche and quesadillas also available.

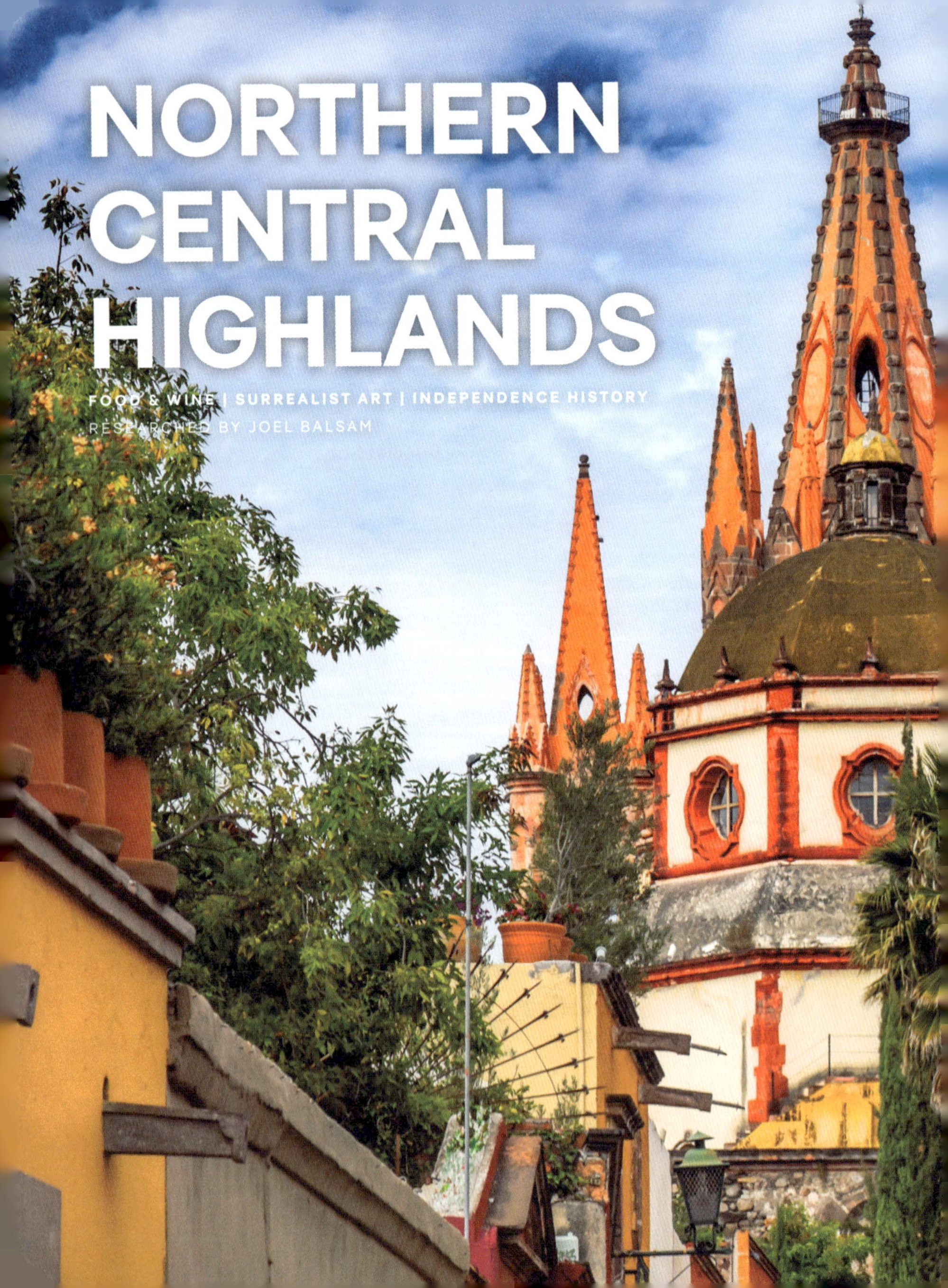

NORTHERN CENTRAL HIGHLANDS

FOOD & WINE | SURREALIST ART | INDEPENDENCE HISTORY

RESEARCHED BY JOEL BALSAM

- **Trip Builder** (p198)
- **Practicalities** (p199)
- **Boho & Beautiful in San Miguel** (p200)
- **Art-chitecture in the Hills** (p202)
- **Wine & Mezcal Tasting** (p204)
- **Guanajuato Alleys & Architecture** (p206)
- **How Mexico Broke Free** (p208)
- **Listings** (p210)

NORTHERN CENTRAL HIGHLANDS
Trip Builder

Explore a vast area of contrasting semi-desert and mountainous forest in a handful of states a few hours north of the capital. Find surrealist and enchanting architecture along with proud traditions of artisanship, wine, mezcal and enchiladas.

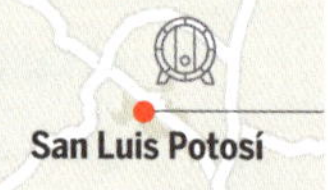

Taste ancestral mezcal and learn how it's made around **San Luis Potosí** (p204)
45min from San Luis Potosí city

Wander alleyways above and underground in **Guanajuato** (p206)
4hr from Guadalajara

Visit the birthplace of the Mexican independence movement, **Dolores Hidalgo** (p208)
45min from San Miguel de Allende

Explore Edward James' trippy surrealist architecture (pictured above) outside **Xilitla** (p202)
7hr from Querétaro

Shop for art and home decor in **San Miguel de Allende** (p200)
1½hr from Guanajuato

Go winery hopping around **Bernal** and **Tequisquiapan** (p204)
1hr from Querétaro

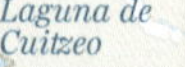
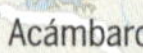

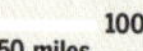

Practicalities

ARRIVING

Aeropuerto Internacional de Guanajuato and **Aeropuerto Internacional de Querétaro** host domestic and international flights. Bus travel is a more affordable alternative, and 1st class buses are comfy.

CONNECT

Buy a Telcel or other SIM card for internet access. Reception can be spotty outside cities, particularly in the Sierra Madre Oriental hills.

MONEY

Carry pesos for taxis, street food and museums. Local markets are a good bet for affordable, delicious food.

WHERE TO STAY

Neighborhood	Pros/Cons
San Miguel de Allende	Plenty to see and do. Touristy, but worth it.
Guanajuato	Colorful and walkable. Also touristy, but with Mexicans.
Querétaro	Art and wine. Relatively few attractions.
San Luis Potosí	Close to mezcal and waterfall tours. City is only good for a day or two.

GETTING AROUND

Bus 1st and 2nd class buses link cities, but not small towns. Urban buses rarely exceed M$8. However, times are irregular.

Car Rent a car to go beyond cities to small towns and wineries. Or hire a local taxi to arrange drop-off and pick-up. DiDi is more common than Uber. Or book a tour to make things simpler.

TOP: GUAJILLO STUDIO/SHUTTERSTOCK
BOTTOM: RUBI RODRIGUEZ MARTINEZ/SHUTTERSTOCK

EATING & DRINKING

This region is popular for its local takes on enchiladas (tortillas bathed in red pepper sauce topped with veggies, cheese and meat; pictured top left).

Querétaro is the second-largest wine-producing region in Mexico after Baja California. Guanajuato is the third. Or go to San Luis Potosí to taste mezcal.

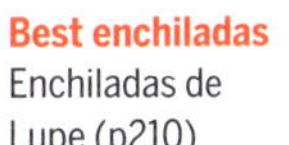

Best enchiladas
Enchiladas de Lupe (p210)

Must-try natural wine
Octagano (p205)

MAY–JUL
Escape hot beaches for blissful highlands. Also prime wine-tasting season.

AUG–OCT
Celebrate **Fiestas Patrias** for two months around Mexican Independence Day (Sep 16).

NOV–FEB
Dry season; cooler temperatures but not freezing. Avoid Christmas if possible.

34 Boho & Beautiful in SAN MIGUEL

ENCHANTING STREETS | ART & DESIGN | FOOD & BARS

Walking around San Miguel de Allende feels like stepping into a painting. Ancient cobblestone streets are lined with buildings bursting with terracotta hues and accented by crawling bougainvilleas. And then there are its spectacular churches, including the Sagrada Família–esque **Parroquia de San Miguel Arcángel**. Enter a shop to find art that'll make your own home that much more paintable.

How to

Getting here San Miguel is a few hours' bus trip or drive from CDMX. Or fly into either the Guanajuato or Querétaro international airports.

When to go It's blissfully mild year-round, but go between November and April for the least rain.

Hidden gem Enter through the wildly decorated facade to **El Águila Imperial**, where artist Raul Reyna *(442-835-5816)* has been cobbling together extraordinary antiquities and his own creations for decades.

'GI Paradise' Americans first caught wind of San Miguel when a 1948 *Life* magazine story called it a 'GI Paradise' because of its peacefulness, mountain temperatures and charming architecture. It has become an expat hub ever since, particularly amongst liberal artsy types. These North American artists, along with a rich tradition of local artisanship, have helped transform San Miguel into one of the best places to shop for clothing, paintings and precious home decor.

Arting Around San Miguel's **Mercado de Artesanías** has dozens of artisan vendors selling everything from Oaxacan *alebrijes* to string cheese – but don't stop there. Try on patented hats from proud rancher **Suki Palomina** *(sukipalomina.com)*. Grace your face with a pair of sunglasses with handmade arm chains at **Maktub** by Las Jaras *(instagram.com/las*

JOEL BALSAM

jaras.studio). And to make your home as gorgeous as the ones in San Miguel, check out decor shops like **Mixta** *(instagram.com/mixtasma)* or **Atemporal** *(instagram.com/@atemporal_7)*.

Art Factory Find the echelon of top San Miguel art and design at **Fábrica La Aurora** *(fabricalaaurora.com)*, a former raw cotton factory with dozens of contemporary art galleries. You can spend hours there gazing at the beautiful (but pricey) artwork. Take breaks at one of its excellent cafes.

Bargains Galore On Tuesdays and Sundays, scour San Miguel's **Tianguis** outdoor market for clothing at rock-bottom prices. Some savvy scavengers have allegedly found luxury brands like Loro Piana in the heaps.

San Miguel's Best Bites & Bars

Tostévere A cute little spot for tostadas and cocktails. Try the smoky mezcal cocktail with coconut foam and burnt rosemary.

El Manantial Great music and vibe with a good tequila selection. Sit at the bar and you'll meet some interesting people.

El Compita The best *tortas* in town/Mexico – my go-to is the *milanesa de pollo*. I eat here at least twice a week!

Tacos Don Felix Family-run restaurant known for its enchiladas and dangerous giant margaritas.

Brutal Stylish and intimate wine bar with a large range of wine and knowledgeable wine specialists.

Recommended by Teu Campbell, *co-owner of Inside Cafe* *@insidecafe.mx*

Above Smoky mezcal cocktail at Tostévere

35 Art-chitecture in THE HILLS

SURREALISM | JUNGLE | WATERFALLS

On the steep slopes of the Sierra Madre Oriental hills, find a magical labyrinth of surreal structures born from the imagination of eccentric Brit Edward James. Covering 36 hectares and more than 200 sculptures amidst thick idyllic jungle, El Jardín Escultórico Edward James (Sculpture Garden) aka **Las Pozas** *(The Pools; laspozasxilitla.org.mx)* is an experience that's as surreal as the art itself.

How to

When to go It drizzles year-round. If you don't want to get drenched, avoid rainy season (May–Sep).

Getting there Buses and shared taxis wind up to Xilitla from San Luis Potosí and Querétaro.

Advance tickets Buy online up to 60 days ahead for M$150. Seniors and kids aged 6–12 cost M$100.

Guided tours They're obligatory. English tours (M$60) are at 10am and 3pm. Spanish tours (M$30) run between 9am and 4pm.

Secret Gardens When asked what he was up to when he disappeared for days at a time, Edward James would say he was in his 'Garden of Eden.' A wealthy descendant of British aristocrats (King Edward VII was allegedly his grandfather), James found himself in the town of Xilitla in the 1940s and decided to build himself a set of structures to add to his collection of surrealist art.

Imagination to Reality James hired his Mexican bodyguard and driver Plutarco Gastelum along with 150 local workers to bring his drawings to life. They carved wooden molds and filled them with concrete to create peculiar pillars that unfurl like flower petals, winding staircases to tower over the trees, and a set of pools (Las Pozas) for the locals to enjoy. James also filled his garden with rare plants and exotic animals like ocelots, macaws and boa constrictors.

FITOPARDO/GETTY IMAGES

Xilitla Must-sees

Plutarcos One of the few Edward James structures in town – he stayed when he spent long periods in Xilitla. It's now a restaurant with the best drinks and the food is really good.

El Arca Very cheap tacos and *gringas* (flour tortillas with cheese and meat) and good *sazón* (seasonings).

Posada James Makes you feel at home with one of the best views in Xilitla.

Cascada la Cebolla Near Hostal Casa Verde, this is one of the most beautiful waterfalls in the area and it has no cost to enter.

Recommended by Rodolfo Carlos Diaz de León, *Xilitla local*

@xilitla_caracol

Tour Before It's Too Late

After James died in 1984, there wasn't the financial backing to continue the project and it was later turned over to a foundation. Today you can visit Las Pozas on daily 1½-hour tours in either English or Spanish. Wandering the 236 or so structures is a magical experience, especially as the green tentacles of the forest are slowly subsuming them. Don't miss the nearby waterfalls and the hub town of Xilitla's **Museo Leonora Carrington**, which has a collection of spectacular surrealist sculptures.

Above Las Pozas

36 Wine & Mezcal TASTING

HIGH ALTITUDE | CUTE TOWNS | TASTINGS

Sprouting from the volcano-enriched soil in Querétaro and Guanajuato states are some mighty fine grapes used to produce enticing wines. The two regions rank first and second respectively in total Mexican wine production. Go on a tasting tour at a winery, or several, and/or head to San Luis Potosí to learn about its historic mezcal production process.

How to

Tours Try several producers (without driving drunk) on a tour from one of the nearby towns.

When to go May's **Feria Nacional del Queso y del Vino** wine and cheese festival in Tequisquiapan features tastings and live concerts.

Don't miss International award-winning sheep cheese at **Rancho San Josemaría** *(@ranchosan josemaria)*. **Bike Tour Querétaro** *(@biketour queretaro)* can take you there on a driving tour from Querétaro.

Long Tradition Spanish conquistadors ordered the first wine grapes planted in this region in the first half of the 16th century. Since then, a proud wine-producing tradition has been established that is second only in total production in Mexico to Baja California.

Wine & Cheese Trail Embark on Querétaro's **Ruta de Vino y Queso** (Wine and Cheese Trail) to visit internationally renowned and smaller Mexican wineries and explore their vineyards. Most of the wineries are conveniently located near *pueblos mágicos* Bernal and Tequisquiapan.

Guanajuato State Wineries Guanajuato towns Dolores Hidalgo and San Miguel de Allende are surrounded by more than a dozen wineries. Some of the top include **Cuna de Tierra** *(cunade tierra.com)*, **Tres Raíces** *(viñedotresraices.com)*, **Dos Búhos** *(dosbuhos.com)* and

RUBI RODRIGUEZ MARTINEZ/SHUTTERSTOCK

Viñedo San Miguel *(vinedo sanmiguel.com.mx)*.

Or stick around in San Miguel to do a natural wine and mezcal tasting with an elaborate spread of snacks at **Octagano** *(visitas.elnidal.com.mx)*. Expect to leave good and wasted.

Ancestral Mezcal While Oaxaca understandably gets most of the attention for its mezcal, San Luis Potosí also has a rich tradition of producing the smoky agave spirit and was one of the first states to be listed with a Mexican Denomination of Origin. Learn about ancestral mezcal production and meet the producers on a tour with experienced English-speaking guide Miguel Galarraga Robledo of **Auténtico San Luis** *(autenticosanluis.com)*.

Top Wineries

Freixenet One of the most iconic and oldest vineyards in our state. Famous for its underground cellar.

La Redonda Developed Mexican-run winery that's the most affordable of them all.

Vinaltura Eat a high-quality lunch and enjoy their beautiful views in a not-so-busy ambiance.

Bodegas de Cote Also wins lots of awards. Has great food and activities in their vineyard. Located right next to Freixenet.

San Juanito Represents Mexico in a lot of international wine contests, but not as developed, or as worth visiting, for tours.

Recommended by Uriel Peña, *Bike Tour Querétaro guide. @biketourqueretaro*

Above Tequisquiapan, Querétaro

37 Guanajuato Alleys & ARCHITECTURE

COLORFUL | PARIS-INSPIRED | MINING HISTORY

Centuries of silver-mining success has left Guanajuato with an intricate network of *callejones* (alleyways) that feel like Southern Spain or Morocco. Tack on a marvelous display of colorful cathedrals, theaters and museums and you're guaranteed to get your steps in.

GALYNA ANDRUSHKO/SHUTTERSTOCK

Trip Notes

Getting around Avoid driving in Guanajuato. Confusing one-way roads can send you in the wrong direction for a while.

When to go Guanajuato fills up for the popular annual performing artists extravaganza **Festival Internacional Cervantino**. Avoid it to find lower prices – or come to see a thriving Mexican festival.

Drinks with a view Observe where you've walked at a high-elevation bar like **Bartola** *(@bartolaskybar)* or **Xolazul** *(@xolazul)*.

Sunset Spot

Take a six-pack of beer up to **Monumento Al Pípila** lookout point and watch the city slowly turn on its night lights as the sun goes down.

Recommended by DJ Barnes Umaña, *guide with Mexico Street Food Tours. mexicostreetfood.com*

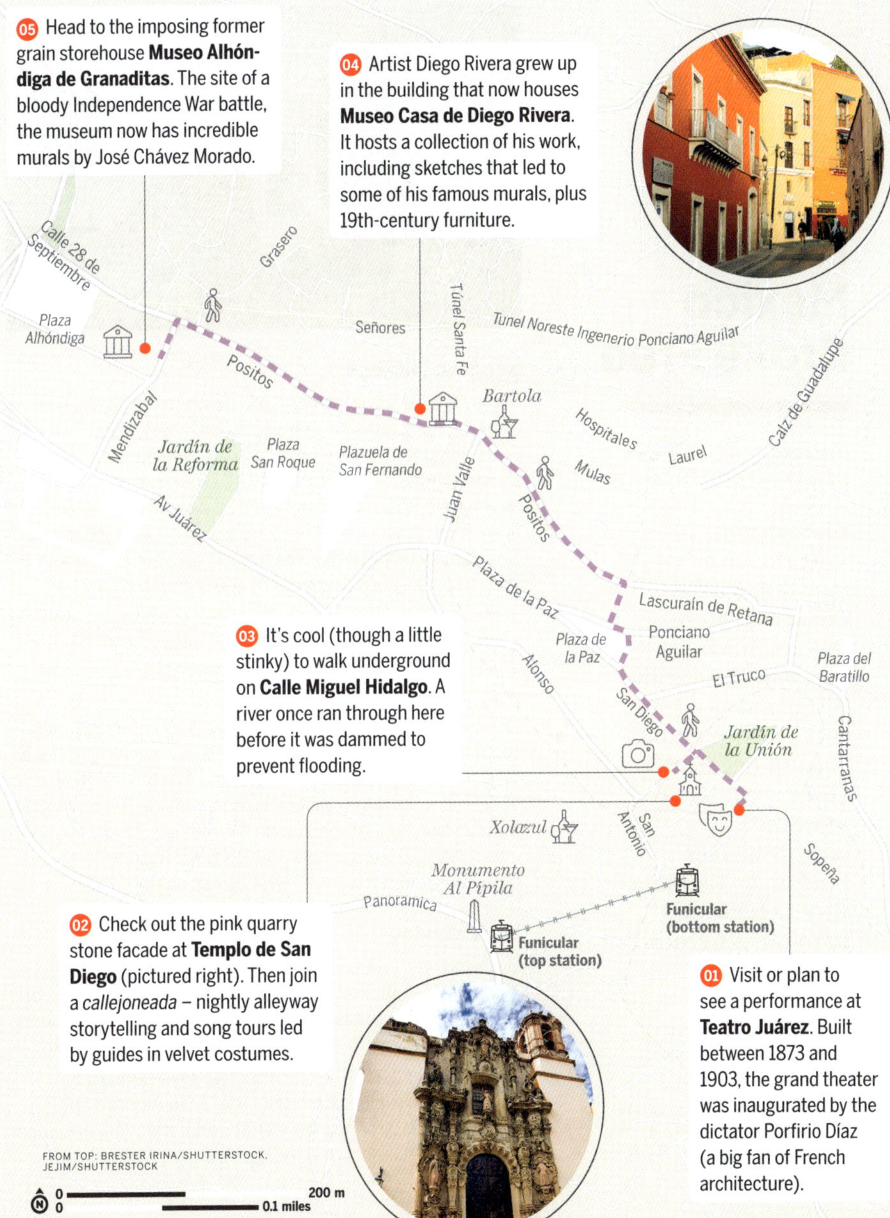

05 Head to the imposing former grain storehouse **Museo Alhóndiga de Granaditas**. The site of a bloody Independence War battle, the museum now has incredible murals by José Chávez Morado.

04 Artist Diego Rivera grew up in the building that now houses **Museo Casa de Diego Rivera**. It hosts a collection of his work, including sketches that led to some of his famous murals, plus 19th-century furniture.

03 It's cool (though a little stinky) to walk underground on **Calle Miguel Hidalgo**. A river once ran through here before it was dammed to prevent flooding.

02 Check out the pink quarry stone facade at **Templo de San Diego** (pictured right). Then join a *callejoneada* – nightly alleyway storytelling and song tours led by guides in velvet costumes.

01 Visit or plan to see a performance at **Teatro Juárez**. Built between 1873 and 1903, the grand theater was inaugurated by the dictator Porfirio Díaz (a big fan of French architecture).

FROM TOP: BRESTER IRINA/SHUTTERSTOCK, JEJIM/SHUTTERSTOCK

How Mexico Broke Free

HIDALGO AND THE CRY FOR INDEPENDENCE

On September 16, 1810, church bells rang through the Guanajuato town of Dolores. It was time to revolt. The ensuing War of Independence led to Mexico exiting Spanish rule in 1821. Learn about Mexico's independence movement, then head to the Northern Central Highlands to travel its freedom trail.

Left Mexican flag **Centre** Parroquia de Nuestra Señora de Dolores **Right** Statue of Ignacio Allende, Museo Histórico Casa de Allende

AVFOTOVIDEO/SHUTTERSTOCK

Seeds of Dissent

'Down with bad government and death to the *gachupines* (a derogatory term for Spanish ruling class),' cried Catholic priest Miguel Hidalgo y Costilla in the town later renamed Dolores Hidalgo. 'El Grito' (The Cry) sparked a revolution against the Spanish Crown, led by a partnership of Mexico's poor and indigenous groups along with criollos (people of Spanish ancestry born in Mexico). Both were fed up with their Spanish-born overlords in and out of the country.

Hidalgo, a criollo, had already been discussing revolution with Ignacio José de Allende y Unzaga, a weapons aficionado from San Miguel – but their plot was discovered, prompting immediate action.

Action came less than two weeks later when Hidalgo led thousands of rural workers and miners marching to the silver mining city Guanajuato, resulting in a bloody massacre of Spanish Crown loyalists shored up inside the city's grain storage building, Alhóndiga de Granaditas. Three months later, Hidalgo declared his advocacy for Mexico to abolish slavery (though it wasn't formally ended until 1837).

Viva México

But Hidalgo's independence movement didn't last long – at least not with him at the helm. Four months after El Grito, Hidalgo was defeated by New Spain's governing forces outside Guanajuato and he was captured shortly after.

As a warning to other prospective revolutionaries, Hidalgo and fellow leaders Allende, Juan Aldama and José Mariano Jiménez were shot and beheaded, and their heads were hung from birdcages outside Alhóndiga de Granaditas.

ROBERTO GALAN/SHUTTERSTOCK

ELENI MAVRANDONI/SHUTTERSTOCK

But the independence movement wouldn't end there. After Hidalgo was killed, another priest, José María Morelos y Pavón (the namesake of Michoacán's Morelia), took over and drafted a constitution for a new country – but he too was killed in 1815.

Revolts were dispersed throughout the country for the next five years, but the tables finally turned in 1821 when Agustín de Iturbide, a royal officer, joined the independence movement and created a plan with then-rebel leader Vicente Guerrero. Plan de Iguala promised equality and preservation of the Catholic church's status in an independent Mexico.

> Mexico celebrates its independence on September 16 – the day of El Grito – with Fiestas Patrias.

With Mexico City surrounded by rebel troops, government leader Juan O'Donojú met with Iturbide on August 24, 1821, to sign a treaty granting Mexico independence.

Fiestas Patrias

Mexico celebrates its independence with Fiestas Patrias on September 16 – the day of El Grito – rather than the day the treaty was signed. (No, Mexico's Independence Day isn't Cinco de Mayo. That's to celebrate a Mexican military victory over the French on May 5, 1865, and is a much bigger deal in the US than in Mexico.)

Take to the streets anywhere in the Northern Central Highlands on the evening of September 15 through to the big day to celebrate with fireworks, food and dancing. Celebrations for Fiestas Patrias can last for two months, especially in lively San Miguel de Allende.

Independence Trail Stops

Parroquia de Nuestra Señora de Dolores Where Miguel Hidalgo rang church bells and cried for independence.

Museo de la Independencia Hidalgo freed prisoners here in Dolores Hidalgo.

Santuario de Atotonilco Hidalgo gathered rural and indigenous people for battle at this UNESCO-recognized church north of San Miguel.

Museo Histórico Casa de Allende Independence general Ignacio Allende lived in this San Miguel building (now a museum) and studied nearby at **Colegio de Sales**.

Museo Alhóndiga de Granaditas Where Hidalgo's rebels won their bloodiest victory. Also in Guanajuato, **Monumento Al Pípila** honors the miner who burned the door down.

Listings

BEST OF THE REST

Star-worthy Eats

Inside $$

'Sexy' Mexican breakfasts, grilled cheese that's the world's tastiest (some say), and *café de olla* lattes. Come after 4pm for Xam Xam Asian eats or tacos on Tuesdays.

Nudol $$$

Instant favorite since opening in San Miguel in 2024 with devourable fried chicken bao buns and ramen bowls. Eat at the long bar while a DJ spins vinyl records.

Dos Chingones $$

Peer over Guanajuato's La Presa (dam) while trying to get your mouth around huge, gourmet fish tacos filled with marlin, tuna, *aguachile* and more. Two is plenty.

Enchiladas de Lupe $

This tiny hole-in-the-wall spot in Guanajuato is always full as diners tuck into the city's best enchiladas mineras.

Lxs de Abajo $

Young people-powered bar and restaurant in Zacatecas with plant-based bites including cauliflower wings, veggie burgers and huge beers.

Tikua $$$

Querétaro's best restaurant, serving authentic southeastern Mexican cuisine you won't find anywhere else. Taste rare ingredients including various insects.

Plutarcos $$

Edward James, the eccentric poet and dreamer behind **Las Pozas** (p202), designed this building. It's now a restaurant serving Italian food with occasional live music.

Local Watering Holes

Los Lobos

Join students drinking giant beers at this rock-themed bar in Guanajuato. Pool tables and a big patio. Gay-friendly.

Cantina La Hiedra

Traditional cantina (1907) in Dolores Hidalgo. It was a former hang-out of hometown hero José Alfredo Jiménez, aka El Rey (The King) of *ranchera* (Mexican 'country music').

Mina Club

A literal hole in a Zacatecas mountain, home to one of Mexico's most unique nightlife venues. Open Thursdays to Saturdays, the club can fit 400 people.

Tampico

Cheers with locals at this typical San Luis Potosí cantina. Drinks come with free *botanos* (snacks). Mexican music will prompt sing-alongs.

El Faro

This Querétaro bar is oozing with ambiance. It's been around for more than a century – probably the oldest bar in the historic center. Amazing art-filled decor.

Must-visit Museums

Museo Pedro Coronel

Bet you didn't know Zacatecas has Picasso, Goya and Miró paintings. Find them at this museum occupying a former Jesuit college.

Museo de las Momias

Guanajuato's most popular, and creepiest, museum, holds more than 100 mummified corpses. Find it a 10-minute drive west of the center.

Museo José Alfredo Jiménez

Updated museum in Dolores Hidalgo dedicated to 'The King' of *ranchera* music. Immersive augmented reality brings a painting and recreation of La Hiedra cantina to life.

Centro de las Artes Centenario

San Luis Potosí's best museum, occupying a former prison, contains sculptures and paintings from surrealist Leonora Carrington.

MUCAL

Stunningly restored *casona* (mansion) in Querétaro filled with quirky, and sexy, retro calendars and the paintings printed onto them. Stay for a drink in the garden cafe.

Museo José Guadalupe Posada

Aguascalientes museum dedicated to the local illustrator who created Mexico's most recognizable image: *La Calavera de la Catrina* (skeleton in women's clothing).

 Amazing Architecture

Parroquia de San Miguel Arcángel

It's not an over-estimation to compare this marvelous San Miguel church to Barcelona's La Sagrada Família. It was designed by a then-unknown stonemason.

Santuario de Jesús Nazareno de Atotonilco

Some call this church north of San Miguel Mexico's Sistine Chapel. It has exquisite folk murals that communicate Bible stories.

Ranchito Cascabel

A psychedelic wonderland of mosaic snakes, giant mushrooms, flirting aliens and curvaceous buildings that bloom like flowers and metamorphose like butterflies. Find it north of San Miguel.

FERKAD/SHUTTERSTOCK

Peña de Bernal

Templo de la Purísima Concepción

Impressive neoclassical church in a mining boom town that whittled down to ghost town status. The town, Real de Catorce, is a popular trip from San Luis Potosí. However, it's not easy to get here without a car.

 Outdoor Adventures

Mayan Baths

Glamorous hot springs near San Miguel that feature cave accommodations, spa treatments and waiters swimming to deliver drinks – but it'll cost you.

Peña de Bernal

Querétaro shelters one of the world's largest monoliths surrounded by a *pueblo mágico*. You can climb most of the way up.

Cascada de Tamul

One of many spectacular aquamarine waterfalls in La Huasteca Potosina region of San Luis Potosí. Ideal to visit it, along with other wonderful swimming holes, on a tour.

Reserva de la Biosfera Sierra Gorda

Querétaro state's giant green jewel has it all: expansive wilderness, deep caves and explorable caverns, massive populations of macaws and parrots and gushing waterfalls.

BAJA PENINSULA

BEACHES | WINE | WILDLIFE

RESEARCHED BY JOHN HECHT

- **Trip Builder** (p214)
- **Practicalities** (p215)
- **Hit the Wine Trail** (p216)
- **Venture Off Baja's Beaten Path** (p218)
- **Listings** (p220)

BAJA PENINSULA

Trip Builder

Ready for a digital detox? Reconnect with nature here as you experience unforgettable turquoise beaches, desert hot springs, vivid underwater worlds and epic whale encounters. And what better place to celebrate Baja's overpowering beauty than in wine country's hillside vineyards...

SHERRY V SMITH/SHUTTERSTOCK, PREVIOUS SPREAD: CORSEYE/SHUTTERSTOCK

Practicalities

ARRIVING

Aeropuerto Internacional de Los Cabos The main entry point for Baja as well as airports in Tijuana and La Paz. By land, you can cross into border cities Tijuana, Tecate and Mexicali.

CONNECT

In the remote villages, you can usually access wi-fi but many such places have no phone signal.

MONEY

Always carry cash when visiting small towns. Paying with credit cards is possible in most but not all places.

WHERE TO STAY

Place	Pros/Cons
Ensenada & Valle de Guadalupe	Historical sites and vineyards. Cruise-ship frenzies.
Cabo Pulmo	Best off-grid experience. Limited services.
La Paz	Spectacular beaches. Scorching summer months.
San José del Cabo	Convenient base for day trips. Winter high season brings overtourism.

GETTING AROUND

Car A rental vehicle is your best option to explore spread-out or hard-to-reach areas with limited or no bus service.

Bus Buses run frequently between San José del Cabo and La Paz but do not serve most of the remote towns. 'Playa Bus' in La Paz will get you close to the Tecolotito trailhead.

TOP: ROBERT BRIGGS/SHUTTERSTOCK BOTTOM: VOR/SHUTTERSTOCK

EATING & DRINKING

Try fruit-forward local wines and hoppy craft beers.

Fish tacos (pictured top left), battered and fried to perfection, are a Baja specialty.

Sample Baja Med cuisine – Baja Californian and Mediterranean fusion fare.

Best wine and dine experience Finca Altozano (p221)

Must-try fish tacos Taco Fish (p221)

JAN–MAR
Height of whale-watching season; swim alongside whale sharks.

APR–JUN
Crowd-free months between US spring break and Mexican vacation periods.

JUL–SEP
Celebrate the midsummer grape harvest fest in wine country.

OCT–DEC
November brings cooler weather and the Día de Muertos.

38 Hit the WINE TRAIL

WINING | DINING | TOURS

Baja's wine country makes for an unforgettable getaway, even if you don't consider yourself much of a connoisseur. With some 150 wineries scattered across Valle de Guadalupe's scenic rolling hills, not to mention top-notch restaurants specializing in Baja Med cuisine and gourmet fare, it's the quintessential wining and dining experience in rural-chic fashion. Think Napa in the desert.

How to

When to go The midsummer Harvest Festival in late July and early August is a big draw but rooms go fast.

Getting there Vineyards are spread out so you'll need a car. Alternatively, there's no shortage of taxis and tour companies willing to be your designated driver. **Baja Winery Tours** *(bajawinerytours.com)* provides private transportation and pricier all-inclusive tours.

Need to know Some of the larger wineries require reservations for tastings.

The **Ruta del Vino** (Wine Route) is an intoxicating blend of luxury lodging, wine tasting and fine dining in laid-back rural areas with dirt roads and cacti amid the grapevines. It attracts a hip crowd of 20- to 40-somethings looking to relax and indulge in the finer things and it's one of the oldest wine-producing regions in the Americas.

Crash course Before diving into the tastings, get some background on the history of wine in the region to make it a more enriching experience. The exhibits at **Museo de la Vid y El Vino** explain the winemaking process and much more.

Go big and small To see how the wineries operate, start with a visit to a low-key family-run vineyard, where you're sure to get more personal attention, like **Casa Magoni** or **Trevista**. It's also fascinating to get a glimpse

SHERRY SMITH/GETTY IMAGES

of the inner workings of the larger, more industrialized setups at wineries such as **Monte Xanic**, but remember to make an appointment beforehand.

The route less traveled

When most people think of wine country in Baja, Valle de Guadalupe comes to mind. But did you know there's also a Ruta Antigua (Old Route) that runs south of Ensenada? Granted, you won't find much in the way of boutique hotels and acclaimed restaurants in the area but several vineyards, including industry giant **Santo Tomás**, are often pleasantly uncrowded.

Unique Wine Experiences

Vena Cava Not only produces excellent organic wines, such as sauvignon blanc, but also has one of the valley's quirkiest vineyards, with its high tasting-room ceilings fashioned from repurposed fishing boats.

Adobe Guadalupe Oozing with hacienda-style charm, here you can taste the lauded red blend, Rafael, in a replica adobe mission complete with a white facade and church bell. It also breeds Azteca horses and offers horseback riding.

Clos de Tres Cantos This petite winery is built almost entirely of recycled materials, creating a space that's at once old-world yet modern. Sip the praiseworthy grenache.

Above Adobe Guadalupe

39 Venture off Baja's BEATEN PATH

NATURE ENCOUNTERS | BEACHES | WATER ACTIVITIES

Leave behind the party scene and cruise-ship crowds and embrace southern Baja's serene off-grid beach towns, stunningly gorgeous desert oases, biodiverse reefs and life-affirming hikes and nature encounters that make it a joy to be alive.

LEONARDO GONZALEZ/ SHUTTERSTOCK

Trip Notes

When to go November to March bring ideal kitesurfing conditions in La Ventana; it's also a good time to spot migrating whale sharks.

Getting around You'll need a car to visit most of these places. Cabo Pulmo is best approached from the north road, heading south from La Ribera.

Top tip Monitor weather conditions closely: poor water visibility or problematic muddy roads can really put a damper on things.

La Ventana Diving Sites

La Reina World-class seamount with giant mantas and playful sea lions.

Punta Norte Drift-dive over coral loaded with fish schools.

La Reinita Sea-life-encrusted pinnacle with octopuses and seahorses.

Tacote Videographer's dream with bright coral and turtles.

JOHN HECHT

Recommended by Tim Hatler, *owner of resort Palapas Ventana. @palapasventana*

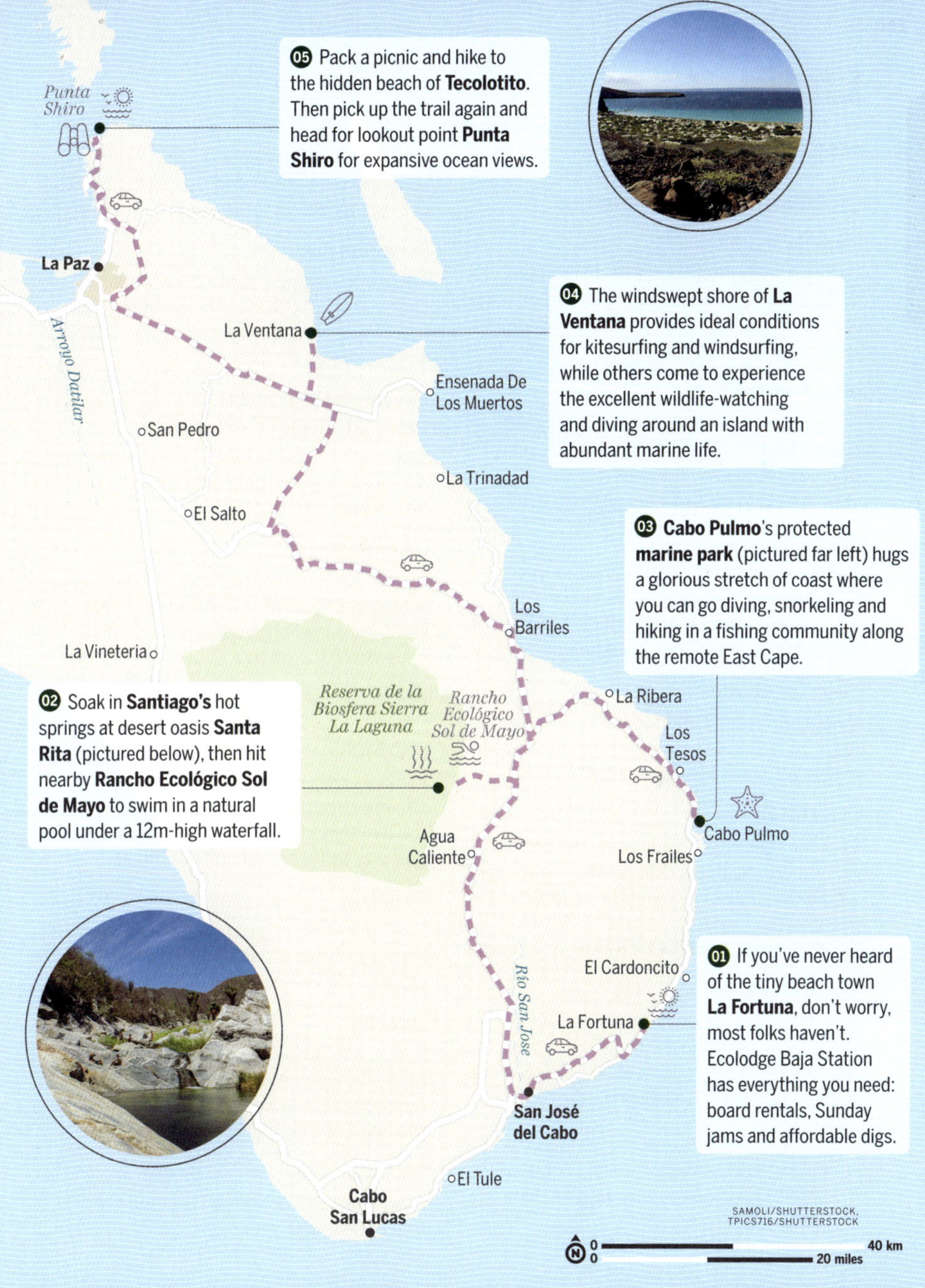

SAMOLI/SHUTTERSTOCK, TPICS716/SHUTTERSTOCK

Listings

BEST OF THE REST

Blissful Beach-Bumming

Playa Balandra

The most beautiful in a series of beaches north of La Paz, Playa Balandra is an enclosed cove with shallow azure waters and a famous mushroom rock formation.

Playa Santispac

Hugging the gorgeous Bahía Concepción coast, north of Loreto, this beach has a crowd-free hidden cove on the east end where you'll likely have the white sands all to yourself.

Playa Chileno

Delight in incredibly calm waters at this Los Cabos wheelchair-accessible beach, then dine at oceanfront restaurant Comal. Decent snorkeling on the beach's east end.

Playa Los Cerritos

Take a surf lesson, then snack on amazing fish tacos at Barracuda Cantina. The most swimmable waters in the Todos Santos area.

Playa El Arbolito

Popular sunbathing spot along the East Cape, in Cabo Pulmo. A cliffside trail runs out to an isolated rocky point called Cabo del Shiro.

Cerveza, Craft Cocktails & Mezcal

Baja Brewing Co

A buzzy pub-style environment pouring local microbrews produced on site in San José del Cabo, or swig *cerveza* at their oceanfront rooftop cantina in Cabo San Lucas.

Hussong's Cantina

The oldest and perhaps liveliest cantina in the Californias has been serving tequila since 1892. Claims to have invented the margarita cocktail, as does another nearby Ensenada bar.

Dandy Del Sur

This atmospheric Tijuana dive bar has changed very little since it opened its doors nearly seven decades ago, and we mean that in a good way.

Mezcalería La Miserable

Intimate La Paz mezcal bar where you can sip agave spirits hailing from Oaxaca, Guerrero and other regions, but be careful: the potent drinks pack a punch.

Green Room

This Todos Santos beach bar is a bit of a schlep but once you dig your toes in the sand with a cocktail in hand – especially at sunset – it's worth the effort.

For Coffee Lovers

Baja Beans

Pleasant coffee shop near Todos Santos serving strong Mexican-grown coffee in all the fancy ways. On Sundays, its outdoor patio hosts a crafts market and live music.

Gratitude

You'll feel serious gratitude when you try the high-quality java roasted here. An ideal spot to tap into the La Paz cultural scene.

Taller 17

The strong coffee, organic matcha and freshly made brownies and cookies will make you happy to wake up in Todos Santos. Smack in the heart of the pretty historic center.

Doce Cuarenta

Downtown La Paz coffee shop and bakery that deservingly gets high praise for gourmet coffee and glazed cinnamon rolls, a delight while sitting in the sunny rear patio.

Nomádico

A transplant hailing from the coffee region of Chiapas prepares rich gourmet coffee and high-quality tuna tostadas at this beachside cafe on Playa Burro.

Amazing Accommodations

Acre

Channel your inner Tarzan at this trendy treehouse village. Rather than deep jungle, you get farm-to-table gardens and the full boutique treatment. Afternoon mezcal tastings add agave-fueled oomph.

Camp Cecil

On the uninhabited island of Espíritu Santo near La Paz. Sleep under the stars in large dome tents with beds. Rates include meals, transportation, kayaking and snorkeling equipment and cocktails.

Campo Archelon

Campground and former turtle research center on a gorgeous patch of sand in Bahía de los Ángeles. The seascape is deeply relaxing, with awe-inspiring sunrises, and the onsite cafe rules.

Iconic Eats

Taco Fish $

Many consider these battered fish and shrimp tacos the tastiest in La Paz. The extra battered, crispy fish style is reminiscent of an outstanding British fish and chips.

Caesar's $$

Step inside and be transported to the 1950s. The signature Caesar salad, prepared with panache at your table, was apparently invented here by the Tijuana restaurant's founder, Caesar Cardini.

FOTO PARA TI/SHUTTERSTOCK

Seals, Parque Nacional Bahía de Loreto

La Guerrerense Carreta $$

Sabina Bandera's award-winning Ensenada seafood stand dates from the 1960s and attracts long lines with its outstanding ceviche. Renowned chef Anthony Bourdain sang its praises in 2018.

Finca Altozano $$$

Our favorite of celebrity Mexican chef Javier Plascencia's restaurants, this place in Valle de Guadalupe looks out over vineyards and has a tantalizing menu featuring exceptional oysters and wood-fired mains.

Outdoor Thrills

Parque Nacional Bahía de Loreto

This park makes Loreto a world-class destination for all types of outdoor activities, from kayaking and diving to stand-up paddleboarding (SUP) and snorkeling. Aside from the gray whales that frequent the Sea of Cortez, this is the best place to see ginormous blue whales.

Isla Espíritu Santo

A treasure trove of shallow azure inlets and sorbet-pink cliffs, Espíritu Santo is a La Paz marvel. Most folks visit the wildlife-rich island on day trips but glamping grounds are available, too.

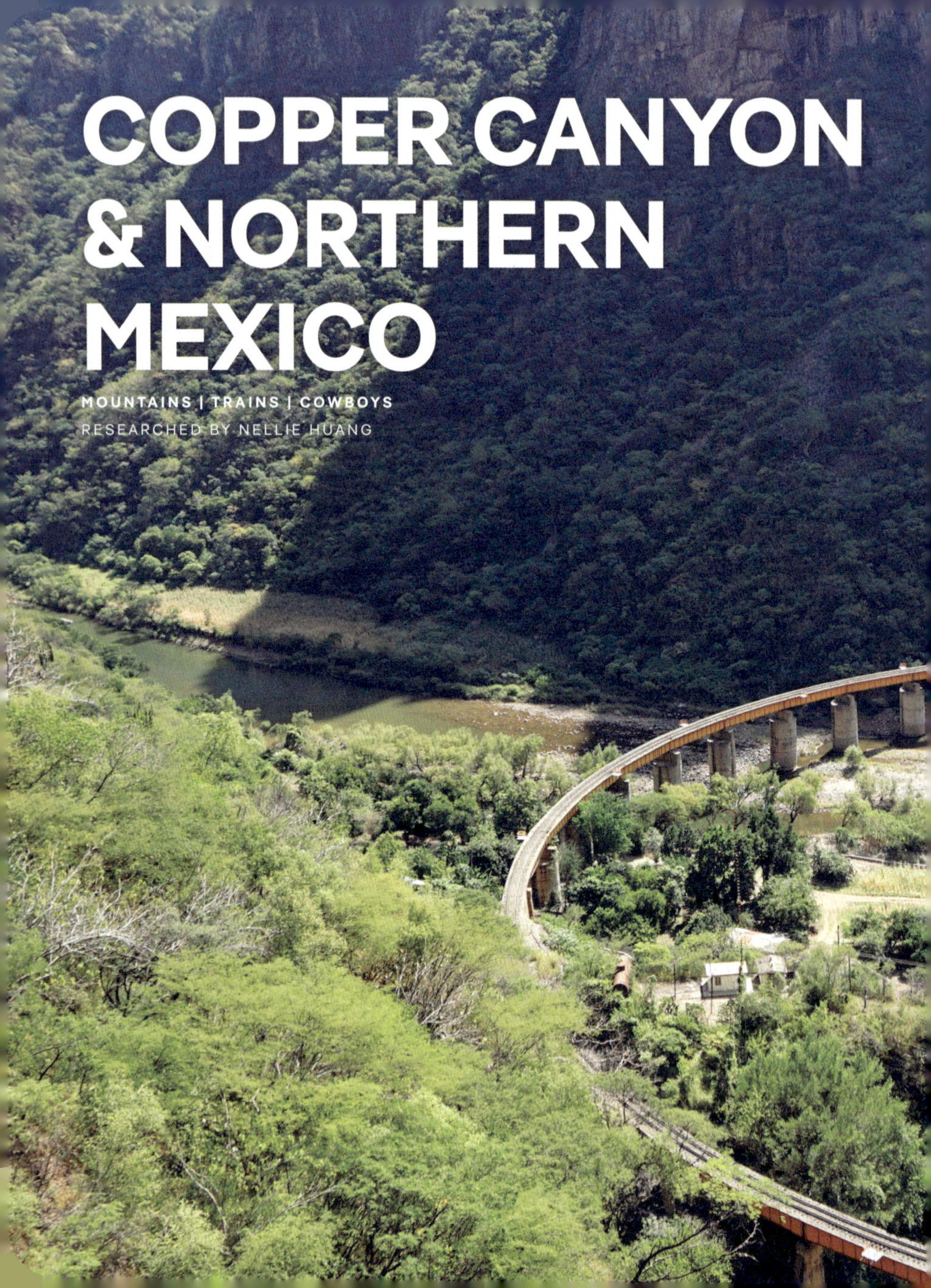

COPPER CANYON & NORTHERN MEXICO

MOUNTAINS | TRAINS | COWBOYS

RESEARCHED BY NELLIE HUANG

- **Trip Builder** (p224)
- **Practicalities** (p225)
- **All Aboard the Chepe Train** (p226)
- **Pancho Villa's Mexico** (p228)
- **Northern Mexico's Natural Landmarks** (p230)
- **The Evolution of Monterrey** (p232)
- **Listings** (p234)

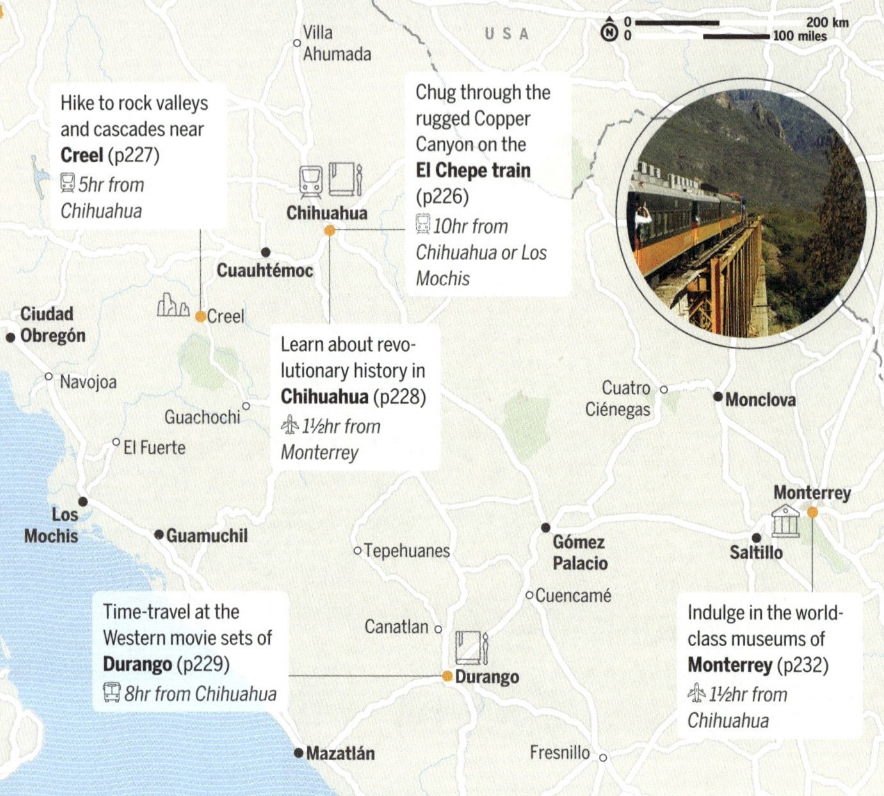

COPPER CANYON & NORTHERN MEXICO
Trip Builder

Northern Mexico is a magical canvas of vast deserts, rugged canyons and mining towns. This often misunderstood part of Mexico encompasses some of the country's biggest states. Take your time to hike, bike and chug your way through this frontier land.

Practicalities

ARRIVING

Chihuahua International Airport The main gateway to the Copper Canyon, and the start/end of the Chepe train journey. Taxis to the city center cost M$260; get your ticket at Arrivals.

MONEY

Most hotels accept credit cards but carry pesos for food and tips because the number of ATMs is limited in the Copper Canyon.

CONNECT

In parts of the Copper Canyon, there's no phone signal – but most hotels have stable wi-fi.

WHERE TO STAY

Place	Pros/Cons
Chihuahua	Easy transport access and a variety of accommodations options. Not an attractive city.
Creel	Small town with a handful of *cabañas* (cabins). Need a car or tour to explore the surroundings.
Monterrey	Widest selection of accommodation. Great transport network.
Durango	Good budget options. Easy to explore on foot.

GETTING AROUND

Train El Chepe connects various mountain towns in Copper Canyon, starting and ending at Creel and Los Mochis.

Bus Northern Mexico is well connected by bus; Chihuahuenses (*chihuahuenses.com.mx*) and Rápidos Cuauhtémoc (*rapidoscuauhtemoc.mex.tl*) are the most popular companies.

Car The easiest way to explore the natural attractions surrounding Monterrey, Chihuahua and Durango.

TOP: GUAJILLO STUDIO/SHUTTERSTOCK
BOTTOM: FABIAN MONTANO HERNANDEZ/SHUTTERSTOCK

EATING & DRINKING

Northern Mexico is famous for having the best beef. Vegetarians will still find plant-based options.

Chile pasado Mashed chilaca chilies topped with Chihuahua cheese.

Machaca Spiced, air-dried beef usually eaten with scrambled eggs (pictured top left).

Tesgüino A Rarámuri traditional beer brewed from malted corn (pictured bottom left).

Best cabrito al pastor (roast kid goat)
El Rey del Cabrito (p235)

Must-try carne asada (grilled steak)
La Cabaña (p235)

SEP–NOV
Mild temperatures and sunny days, perfect for mountain hikes.

JUN–AUG
Rainy season, with occasional afternoon thundershowers.

DEC–FEB
Sub-zero temperatures at the canyon rim, with possible snowfall.

APR–JUN
Driest time of the year, with water shortages in some towns.

40 All Aboard the CHEPE TRAIN

CANYONS | HIKING | PANORAMAS

Hop on board El Chepe train for the ride of a lifetime, through pine-clad ridges and vertiginous cliff-drops. The train climbs up the dramatic mountains of Chihuahua and zigzags through the theatrical Copper Canyon on one of the world's most scenic train journeys.

DAVID COLIN/SHUTTERSTOCK

Panoramic Railway

Nicknamed El Chepe, the **Ferrocarril Chihuahua Pacífico** trundles between Chihuahua and Los Mochis, reaching over 2400m in altitude as it teeters on the cusp of the Copper Canyon. You *can* actually ride the train all the way through in 10 hours – but you'll miss out on the chance to explore one of Mexico's wildest regions.

Trip Notes

Getting around The railway operates two trains: the fast **Chepe Express** *(chepe.mx)* and the slower **Chepe Regional**, which can be booked by email *(chepe@ferromex.mx)*.

When to go The best time to go is from September to November, when the weather is mild.

Top tips Both directions promise striking scenery. If you travel east (Los Mochis to Chihuahua), book a seat on the right side for the best views (left when westbound).

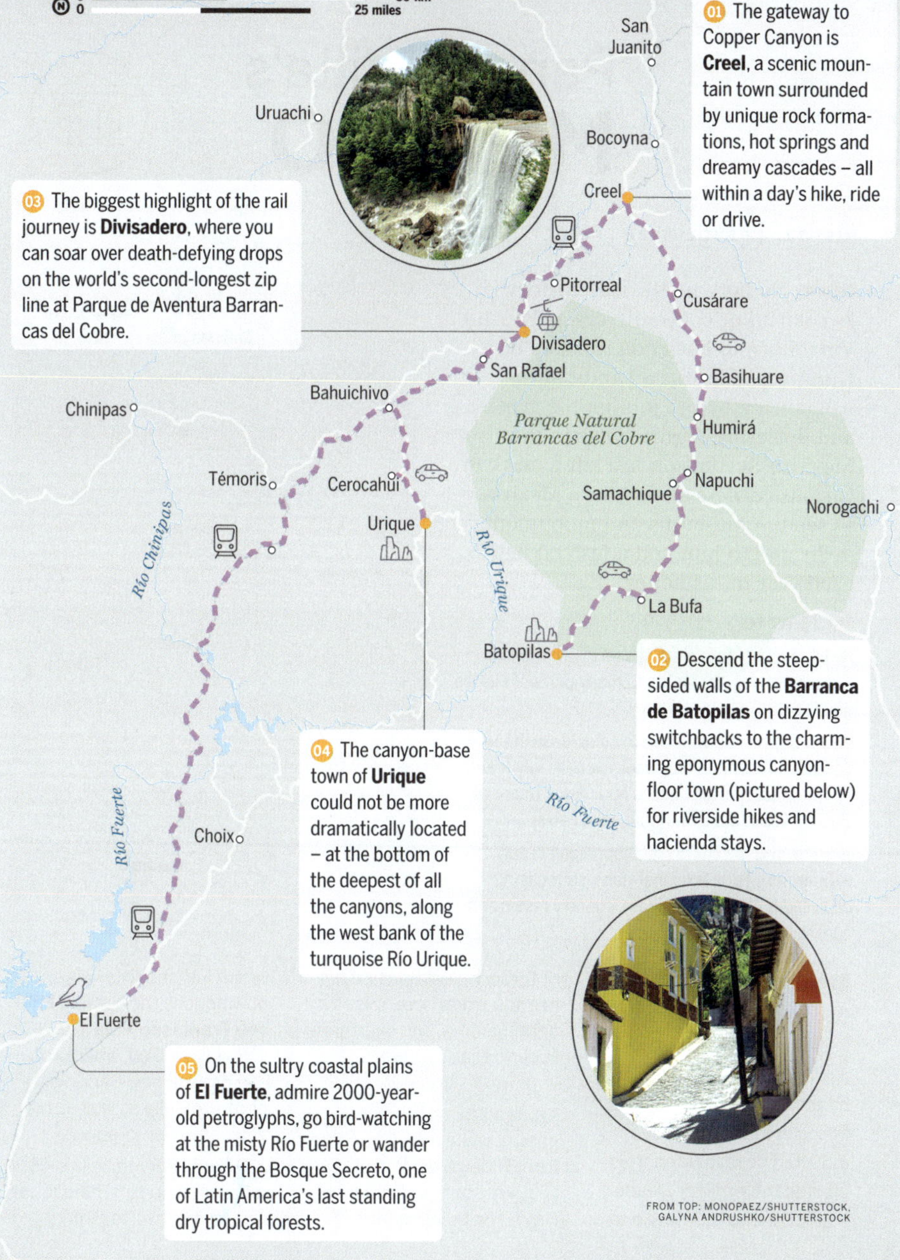

FROM TOP: MONOPAEZ/SHUTTERSTOCK, GALYNA ANDRUSHKO/SHUTTERSTOCK

41 Pancho Villa's MEXICO

HISTORY | REVOLUTION | PRIDE

No hero in Mexico's history is as colorful or contradictory as Pancho Villa. Born to hacienda workers in Durango, Villa was a bandit and womanizer, before joining the army and defeating Porfirio Díaz in the Mexican Revolution. He left a mark in various corners of Northern Mexico, as seen in museums and monuments dedicated to him and a festival held each year in his honor.

How to

Getting here Chihuahua has an international airport with regular flights to many parts of Mexico and the US.

When to go Time your trip to coincide with the Jornadas Villistas, a one-week event in July featuring theatrical performances and reenactment of Pancho Villa's death in Hidalgo del Parral.

Rodeos and ranchers Also happening in July is Durango's Feria Nacional (fair), showcasing *charreadas* (Mexican rodeos), country music and carnival rides.

Mexico's Biggest Hero

Once the key city in Nueva España, Chihuahua played a pivotal role in Mexico's history. It was here that the Mexican Revolution began in 1910. The revolutionaries elected their military leaders – and Pancho Villa was one of them. He established his headquarters here, raised a fighting force, and overthrew Porfirio Díaz's regime.

In 1923, Villa was assassinated amid a barrage of gunfire while traveling home from Hidalgo del Parral (230km south of Chihuahua City). The building from which Pancho Villa was shot now houses the humble **Museo Francisco Villa** *(adult/child M$44/28)*, where you can browse black-and-white photos of Villa as well as his guns and memorabilia.

After his death, Villa's 48-room mansion in Chihuahua was also converted into a museum. **Museo Historico de la Revolución** *(adult/child M$20/10)* now has the biggest collection of Villa's personal belongings, loaded with Hollywood-style stories of crime and stakeouts. The front section was Villa's bedroom, kitchen and dining area; at the back stands the bullet-riddled Dodge that Villa was murdered in.

The best place to take a deep dive into Villa's past is in his birthplace, Durango (400km south of Parral). A block from Plaza de Armas stands **Museo Francisco Villa**, with interactive digital exhibits and extensive information on Villa and his army. Dating back to 1800, the building itself is a work of art, embellished with mural art from famous Durango artists.

Durango's Local Favorites

Paseo Túnel de Minería In Plaza de Armas, descend to the dark yet intriguing underground passage to learn about the city's mining history and legends.

Paseo Teleférico Hop onto the cable car at Cerro del Calvario to reach the viewpoint for dazzling views of the city.

Cielo Rosa Dine alfresco while enjoying the sunset at this atmospheric, hilltop restaurant by the cable car station.

Botica Cocina Bar End the night at this gastro bar for creative cocktails served in laboratory flasks and test tubes.

By Paulina Berenice, *owner of Hotel Boutique Casona los Pavorreales*

Above Paseo Teleférico

Northern Mexico's

NATURAL LANDMARKS

01

02

04

05

01 Cascada de Basaseachi
Mexico's highest full-time waterfall tumbles 246m to its azure pool, which is surrounded by a national park where cougars and white-tailed deers roam.

02 Valle de los Monjes
Just outside Creel sprawls the Valle de los Monjes, a rock valley dotted with vertical out-crops that rise imposingly above the pine forests.

03 Mirador de Divisadero
The highlight of El Chepe train is Divisadero, where you can feast on jaw-dropping canyon views from a viewpoint outside the train station.

04 Barrancas de Urique
A series of hairpin bends descend the steep Barrancas de Urique to reach the canyon-bottom eponymous town, where riverside walks await.

05 Bosque Secreto
Surrounding the coastal plains of El Fuerte is the Bosque Secreto, one of Latin America's last standing dry tropical forests.

06 Cuatro Ciénegas
Located in Coahuila, this protected area is an 843-sq-km nature reserve bespeckled with shimmering cerulean *pozas* (natural pools).

07 Desierto Chihuahuense
This is the largest hot desert in North America and is considered the most biologically diverse desert in the world by WWF.

08 Cerro de Silla
Monterrey's iconic Cerro de Silla (Saddle Hill) has an abandoned cable car esplanade that offers panoramic views of the city.

09 Parque Ecológico Chipinque
Looming over the metropolis of Monterrey is a mountaintop reserve with fantastic hiking and mountain biking trails.

10 El Potrero Chico
Just 45km northwest of Monterrey is Mexico's rock-climbing capital, featuring vertiginous 600m-high limestone walls.

11 Grutas de García
This impressive cave system near Monterrey extends for more than 3.5km, containing 16 chambers full of stalactites and stalagmites.

01 VERSOCA/SHUTTERSTOCK, **02** ESDELVAL/SHUTTERSTOCK, **03** WAYAK/SHUTTERSTOCK, **04** ADM233KA/SHUTTERSTOCK, **05** HEMIS/ALAMY STOCK PHOTO, **06** MARCO PORTAL URBINA/SHUTTERSTOCK, **07** WITOLD SKRYPCZAK/ALAMY, **08** PAC-05/SHUTTERSTOCK, **09** JUAN PABLO HINOJOSA/SHUTTERSTOCK, **10** ANNYSFOTOGRAFA/SHUTTERSTOCK, **11** IGNACIO LAZO ARTEAGA/SHUTTERSTOCK

The Evolution of Monterrey

HOW MEXICO'S POWERHOUSE IS REWRITING ITS PAST

Once the backdrop to violent narco wars, Monterrey is slowly cleaning up its act and rising from the ashes. A place of riches and wealth, the metropolitan city is now Mexico's financial capital, with a mishmash of high-rises, noisy and sweaty industries, and a bustling central district that is undergoing a revival.

Left Barrio Antiguo **Centre** Parque Fundidora **Right** Paseo Santa Lucía

ELE96REBREA/SHUTTERSTOCK

Just 240km from the US border, Monterrey has always enjoyed a strategic geographical location that made it a nerve center in Northeast Mexico. The 'Sultan of the North' is one of Mexico's wealthiest cities, thanks to a variety of light and heavy industry, international businesses and agriculture.

Yet behind the shiny facade of high-rises and wealthy suburbs lies a dark history that *regios* (Monterrey locals) know all too well. As recently as 2012, Monterrey battled the drug wars up close. Its commercial district and historic downtown, Barrio Antiguo, witnessed a dismal amount of violence and was besieged by mass murders and bombings.

During the turf war between the Zetas and the Gulf Cartel, high-power firefights erupted along the main boulevards. Blockades controlled by the cartels' gunmen paralyzed the city for days, and mutilated bodies were displayed like trophies in city squares. Police stations, the statehouse and the US consulate were attacked with explosives. What was originally the cultural center of Monterrey was practically abandoned in the early 2000s.

Reaching its Lowest Point

In 2010, Monterrey's business elite sent an open letter to President Felipe Calderón and Nuevo León's governor. By the time the letter was published in the major newspapers, Calderón had dispatched more than 45,000 troops in counternarcotics operations across Mexico. Employing the military's help proved ineffective at first – with the number of homicides skyrocketing alongside reports of human rights violations by soldiers. By 2012, Mexico's

JJAF/SHUTTERSTOCK

GABRIELBAHENA/SHUTTERSTOCK

drug violence sunk the downtown to the very bottom when it became a no-go zone.

More than a decade later, the situation in central Monterrey has stabilized and narco-related violence reduced substantially (though homicides still occur from time to time). Barrio Antiguo and many of the central areas are now considered safe by day and night. The violence that played out in Barrio Antiguo's bars and nightclubs has driven out many businesses from the area, but millions of dollars have since been poured into the district.

Looking to the Future

Things are looking up as a melange of third-wave coffee shops, craft-beer stores and indie boutiques have returned to Barrio Antiguo. Restored buildings splashed in pastel colors stand alongside crumbling, vandalized houses; cracked sidewalks line slick gourmet bars, while open rooftop restaurants overlook empty, abandoned residences. The area is still a work in progress, but there's a spirit of hope in the air.

The main artery of the neighborhood, Calle Morelos, is now lined with characterful bars, beer gardens and indie boutiques. Running perpendicular is the car-free Calle Mina, which transforms into the Corredor del Arte on Sundays with a whimsical collection of antiques, handicrafts and knickknacks. Further south on Calle Jardón is where the city's antique stores converge. The whole district springs to life, especially in the evening, with locals hitting trendy bars and lively nightlife spots that attract a diverse crowd.

Monterrey has never been one to stand defeated. Through the past decades of drug wars, it has endured, grown and evolved. And through it all, it has retained its complex soul.

Best Bars & Music Spots in Monterrey

Café Iguana *(cafeiguana.com.mx)* Catch live music of all genres at this institution where the biggest bands have played.

Almacén 42 *(almacen42.com)* Shipping containers have been converted into an urban bar with a solid menu of craft beer.

Uptown Live Music Bar Jam to live music, ranging from *ranchero* (country) to rock, at this venue.

Saxy Jazz Club Tap your feet to live jazz and Latin music at this hip joint.

TOPAZDeluxe Groove to electronic music at this club that draws in a young crowd.

By David Navas, *dancer and musician who leads TTMDA Mexico*

Listings

BEST OF THE REST

Outdoor Thrills

Parque de Aventura Barrancas del Cobre

Fly across dizzying heights on the ZipRider, the world's second-longest zip line, at this adventure park on the Copper Canyon Rim. Close to the Divisadero station, the park has guided hikes, *via ferrata* routes and a glass-floored restaurant.

Valle de los Monjes

A few kilometers from Creel, this unique rock valley is strewn with imposing vertical outcrops poking high above the adjacent pine forests. The Rarámuri (Tarahumara), indigenous to Copper Canyon, named this area Bisabírachi, meaning 'Valley of the Erect Penises.'

Parque Ecológico Chipinque

Looming over Monterrey is a protected ecological park crisscrossed with fantastic hiking and mountain biking trails through dense deciduous forests where wild bears roam freely.

El Potrero Chico

Just 45km from Monterrey, this is Mexico's rock-climbing capital, featuring steep 600m-high limestone walls. Its well-bolted, multi-pitch spot routes make it an excellent spot for climbers of all levels.

Parque Ecológico La Huasteca

Colossal spines of karst limestone rise sharply above the vertiginous walls of the Cañón de la Huasteca. Adventure seekers can choose from two *via ferrata* routes (Rutas Vertigo and Ignis).

Wet & Wild

Cascada de Basaseachi

Mexico's highest full-time waterfall is surrounded by azure pools and a protected national park, home to the cougar, white-tailed deer and collared peccary.

Aguas Termales Recowata

Blissfully warm bubbling water is channeled into several inviting bathing pools tucked between the gorges, with a river running beneath them. At 35km south of Creel, these hot springs provide an excellent respite after long hikes in the rocky valleys.

Cuatro Ciénegas

In the Desierto Chihuahuense sprawls an 843-sq-km nature reserve bespeckled with cerulean *pozas* (natural pools). It is home to over 75 endemic species and stromatolites, the Earth's oldest living life form.

Exploring Caves

Grutas de García

Extending for more than 3.5km inside the Sierra del Fraile, this is one of Mexico's most impressive cave systems. Take a scenic cable car or hike the serpentine 1.5km trail to get to the cave entrance, before exploring the 16 chambers stacked full of stalactites and stalagmites.

Grutas Nombre de Dios

On the northern edge of Chihuahua City is an underground network of caves boasting impressive stalagmites, stalactites and rock formations. Guides will point out distinctive formations, including the Tower of Pisa and the Heart of the Cave, a vault with an entrance shaped like a heart.

Panoramic Views

Paseo Teleférico

For a bird's-eye view of Durango, hop onto the cable car at Cerro del Calvario, a small hill in the center of Durango. It takes visitors up to a viewpoint just 680m away, the Mirador de los Remedios.

Cerro del Obispado

This large lookout is perched at the top of Bishop's Hill (775m), 4km west of downtown Monterrey, offering spectacular 360-degree vistas of the city and the Sierra Madre Oriental mountains. In the center stands the biggest monumental flag in Mexico, with a pole measuring 100m in height.

Mirador Cerro del Gallego Cañón de Urique

This viewpoint 24km southeast of Cerocahui reveals the Urique Canyon in its full glory. From this elevation, you can see the Urique road zigzagging its way down to the canyon bottom and Río Urique flowing through the Copper Canyon.

Cultural Hits

Museo de Historia Mexicana

The world-class Mexican History Museum in Monterrey transports you through time, from the pre-Hispanic era to the 20th century. More than 1200 artifacts are on display, including Olmec stone heads and a real locomotive.

Horno3

A former steel blast furnace in Monterrey's Parque Fundidora has been ingeniously converted into an impressive high-tech, hands-on museum dedicated to Mexico's steel industry. The highlight is the dramatic furnace show, beamed four times a day from the bulk of Horno3.

Museo Menonita

Get insights into the Mennonite community that has lived in Mexico for over 100 years at this well-curated museum north of Cuauhtémoc. A replica of the traditional Mennonite house, the museum showcases their tools, dresses and other paraphernalia.

Places to Eat

El Rey del Cabrito $$

This local institution is synonymous with Monterrey and serves up its most famous dish: *cabrito* (goat). The signature *cabritos* are slow-roasting over charcoal in the window, and dishes come still sizzling on a bed of onions, with salad and tortillas.

La Cabaña $$

One of the fancier places in town, La Cabaña serves a good *tampiqueña* (steak accompanied by several side orders), as well as tasty salads, grills and local specialties like trout stuffed with shrimp.

Breweries & Wineries

La Sotolería $

A fun cowboy bar serving an overwhelming range of *sotol* and cocktails, plus grilled meat and *botanas* (snacks) in Chihuahua's city center.

Almacén 42 $$

In Monterrey's Barrio Antiguo, try craft beers from all over Mexico at this urban bar, converted from a few shipping containers.

Vinícola Casa Chávez $$

Fourth-generation winemakers produce aromatic wine in the Delicias Valley (one hour from Chihuahua), where you can taste homegrown wines and pair them with classic *norteño* dishes.

Vinos Misión $$$

On the gentle slopes of Cerocahui, Jesuit-grown vineyards from the 6th century have been restored to produce delicious wine. The vineyard runs daily wine-tasting sessions where you get to taste five wines for M$350.

Practicalities

238

240

242

243

244

246

248

LANGUAGE

250

Right Cabo San Lucas (p37), Baja California

EASY STEPS FROM THE AIRPORT TO THE CITY CENTRE

Mexico City, the main point of arrival for most visitors, has two airports: the older Aeropuerto Internacional Benito Juárez (Ciudad de Mexico; MEX) located 11km from the city center; and the newer Aeropuerto Internacional Felipe Ángeles (NLU), 35km from the center. The country's second busiest airport, Aeropuerto Internacional de Cancún (CUN), serves more than 70-plus cities worldwide and experiences a high volume of traffic at peak season.

AT THE AIRPORT

SIM CARDS

SIM cards for unlocked phones are available for purchase at the Telcel (widest coverage in Mexico) or AT&T stores in the airports. eSIMs are a more convenient option that can be purchased online in advance and activated upon arrival.

CASH

Official currency exchange counters are located in the Arrivals hall and baggage claim areas of all airports. It's easy to spot them with their big signs that read 'Cambio Exchange.' It's best to wait to exchange in banks because bank rates are better.

ARKADIJ SCHELL/SHUTTERSTOCK

WI-FI

Free wi-fi is available at all airports. If you're using a ride-hailing app, such as Uber, connect using the Gratis_CDMX_Aeropuerto network.

ATMS

ATMs are available at the Arrivals concourse. ATMs at the airport are more reliable (lower risk of scams) than those on the streets.

CHARGING STATIONS

Free charging stations are available for use at the Departures boarding gates. Keep an eye on your phone while it's charging.

TOURIST PERMITS

It is no longer required to fill out a *forma migratoria múltiple* (FMM; tourist permit) when flying into Mexico. Those traveling by land still need to complete the digital form at inm.gob.mx/fmme. Most visitors get a passport stamp instead. The length of your permitted stay in Mexico, maximum 180 days, is determined by the immigration officer.

GETTING TO THE CITY CENTER

MEX Airport Metro Line 5 has a Terminal Aérea station at Terminal 1; a ride costs only M$5 and takes 35 minutes to the center. Bus Line 4 runs from both terminals to Colonia Buenavista (M$30). Rideshare usually costs M$300 to M$500 to the historic center.

NLU Airport ETN and Estrella Blanca provide bus transfers from this airport to the Terminal Central de Autobuses del Norte (northern bus station) for M$80 each way; the journey takes 1½ hours. A taxi costs around M$800 to downtown Mexico City.

CUN Airport ADO runs regular bus services from the airport to downtown Cancún for M$140; the journey takes 45 minutes. Shared shuttles are available (M$600 per person) dropping you right at your hotel. Those traveling in a group are better off getting a taxi (around M$800).

HOW MUCH FOR A...

TAXIS

The official taxis charge a fixed rate from the airport. Prepay for your ride at the taxi kiosk in the Arrivals hall.

CAR RENTAL

Some agencies have offices at Arrivals, while others provide free shuttles to their offices nearby. Book in advance during peak seasons.

RIDE-HAILING

The pick-up and drop-off areas are directly outside Arrivals for all airports.

OTHER POINTS OF ENTRY

US–Mexico border There are 50 crossings between the United States and Mexico borders, all of which can be crossed by car. Buses link the cities of Chihuahua, Cuauhtémoc, Ciudad Juárez, Matamoros, Monterrey and Nuevo Laredo to many parts of the US. The most reliable bus companies are Chihuahuenses and Noroeste. The busiest crossings are the Ciudad Juárez–El Paso and Tijuana–San Diego checkpoints.

Guatemala–Mexico border Currently there are 10 formal border crossings, with most of them in Chiapas and two in Tabasco. The most used border crossing is the Ciudad Cuauhtémoc–La Mesilla crossing. Tourist shuttles are a popular and convenient way to get from San Cristóbal de las Casas to Panajachel (US$60pp) and Antigua (US$75pp). Boats are an easy way to cross the border from Frontera Corozal, Chiapas to Bethel in Guatemala.

Belize–Mexico border You can cross this border only at two checkpoints, the more popular being the Chetumal–Santa Elena crossing. An ADO bus runs the Cancun–Belize City route twice a day, making stops in Tulum, Bacalar, Corozal and Orange Walk Town. A one-way journey costs M$960 and takes 8 to 9 hours.

TRANSPORT TIPS TO HELP YOU GET AROUND

The best way to explore Mexico in depth is to rent a vehicle. With a set of wheels, you can travel at your own pace and explore hard-to-reach areas that aren't accessible by public transport. Mexican roads are relatively easy to navigate – just be aware of reckless drivers and hard-to-see speed bumps.

CAR RENTAL

Renting a car requires a credit card, a passport and a valid driver's license from your home country. Most rental car rates include unlimited kilometers and liability coverage. Reserve in advance in the peak season, especially if you need an automatic car, which costs extra.

BUS

Mexico has an extensive intercity bus network, throughout the country. Buses are comfortable and equipped with air-conditioning, reclining seats, sometimes USB ports, video screens and free wi-fi. Most major bus lines sell tickets online, some with discounted fares for advance purchases.

DRIVING IN MEXICO

When you get behind the wheel in Mexico, consider this: some drivers have never taken a driver's test! Traffic rules are rarely enforced; drivers might view red lights and speed limits as mere suggestions; and turning left from the middle lane is common. Stay alert, especially when driving on poorly maintained roads, and always be wary of nighttime carjackings and holdups in cities and on non-toll roads.

AIRPLANE

The entire country is well connected by plane and domestic flights are relatively affordable. During the off-season, it can be cheaper to fly than take a long-distance bus. Low-cost carriers like VivaAerobus and Volaris have the best deals. Occasionally you'll find bargains on Aeromexico, Mexico's flagship airline.

FERRY

Foot-passenger and car ferries potter around the Yucatán's Caribbean coast, connecting the mainland with its many islands. Foot-passenger ferries tend to be faster and are usually air-conditioned, comfortable and punctual. They also leave more regularly than the car ferries. Ferry tickets can be booked online in advance.

DRIVING ESSENTIALS

Drive on the right – the steering wheel is on the left.

On narrow roads or single-lane bridges, give way if the red arrow is pointing in your direction of travel.

The speed limit is 110km/h on highways and 50km/h in urban areas unless otherwise posted.

The blood alcohol limit is 0.8g/L (0.08%) in most states.

Carry cash for toll roads.

ROAD CONDITIONS

Many roads in Mexico aren't government regulated and may have large potholes. Stick to the better-maintained toll roads. Most toll roads accept credit cards but always carry cash to be safe. Speed cameras don't exist in Mexico; in their place are speed bumps (look out for the *'tope'* signs), which aren't always painted. Driving at night is best avoided because of poorly lit roads and potential highway robberies.

COLECTIVOS & COMBIS

Shared passenger vans provide cheap transportation along fixed routes within cities and between towns. Most have more regular service than buses but are slower as they make frequent stops. Hail them on any corner, then tell the driver where you want to hop off.

INSURANCE

Whether you are driving your car or a rental, Mexican car insurance is mandatory. By Mexican law, you must have third-party insurance that covers damage to other vehicles if an accident is your fault. Always carry proof of your insurance in your vehicle.

KNOW YOUR CARBON FOOTPRINT

A domestic flight from Mexico City to Cancún emits about 470kg of carbon dioxide per passenger. A car emits around 210kg for the drive, while a bus emits 36.2kg over the same distance, per passenger. Sustainable Travel's carbon calculator tool *(sustainabletravel.org)* can be used to calculate and purchase carbon offsets to contribute to carbon-reducing projects.

ROAD DISTANCE CHART (KM)

	Puerto Vallarta	Cabo San Lucas	Cancún	Chihuahua	Guadalajara	Guanajuato	Mexico City	Monterrey	Oaxaca	Veracruz
Puerto Vallarta	–									
Cabo San Lucas	1256	–								
Cancún	2448	3448	–							
Chihuahua	1307	1268	3046	–						
Guadalajara	310	1288	2145	1179	–					
Guanajuato	581	1604	1950	1137	278	–				
Mexico City	884	1875	1609	1430	539	353	–			
Monterrey	1117	1644	2345	807	812	680	910	–		
Oaxaca	1302	2281	1506	1899	999	803	462	1357	–	
Veracruz	1198	2190	1326	1751	910	714	392	1028	445	–

SAFE TRAVEL

Despite widespread news surrounding its brutal drug war, Mexico remains a relatively safe place to visit. Tourists have been largely spared from decades of violence occurring mostly between rival drug gangs. Avoid buying drugs to steer clear of trouble.

EARTHQUAKES

Sitting in a seismically active region, Mexico is prone to frequent and potentially powerful earthquakes, especially in Oaxaca and Mexico City. Some cities have alert systems that sound when a quake is coming. If you hear the warning, remain calm and move to open spaces away from tall buildings. If you're on the coast, head for higher ground.

INFECTIOUS DISEASES

Viral diseases such as dengue and zika are transmitted by infected Aedes mosquitos and can cause fever, joint pain and extreme fatigue. There are no treatments other than getting plenty of rest and water. Most cases occur in Mexico's rainy southern region. Apply insect repellent and wear long-sleeve shirts to protect yourself.

SCAMS

Always use ATMs located inside banks to avoid having your bank card cloned. If someone offers to clean the bird poop or tomato ketchup on your back, say no. They often swipe your valuables while you're distracted.

Altitude sickness often occurs when people ascend rapidly to altitudes higher than 2500m (Mexico City is at that elevation). Symptoms include dizziness, fatigue, headaches, vomiting and nausea. Overexertion and alcohol can worsen your symptoms.

FONGBEERREDHOT/SHUTTERSTOCK

GUILLERMO APARICIO SERVIN/SHUTTERSTOCK

VOLCANOES

Mexico has 48 active volcanoes. Volcanic ash spews during an eruption and has been known to cause flight disruptions. Use a dust respirator mask and goggles to protect yourself from inhaling the ash.

VACCINATIONS

There's no mandatory vaccination required to visit Mexico, but **CDC** *(cdc.gov)* recommends the following:

Hepatitis A Travelers except children under one year old.

Hepatitis B Long-term travelers.

Measles Infants six to 11 months old.

Rabies Those who may come into contact with animals.

Typhoid All travelers.

Emergency services can be reached 24/7 by dialing 911 for the police, 065 for an ambulance, 068 in case of fire, and 078 for road assistance and towing service.

QUICK TIPS TO HELP YOU MANAGE YOUR MONEY

CREDIT CARDS

Credit cards are widely accepted in large urban centers, especially in malls, hotels and midrange restaurants. You can save on exorbitant ATM fees and poor currency exchange rates by paying with a major credit card. When visiting small towns, always carry cash. Most gas stations accept Visa and Mastercard (not American Express). Some businesses tack on so-called 'commission' fees for credit card payments.

ATMS

There's no shortage of ATMs in cities across Mexico, while it's hit or miss in rural areas. In small towns, machines may run out of money.

BARGAINING

Prices in most stores are fixed, but it's common to bargain with street and market vendors. A few dollars can make a big difference to local vendors.

CURRENCY

Mexican pesos

HOW MUCH FOR A

Taco
M$18–35

Beer
M$40–80

Dinner for two
M$600–1000

PAYING THE BILL

You usually need to ask the waiter to bring the check; it's considered rude to leave the bill before customers are done. Always check the bill; some restaurants tack on a service fee, which is illegal.

TIPPING

Tipping is common in Mexico, but it is voluntary. The standard tip for a restaurant meal is 10% to 15%. Tips for porters and gas station attendants are usually M$10 to M$30.

CASH

Always carry cash in Mexico, as you will need it for tips, transport and street food. Even in big cities, credit card terminals may not work. Carry only what you need for your daily expenses.

VAT The standard VAT (known as IVA in Spanish) is 16% in Mexico (reduced rate of 8%), which applies to most goods and services.

Tax refund You can get a VAT refund if you don't live in Mexico, and your purchase was at least M$1200 and was made in one store with a credit card or cash (not more than M$3000).

Guides Your tour group leader will happily accept tips – the standard rate is 10% of your tour fee.

BUDGET HACKS

Exchange rates Exchange your foreign currency at banks to enjoy the best rates. Forex offices at the airport tend to charge higher fees.

Discount tickets Most archaeological sites, museums and public transport services offer reduced rates to seniors, kids under 12 and families.

POSITIVE-IMPACT TRAVEL

Tips to leave a lighter footprint, support local and have a positive impact on local communities.

ON THE ROAD

Plan a nature-focused trip. Mexico has more than 67 national parks and 40 UNESCO-protected biosphere reserves, with bountiful ecotourism options.

Embrace slow travel. Base yourself in a region like Oaxaca or Chiapas and take time to explore.

Go off the beaten path. Over-tourism and overdevelopment are pressing issues, especially in Tulum and Cabo San Lucas.

Calculate your carbon at sustainabletravel.org. You can also contribute to environmental organizations to offset the impact of your emissions.

Rent bicycles to get closer to nature and local culture. Rent a bike easily in major cities with apps like Ecobici in Mexico City, MiBici in Guadalajara and Biciplaya in Playa del Carmen.

Rent a kayak instead of taking a motorboat – Laguna Bacalar and Huasteca Potosina are options.

Look into the green credentials of accommodations by checking recycling practices, renewable energy sources, energy-efficient appliances, and heating and cooling systems.

DBSOCAL/SHUTTERSTOCK

GIVE BACK

Volunteer with wildlife conservation programs. Assist biologists in their fieldwork at **Centro Ecológico Akumal** *(ceakumal.org)* and **Pronatura** *(pronatura.org.mx)*.

Help local communities through social initiatives. Junax *(junax.org.mx)* does important work with indigenous communities in Chiapas; Casa de los Amigos in Mexico City accepts volunteers who can help with refugees.

Support social enterprises. Seek out social impact cafes that direct a percentage of their earnings toward environmental projects.

Participate in wildlife conservation projects. Release baby turtles (pictured) at **Vive Mar** *(vivemar.com.mx)* in Puerto Escondido and **Tortugueros Las Playitas** *(todostortugueros.org)* on Baja's Playa Los Cerritos.

Book responsible wildlife tours. Spot the blue whale with **Loreto Sea & Land Tours** *(toursloreto.com)*, a reputable operator that prohibits snorkeling with whales.

SUPPORT LOCAL

Eat locally. Mexico has no shortage of cheap *taquerías,* casual *fondas* and bustling markets, where you can get delicious homemade comfort food.

Buy arts and crafts directly from artisans. This empowers local economies and assures that the actual producers get their fair share.

Visit a Saturday market. Try local produce and find handmade textiles or ceramic work.

LEAVE A SMALL FOOTPRINT

Save water. Take shorter and less frequent showers, as Mexico is facing a severe water shortage, especially in the drought-stricken northern region.

Go green. Explore national parks and reserves, and learn about nature preservation programs at botanical gardens dotted around Mexico.

Stick to the trail. Respect Mexico's flora and fauna and protect natural landscapes by keeping to hiking and cycling trails.

Use reef-safe sunscreen. Make sure your sunscreen does not contain oxybenzone and parabens. In many cenotes and waterfalls, it's prohibited to use sunscreen.

JOAO KERMADEC/SHUTTERSTOCK

DOS & DON'TS

Do respect rules at archaeological sites. Use walking paths and don't climb monuments.

Do seek out local perspectives. Check out cultural performances organized by the municipality, like Mérida's reenactment of Pok ta Pok (Maya ball game).

Do be mindful of indigenous customs and traditions. Dress conservatively when visiting homes. Don't wear disguises during Día de Muertos.

CLIMATE CHANGE & TRAVEL

Lonely Planet urges all travelers to engage with their travel carbon footprint, which will mainly come from air travel. While there often isn't an alternative, travelers can look to minimize the number of flights they take, opt for newer aircrafts and use cleaner ground transport, such as trains.

One proposed solution – purchasing carbon offsets – unfortunately does not cancel out the impact of individual flights. While most destinations will depend on air travel for the foreseeable future, for now, pursuing ground-based travel where possible is the best course of action.

The UN Carbon Offset Calculator shows how flying impacts a household's emissions:

The ICAO's carbon emissions calculator allows visitors to analyze the CO_2 generated by point-to-point journeys:

RESOURCES

responsibletravel.org
goabroad.com
transitionsabroad.com
florafaunaycultura.org

UNIQUE & LOCAL WAYS TO STAY

Mexico overflows with a wide spectrum of accommodations ranging from A-framed wooden cabañas (cabins) to charming B&Bs in historic mansions, family-friendly all-inclusives and private villas with stunning vistas. You can still find great bargain deals, especially in the less visited areas, but expect to pay a premium on attractive design concepts, quality food and above-and-beyond service.

PATRYK KOSMIDER/SHUTTERSTOCK

BUDGET BLISS

Mexico has no shortage of cheap dorms, youth hostels and good-value posadas (family-run inns). Hostels often have a convivial vibe and shared amenities, where you can meet other travelers over breakfast and book organized tours with the hosts. Posadas typically fall under budget or midrange categories, providing meals that are usually delicious and affordable.

AIRBNBS & RENTALS

Vacation rentals for short- and long-term stays abound in Mexico and with giants like Airbnb and Vrbo in the picture, it's never been easier to find spacious apartments to stay in. However, not everyone in Mexico sees the rapidly expanding homestay market as a good thing. In Tulum, locals blame Airbnb in part for overtourism; in Mexico City, residents say an influx of deep-pocketed digital nomads are driving rent up and forcing locals out of their neighborhoods. It's a thorny issue but we recommend opting for indie, local alternatives.

GUESTHOUSES & CABAÑAS

For a fine midrange option, book a stay in a *cabaña,* many of which come equipped with full kitchens, dining areas and porches. *Casas de huéspedes* (guesthouses) usually only include a simple room, but breakfast is often provided. Take advantage of the chance to know your host. *Cabañas* without websites usually accept reservations through WhatsApp.

TRASCENDA/SHUTTERSTOCK

MONICA GARZA 73/SHUTTERSTOCK

GLAMPING

The 'glamorous camping' trend has become quite popular in Mexico in recent years. This upscale camping option appeals to those who like to be close to nature but also appreciate a touch of luxe. They run the gamut from stylish, air-conditioned bubble domes with private hot tubs, to bell tents, Mongolian yurts and A-framed cabins with private decks. You can enjoy hotel-like facilities set in scenic natural surroundings, often in seaside locations too. On-site perks sometimes include swimming pools, luxury spas, yoga studios and lounge bars. While it's not cheap, stepping out of your cozy bed and being greeted by fresh mountain air and expansive views is well worth the price.

CAMPING UNDER THE STARS

Some nature reserves and guesthouses provide affordable camping sites, where you can pitch your own tent and sleep under the starry skies. Most will rent sleeping bags and mattresses for a low price. At some campsites, you can even rent barbecue pits to have dinner outdoors. Another budget-oriented sleeping option, mostly for low-key beach destinations, is hammocks. Let the sea breeze lull you to sleep, but make sure to apply plenty of mosquito repellent. If it's too buggy or chilly, some of these spots also rent no-frills cabins.

BOOKING

The best way to find and book accommodations is online and through travel organizations or websites. Be aware that some accommodations options, especially in rural areas, will only have information available in Spanish and only be reserved via WhatsApp.

Room rates peak during the Mexican summer vacation (July and August), as well as during Semana Santa (mid-April), Día de Muertos (first week of November) and Christmas holidays – book as far ahead as possible for these periods. Prices are slightly reduced during the shoulder seasons of January to March and May to June. The daily tourist tax is usually included in the nightly room rate.

Pitch Up *(pitchup.com/campsites/mexico)* Search campsites and glamping spots across the country.

Glamping Hub *(glampinghub.com/mexico)* A booking platform with unique glamping destinations across Mexico.

Vacation Villas of Mexico *(vacationvillasofmexico.com)* Book high-end villas in the popular coastal areas of Mexico.

OMAR MANRIQUE/SHUTTERSTOCK

ECO-FRIENDLY LODGES

Mexico is seeing an increasing amount of ecolodges with sustainable development practices, but do your research when booking an ecolodge. In some trendy spots like Tulum, self-proclaimed 'eco-chic' spots are nothing more than greenwashing.

ESSENTIAL NUTS-AND-BOLTS

TOILETS

Public restrooms are plentiful in urban centers (M$5 to M$10), but not so much outside the city. It's wise to pack hand sanitizer and toilet paper.

SMOKING

It is illegal to smoke in all public places, including hotels and open-air spaces such as beaches and parks. Violators face stiff fines.

TAP WATER

Avoid drinking Mexico's tap water and only consume ice made with *agua purificada* (purified water).

FAST FACTS

Time Zone
GMT-6

Country Code
52

Electricity
120V/60Hz

GOOD TO KNOW

Citizens from more than 70 countries do not need a visa to enter Mexico and can stay for a maximum of 180 days (as determined by the immigration officer).

The legal minimum age to buy alcohol in Mexico is 18. It is illegal to drink alcohol on the streets in Mexico.

Stay on the right when driving, cycling and standing on escalators.

Travelers are entitled to a VAT refund on purchases of at least M$1200.

ACCESSIBLE TRAVEL

Sidewalks with ramps are uncommon; uneven pavements and cobbled streets can prove difficult to navigate in a wheelchair.

Mexico's Blue Flag–designated beaches usually provide at least partial-access wheelchair ramps for people with mobility issues.

Airports in Mexico City and Cancún provide wheelchair service and transport for passengers with reduced mobility.

Larger hotels and modern resorts tend to have wheelchair-friendly amenities, and helpful staff who go out of their way to ensure your comfort.

Wheelchair-accessible vans and shuttles are available in many tourist-oriented destinations like Cancún, Puerto Vallarta and Los Cabos.

Some city buses and modern metro systems in Mexico have wheelchair access, while most train and metro stations have elevators and tactile paving.

Ferries provide free assistance to travelers with mobility issues. Some car ferries have lifts, while passenger ferries are fully accessible.

Wheelchairtraveling.com has a wealth of information about tours, transport and hotels in Mexico.

Wheeltheworld.com is a booking service that lists hotels, tour packages and accessible activities.

INTERNET ACCESS

Wi-fi and 4G are available in most places, though it's difficult to find stable connections in some remote areas.

PUBLIC HOLIDAYS

In urban centers and beach destinations, restaurants and shops remain open on holidays like Christmas Day and Día de Muertos.

GREETINGS

The go-to greeting is a hug and a kiss on the cheek. Handshakes are used for work and formal occasions.

FAMILY TRAVEL

All-inclusive hotels are great for families, providing cots or extra beds in the room, as well as high chairs in their restaurants.

Visitors under 12 often get a discount on their entrance fee to museums, archaeological sites and water parks.

Bus or airline companies usually offer half-off prices for kids aged five to 12.

Child seats are generally not available in taxis or car rentals.

Strollers can be hard to push on the uneven sidewalks and cobblestones of colonial-era towns.

DIGITAL NOMADS & RESIDENTS

Mexico has been drawing in huge influxes of digital nomads. The immigration department is cracking down on those who have overstayed. It's advisable to apply for a temporary residency visa, even if you plan to stay in Mexico only for a few months.

BUSY SUNDAYS

All archaeological sites in Mexico provide free entry for Mexican nationals and foreign residents on Sundays (with ID). That also means Sundays tend to be the busiest day of the week to visit an archaeological site; it's best to visit on a weekday.

VICTOR SG/SHUTTERSTOCK

LGBTIQ+ TRAVELERS

Most of Mexico is open-minded about sexuality and gender identity. The majority of Mexico's 32 states have approved same-sex marriage, but homophobia and hate crimes persist.

Mexico City has the largest LGBTIQ+ scene, especially in the Zona Rosa district and along República de Cuba. It also plays host to the largest Pride parade in the country.

Puerto Vallarta's Zona Romántica is bursting with gay-friendly hotels, restaurants and bars staging drag shows.

Out Adventures *(outadventures.com)* offers gay tours, hotels and general info about Mexico travel.

PHRASES TO GET YOU TALKING

Mexican Spanish pronunciation is easy, as most sounds have equivalents in English. Also, Spanish spelling is phonetically consistent, meaning that there's a clear and consistent relationship between what you see in writing and how it's pronounced. Note that kh is a throaty sound (like the 'ch' in the Scottish loch), v and b are like a soft English 'v' (between a 'v' and a 'b'), and r is strongly rolled. There are also some variations in spoken Spanish across Latin America, the most notable being the pronunciation of the letters ll and y. In some parts of Mexico they are pronounced like the 'll' in 'million', but in most areas they are pronounced like the 'y' in 'yes'.

BASICS

Hello.	*Hola.*	*o*·la
Goodbye.	*Adiós.*	a·*dyos*
Yes.	*Sí.*	see
No.	*No.*	no
Please.	*Por favor.*	por fa·*vor*
Thank you.	*Gracias.*	*gra*·syas
Excuse me.	*Perdón.*	per·*don*
Sorry.	*Lo siento.*	lo *syen*·to

What's your name?
¿Cómo se llama Usted?
ko·mo se *ya*·ma oo·*ste*

My name is ...
Me llamo ... me *ya*·mo ...

Do you speak English?
¿Habla inglés? *a*·bla een·*gles*

I don't understand.
No entiendo. No en·*tyen*·do

TIME & NUMBERS

What time is it?	*¿Qué hora es?*	ke *o*·ra es
It's (10) o'clock.	*Son (las diez).*	son (las dyes)
It's half past (one).	*Es (la una) y media.*	es (la *oo*·na) ee *me*·dya
At what time?	*¿A qué hora?*	a ke *o*·ra
At ...	*A la(s) ...*	a la(s) ...
yesterday	*ayer*	a·*yer*
today	*hoy*	oy
tomorrow	*mañana*	ma·*nya*·na

1	*uno*	*oo*·no	**6**	*seis*	seys
2	*dos*	dos	**7**	*siete*	*sye*·te
3	*tres*	tres	**8**	*ocho*	*o*·cho
4	*cuatro*	*kwa*·tro	**9**	*nueve*	*nwe*·ve
5	*cinco*	*seen*·ko	**10**	*diez*	dyes

EMERGENCIES

Help!	*¡Socorro!*	so·*ko*·ro
Go away!	*¡Vete!*	*ve*·te

Call the police!
¡Llame a la policía! *ya*·me a la po·lee·*see*·a

Call a doctor!
¡Llame a un médico! *ya*·me a oon *me*·dee·ko

I'm lost.
Estoy perdido/a. es·*toy* per·*dee*·do/a (m/f)

Index

A

Acapulco 160, 164-5
accessible travel 248
accommodations 246-7
activities 20-7, *see also individual activities*
air travel 240
alcohol 248
alebrijes 18, 152
altitude sickness 242
animals 12-13, *see also individual animals*
archaeological sites 6-7
  Cacaxtla 75, 76
  Calakmul 15, 98, 110-11
  Cempoala 89, 92-3
  Chalcatzingo 77
  Chichén Itzá 7, 31, 99, 104-5
  Chichén Viejo 105
  Cobá 122
  El Castillo 104
  El Tajín 89
  Great Pyramid of Cholula 76
  Kabah 115
  Labná 115
  Malinalco 77
  Palacio de los Mascarones 115
  Quiahuiztlán 89, 92-3
  Sayil 115
  Tecoaque 77
  Templo de la Virgen del Rosario 169
  Templo de las Inscripciones 133
  Teotenango 77
  Tepozteco 77
  Tula 76
  Uxmal 7, 98, 114-15
  Xochicalco 76
  Xochitécatl 75, 76
  Yaxchilán 7, 133
  Zona Arqueológica Chinkultic 139
  Zona Arqueológica Comalcalco 139
  Zona Arqueológica de Tenam Puente 139
  Zona Arqueológica Guachimontones 194
  Zona Arqueológica Tingambato 194
architecture 56-7
art 52-5, 146-7, 162-3
art galleries, *see* museums & galleries
arts & crafts 18-19, 134-5, 152-3
ATMs 238, 243
axolotls 13
Aztec Sun Stone 60

B

Bacalar 107
Bahía de Banderas 160, 172
Bahías de Huatulco 33
Baja Peninsula 212-21, **214**
  accommodations 215, 221
  drinking 215, 220-1
  driving tours 218-19, **219**
  food 215, 221
  itineraries 36-7, 218-19, **36-7**, **219**
  money 215
  planning 214
  travel seasons 215
  travel to & within Baja Peninsula 215
  wi-fi 215
bargaining 243
Barranca de Batopilas 227
Barrancas de Urique 230
bathrooms 248
bats 111
beaches 10-11, 173, 220
  Isla Blanca 106
  Majahuitas 173
  Playa Balandra 11, 220
  Playa de las Ánimas 179
  Playa de los Muertos 172
  Playa de Quimixto 173
  Playa Escobilla 149
  Playa Icacos 179
  Playa La Mancha 11, 89
  Playa La Ropa 174, 175
  Playa La Saladita 179
  Playa Las Gatas 174, 175
  Playa Madera 174, 175
  Playa Municipal 174
  Playa Norte 179
  Playa Olas Altas 171
  Playa Pescadores 99, 107
  Playa Sayulita 179
  Punta Esmeralda 99, 106-7
  Tecolotito 214, 219
  Tecolutla 89
Bernal 198
bicycle travel 204-5, 234, 244
biosphere reserves, *see* national parks, national reserves & biosphere reserves
bird-watching 13, 227
blogs 43
boat travel 169, 172, 240
Bonampak 133
books 42
border crossings 239

Bosque Secreto 230
bus travel 240
butterflies 13, 186-7

C

cabañas 246
cable cars 229, 234
Cabo Pulmo 214, 219
cacao 117, 131
Cacaxtla 75, 76
Calakmul 15, 98, 110-11
Campeche 30
camping 247
Cancún 31
Cañón del Sumidero 128
car travel 239, 240, 248
Carnival 25
Casa Azul 53-4
Casa de los Azulejos 57
Casa de Montejo 113
cash 238, 243
cathedrals, *see* churches & cathedrals
caves 9, 234
ceiba tree 114, 116
Cempoala 89, 92-3
cenotes 8, 9, 108-9, 116-17
  Cenote Sagrado 105
  Dos Ojos 99, 109
  Dzonbakal 109
  Hacienda Mucuyché 109
  Sacred Cenote 105
  Siete Bocas 99, 109
  X'Batún 109
Central Highlands, see Northern Central Highlands, Western Central Highlands
Central Pacific Coast 158-79, **160**
  accommodations 161
  drinking 161
  food 161, 178
  itineraries 34-5, 174-5, **175**
  money 161
  planning 160
  shopping 178-9
  surfing 179
  travel seasons 161
  travel to & within Central Pacific Coast 161
  walking tours 174-5, **175**
Centro Histórico 56-7
Cerocahui 39
Cerro de Silla 231
Chaac 117
Chac Mool 116
Chalcatzingo 77
charreadas 190
Chiapas 124-39, **126**
  accommodations 127
  arts & crafts 134-5
  drinking 127, 139
  driving tours 132-3, **133**
  festivals 138
  food 127, 130-1, 138
  history 132-3
  itineraries 30-1, 132-3, **30-1**, **133**
  money 127
  planner 126
  shopping 139
  travel seasons 127
  travel to & within Chiapas 127
Chichén Itzá 7, 31, 99, 104-5
Chichén Viejo 105
Chihuahua 39, 224, 228-9
children, travel with 40, 249
churches & cathedrals
  Catedral de Morelia 194
  Catedral de San Ildefonso 113
  Mazatlán cathedral 171
  Parroquia de Nuestra Señora de Dolores 209
  Parroquia de San Miguel Arcángel 200, 211
  Santuario de Atotonilco 209
  Santuario de Jesús Nazareno de Atotonilco 211
  Templo de la Purísima Concepción 211
  Templo de San Diego 207
Cinco de Mayo 27
cliff divers 164-5
climate 20-7, 40
Coatepec 91
coatis 122
coffee 90-1, 130-1
colectivos 241
Comala 194
Comitán de Domínguez 130
Copper Canyon 222-35, **224**
  accommodations 225
  drinking 225, 235
  food 225
  internet access 225
  itineraries 38-9, 226-7, **38-9**, **227**
  money 225
  planning 224
  travel seasons 225
  travel to & within Copper Canyon 225
  wi-fi 225
Cortés, Hernán 92-3
country code 248
courses 67, 167
Cozumel 99, 102-3
credit cards 243
Creel 39, 224, 227
crocodiles 168, 169
Cuajimoloyas 143, 151
Cueva de los Murciélagos 111
cultural experiences 14
currency 243
cycling 204-5, 234, 244

D

dancing 51, 56, 112
dangers 242
Danzantes Aztecas 56
Desierto Chihuahuense 231

000 Map pages

Día de Muertos 23, 154-5
Día de Revolución 23
disabilities, travelers with 248
discount tickets 243
diseases 242
distilleries 185
diving & snorkelling 122, 173
  Cozumel 99, 102-3
  Dos Ojos 99
  La Ventana 218, 219
  Puerto Vallarta 172-3
Divisadero 38, 227
Dolores Hidalgo 29, 198, 208
drinking, *see individual locations*
driving 239, 240, 248
driving tours
  Baja Peninsula 218-19, **219**
  Chiapas 132-3, **133**
  Veracruz 88-9, **89**
  Yucatán Peninsula 114-15, **115**
drug wars 232-3
Dulcería de Celay 57
Durango 224, 228-9

E

earthquakes 242
El Chepe train 224, 226-7
El Fuerte 38, 227
El Potrero Chico 231, 234
El Tajín 89
electricity 248
emergencies 242
Ensenada 36
environmental issues 9, 12
events 20-7, 40
exchange rates 243

F

family travel 249
Faro Carranza 86-7
Feria de Chiapas 138
Feria de Tabasco 138
Feria Huamantla 21
Ferrocarril Chihuahua Pacífico 226
festivals 20-7, 40, 163, 206, *see also individual festivals*
Fiesta Grande de Enero 25, 129, 138
Fiestas Patrias 209
films 43
fireflies 74
food 16-17, *see also individual locations*
forts 87, 169, 177

G

gardens, *see* parks & gardens
gay travelers 51, 249
glamping 247
Gran Hotel Ciudad de México 57
greetings 249
Guadalajara 35, 182, 190-1
Guanajuato 28, 198, 206-7, **207**
Guelaguetza 20
Guerrero Negro 37
guesthouses 246

H

handicrafts 18-19
Hidalgo y Costilla, Miguel 208-9
hiking
  Needa-Naa-Lagashxi 151
  Nevado de Colima Solo 189
  Parque Ecológico Chipinque 234
  Parque Nacional Volcán Nevado de Colima 188-9
  Ruta Cañón Latuvi-Lachatao 151
  Ruta Loma de Cucharilla 151
  Sierra Norte 143, 150-1
  Zapotec 150-1
history 92-3
  Acapulco 176-7
  Aztecs 78-9
  cenotes 105
  Chiapas 132-3
  jaguars 121
  Manila Galleon 176-7
  Maya people 132-3
  Mesoamerican artifacts 60-1
  Olmec, the 136-7
  Veracruz 87, 92-3
  War of Independence 208-9
hostels 246
hot springs 211, 234
Huamantla 70, 75
Huasteca Potosina 9, 15, 211
huipiles 153-4
hurricanes 11, 22

I

indigenous crafts 134-5
indigenous peoples 14, 15
Instituto Cultural Hospicio Cabañas 191
insurance 241
internet access 249
Isla Blanca 106
Isla Contoy 122
Isla Espíritu Santo 221
Isla Holbox 11, 122
Isla Mujeres 122
itineraries 28-39, **28-9**, **30-1**, **32-3**, **34-5**, **36-7**, **38-9**
  Baja Peninsula 218-19, **219**
  Central Pacific Coast 174-5, **175**
  Chiapas 132-3, **133**
  Copper Canyon 226-7, **227**
  Mexico City 56-7, 58-9, **57**, **59**
  Mexico City region 74-5, **75**
  Northern Central Highlands 206-7, **207**
  Oaxaca 150-1, **151**
  Ruta Puuc 114-15, **115**
  Veracruz 88-9, **89**
  Western Central Highlands 190-1, **191**
  Yucatán Peninsula 112-13, 114-15, **113**, **115**
Ixchel 117

J

jaguars 120-1
Jalatlaco 143
James, Edward 202-3
jicaras 153
Jornadas Villistas 20
jungle adventures 15

K

Kabah 115
Kahlo, Frida 52-5
kitesurfing 173, 214, 219
Kukulkán 116

L

La Fortuna 219
La Malinche 92-3
La Paz 37
La Quebrada 164-5
La Ventana 219
Labná 115
Lacandón peoples 15
Lacanjá Chansayab 133
Lago de Pátzcuaro 19, 35
Laguna Bacalar 107
language 41, 250
Las Posadas 24
Latuvi 151
LGBTIQ+ travelers 51, 249
literature 20, 42
Loreto 36
Los Arcos 163
Los Cabos 37
Los Chiapa 129
Los Mochis 39
Los Reyes Magos 24

M

Magellan 176
maize 116, 118-19
malecón 86-7
Malinalco 77
Manila Galleon 176-7
mariachi music 21, 190
markets
  Mercado de Artesanías (Oaxaca) 142
  Mercado de Artesanías (Pátzcuaro) 192
  Mercado de Artesanías (San Miguel de Allende) 200
  Mercado San Juan de Dios 191
  Tianguis 201
masks 19
Maya icons 116-17
Maya people 14, 118-19, 132-3
Maya sites 6-7, *see also* archaeological sites
Mazatlán 170-1
Mérida 31, 112-13
Mesoamerican artifacts 60-1
Mexican Independence Day 22
Mexico City 29, 44-67, **46-7**
  accommodations 49
  architecture 56-7
  courses 67
  discounts 49
  drinking 49, 63-4, 66-7
  entertainment 50-1
  food 49, 58-9, 62-3, 65-6
  internet access 49
  itineraries 56-7, 58-9, **57**, **59**
  money 49
  planning 46-7
  shopping 64-5
  travel seasons 48
  travel to & within Mexico City 48
  walking tours 56-7, 58-9, 67, **57**, **59**
  wi-fi 49
Mexico City region 68-81, **70**
  accommodations 71
  drinking 71, 80-1
  food 71, 80
  itineraries 74-5, **75**
  money 71
  planning 70
  shopping 81
  travel seasons 71
  travel to & within Mexico City region 71
mezcal 204-5
Minas de Tiza 70, 75
Mirador de Divisadero 230
monarch butterflies 186-7
money 238, 243
Monte Albán 6
Monterrey 224, 232-3
Monumento Al Pípila 206, 209
Morelia 35, 182
mountain biking 234
museums & galleries
  Casa de la Cultura 169
  Centro de las Artes Centenario 211
  Centro de Textiles del Mundo Maya 19
  Centro Fotográfico Manuel Álvarez Bravo 146
  El Jardín Escultórico Edward James 202-3
  Fábrica La Aurora 201
  Galería Colectika 162
  Galería Corsica 162
  Galería Omar Alonso 162
  Galerie des Artistes 162
  Gran Museo de Chichén Itzá 123
  Gran Museo del Mundo Maya 123
  Horno3 235
  Las Pozas 202-3
  Manmade México 162
  MUCAL 211
  MUSA Museo de las Artes 195
  Museo Agustín Lara 95
  Museo Alhóndiga de Granaditas 207, 209

000 Map pages

Museo Amparo 81
Museo Arqueológico de la Costa Grande 179
Museo Casa de Diego Rivera 207
Museo Casa Estudio Diego Rivera y Frida Kahlo 54
Museo de Arte Contemporáneo de Oaxaca 146
Museo de Arte Moderno 55
Museo de Artes e Industrias Populares 195
Museo de Historia Mexicana 235
Museo de la Independencia 209
Museo de la Orquídea 94
Museo de la Vid y El Vino 216
Museo de las Momias 115, 210
Museo de los Pintores Oaxaqueños 146
Museo del Danzante Xiqueño 94
Museo del Pulque 75
Museo del Vestido de Santa María Magdalena 95
Museo El Café-tal Apan 91
Museo Francisco Villa (Chihuahua) 228
Museo Francisco Villa (Durango) 229
Museo Frida Kahlo 53-4
Museo Histórico Casa de Allende 209
Museo Histórico de Acapulco 177
Museo Historico de la Revolución 229
Museo José Alfredo Jiménez 211
Museo José Guadalupe Posada 211
Museo Leonora Carrington 203
Museo Maya de Cancún 123
Museo Menonita 235
Museo Morelense de Arte Contemporáneo Juan Soriano 81
Museo Mural Diego Rivera 55
Museo Nacional de Antropología 60
Museo Nacional de Arte 57
Museo Naval 179
Museo Pedro Coronel 210
Museo Regional Michoacano 195
Museo Robert Brady 81
Museo Subacuático de Arte 122
Museo Textil de Oaxaca 142, 146
Museo Vivo del Muralismo 55
Observatorio 1873 179
Paseo Amor Eterno 165
music 21, 42

N

Nahua people 14
Nanacamilpa 70
national parks, national reserves & biosphere reserves
  Cabo Pulmo 214, 219
  Cañón del Sumidero 128
  Cuatro Ciénegas 230, 234
  La Tovara National Park 169
  Los Arcos National Marine Park 173
  Parque del Jaguar 123
  Parque Ecológico Chipinque 231, 234
  Parque Ecológico La Huasteca 234
  Parque Nacional Bahía de Loreto 221
  Parque Nacional Lagunas de Montebello 139
  Parque Nacional Volcán Nevado de Colima 182, 188-9
  Punta Sur 11, 102
  Reserva de la Biosfera Calakmul 99, 110-11
  Reserva de la Biosfera Sierra Gorda 15, 211
  Reserva Mariposa Monarca 35
  Ría Celestún 123
  Ría Lagartos 122
  Sian Ka'an 122
  Tsúuk Akumal Parque Natural 122
  Yum Balam Nature Reserve 122
newspapers 43
Nochevieja 24
Northern Central Highlands 196-211, **198**
  accommodations 199
  drinking 199, 210
  food 199, 210
  itineraries 28-9, 34-5, 206-7, **28-9**, **34-5**, **207**
  money 199
  planning 198
  travel seasons 199
  travel to & within Northern Central Highlands 199
  walking tours 206-7, **207**
Northern Mexico, *see* Copper Canyon

O

Oaxaca 32, 140-57, **142-3**
  accommodations 145
  arts & crafts 152-3
  drinking 145
  food 145
  internet access 145
  itineraries 32-3, 150-1, **32-3**, **151**
  money 145
  planning 142-3
  travel seasons 144
  travel to & within Oaxaca 144, 145
  wi-fi 145
Old Mazatlán 160
Olmec, the 136-7
Orizaba 33

P

Palenque 31
Parachicos 129
parks & gardens
  El Jardín Escultórico Edward James 202-3
  Jardín Botánico Dr Alfredo Barrera Marín 122
  Las Pozas 202-3
  Parque de Santa Lucía 113
  Ranchito Cascabel 211
Parque Ecológico Chipinque 231, 234
Pátzcuaro 182, 192-3
Peña de Bernal 211
pesos 243
planning, *see individual locations*
Playa La Mancha 11, 89
Plazuela Machado 170
podcasts 42
Posada James 203
public holidays 249
public transport 239
Puerto Escondido 11, 32
Puerto Vallarta 34, 162-3, 172-3
pulque 51, 75, 78-9
Punta de Mita 179
Punta Laguna 122
Punta Sur 11, 102

Q

Querétaro 29
Quiahuiztlán 89, 92-3

R

responsible travel 149, 244-5
ride-share 239
Río Bec 111
Rivera, Diego 52-5
Riviera Maya 106-7
road distances 241

000 Map pages

rock climbing 231, 234
Ruta de los Cenotes 109
Ruta de Vino y Queso 204-5
Ruta del Cacao 131
Ruta del Vino 216
Ruta Puuc 114-15, **115**

S

safe travel 242
San Blas 160, 168-9
San Cristóbal de las Casas 30
San José del Pacífico 33
San Luis Potosí 198, 204
San Miguel de Allende 28, 198, 200-1
Santa Elena 115
Santa Rita 219
Santiago 214, 219
sargassum seaweed 10
Sayil 115
Sayulita 34
scams 242
sculpture 163
Semana Santa 26
shopping, *see individual locations*
SIM cards 238
slow travel 244
smoking 248
social etiquette 41
sombreros 190
Spanish language 250
Spring Equinox 26
stand-up paddleboarding 172-3
street art 146-7
sunscreen 9, 101, 109
surfing 166-7, 179
swimming 173

T

Tabasco, *see* Chiapas
tacos 58-9, 62, 178, 195
Talavera pottery 19
tap water 248
Tapalpa 194
taxis 239
Tecoaque 77
television shows 43
temascals 14, 143, 151
Teotenango 77
Teotihuacán 6, 29
Teotitlán del Valle 19, 152, 156
Tepozteco 77
Tepoztlán 70, 72-3, **75**
tequila 184-5
Tequila 35, 182, 184-5
Tequisquiapan 198
theaters 170, 191, 207
Tijuana 36
time zone 248
tipping 41, 243
tlaltequeadas 73
Tlaxcala 74-5
Todos Santos 37
toilets 248
tortillas 75
tourist information 43
tours, *see also* driving tours, walking tours
  mezcal 205
  tequila 185
  wineries 216
train travel
  El Chepe train 224, 226-7
  Ferrocarril Chihuahua Pacífico 226
travel seasons 20-7, 40, *see also individual locations*
travel to/from Mexico 238-9
travel within Mexico 240-1
trekking, *see* hiking
Troncones 166-7
tropical storms 11, 22
Tula 76
Tulum 31
turtles 13, 142, 148-9

U

Urique 39, 227
Uxmal 7, 98, 114-15

V

vacations 249
vaccinations 242
Valle de Guadalupe 37, 214
Valle de los Monjes 230, 234
Valle de Zimatlán 19, 156
VAT 243, 248
vegetarian & vegan travelers 62-3
Veracruz 33, 82-95, **84**
  accommodations 85
  drinking 85, 86, 94
  driving tours 88-9, **89**
  festivals 91
  food 85, 95
  history 92-3
  itineraries 32-3, 88-9, **32-3**, **89**
  money 85
  planning 84
  shopping 86, 94
  travel seasons 85
  travel to & within Veracruz 85
viewpoints
  Cerro de las Culebras 94
  Cerro del Obispado 235
  Mirador Cerro del Gallego Cañón de Urique 235
Villa, Pancho 20, 228-9
visas 238, 248, 249
voladores 88
volcanoes 70, 188-9, 242
volunteering 244

W

walking, *see* hiking
walking tours
  Central Pacific Coast 174-5, **175**
  Guanajuato 206-7, **207**
  Mexico City 56-7, 58-9, 67, **57**, **59**
  Northern Central Highlands 206-7, **207**
  Western Central Highlands 190-1, **191**
  Yucatán Peninsula 112-13, **113**
War of Independence 208-9
waterfalls 138
  Cascada de Basaseachi 230, 234
  Cascada de Tamul 211
  Cascada la Cebolla 203
weather 20-7, 40
websites 247
Western Central Highlands 180-95, **182**
  accommodations 183, 195
  arts & crafts 192-3
  drinking 183
  entertainment 194
  food 183, 195
  history 192-3
  internet access 183
  itineraries 28-9, 34-5, 190-1, **28-9**, **34-5**, **191**
  money 183
  planning 182
  shopping 194
  travel seasons 183
  travel to & within Western Central Highlands 183
  walking tours 190-1, **191**
  wi-fi 183
whale sharks 13, 27
whale watching 13, 160, 172
wi-fi 238, 249
wildlife 12-13, 120-1, 214, 219, *see also individual animals*
wildlife sanctuaries
  Centro Ecoturístico Escobilla 143
  Centro Mexicano de la Tortuga 143, 149
  Playa Escobilla 149
  Reserva Mariposa Monarca 186
  Santuario de las Luciérnagas 74
  Vida Milenaria 89
windsurfing 219
wine 204-5, 216-17, 235

X

Xalapa 32
Xico 91
Xilitla 198, 203
Xochicalco 76
Xochitécatl 75, 76

Y

Yaxchilán 7, 133
Yucatán Peninsula 96-123, **98-9**
  accommodations 101
  drinking 101, 123
  driving tours 114-15, **115**
  food 101, 123
  internet access 101
  itineraries 30-1, 112-13, 114-15, **30-1**, **113**, **115**
  money 101
  planning 98-9
  travel seasons 100
  travel to & within Yucatán Peninsula 100
  walking tours 112-13, **113**
  wi-fi 101

Z

Zapotec 150-1
Zihuatanejo 160, 174-5
zip lines 227, 234

'That time I unknowingly visited Durango during Mexico's Revolution Day, I crashed the town's parade and joined in its celebrations.'

NELLIE HUANG

'Crawling out of the temascal (steam bath), dripping with sweat, covered in bits of medicinal leaves, I felt totally alive.'

LIZA PRADO

'When a fried grasshopper's leg snagged my lip and I washed it away with a kissing-sip of mezcal, I felt at home.'

PHILLIP TANG

'In Tócuaro, a mask-maker let me sit quietly in the corner and watch him as he painstakingly carved intricate detail into a wooden mask depicting a snarling devil visage.'

ANNA KAMINSKI

'There's nothing quite like road-tripping in Baja with its surreal, Seussian desert landscapes and dramatic, cliffside coast highways.'

JOHN HECHT

'That time I saw Veracruz City come alive on a Saturday night, the main square packed with dancers moving in time to the danzón beat.'

IAIN STEWART

FROM TOP: CINOQ/SHUTTERSTOCK, DANIELCZSHUTTERSTOCK

THIS BOOK

Destination editor
Lauren Keith

Production editor
Katie Connolly

Cartographer
Daniela Machová

Book designer
Catalina A

Coordinating editor
Anita Isalska

Assisting editors
Maura Murphy, Maja Vatrić

Assisting cartographers
Vojtěch Bartoš, Dorothy Davidson

Cover researcher
Daisy Korpics

Thanks
Andrea Dobbin, Jenna Myers, Kat Rowan